Unobtrusive methods in
social research

Understanding Social Research

Series Editor: Alan Bryman

Published titles

Unobtrusive Methods in Social Research
Raymond M. Lee

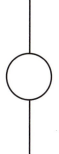

Unobtrusive methods in social research

RAYMOND M. LEE

Open University Press
Buckingham · Philadelphia

Open University Press
Celtic Court
22 Ballmoor
Buckingham
MK18 1XW

email: enquiries@openup.co.uk
world wide web: http://www.openup.co.uk

and
325 Chestnut Street
Philadelphia, PA 19106, USA

First published 2000

A catalogue record of this book is available from the British Library

ISBN 0 335 20051 6 (pb)   0 335 20052 4 (hb)

Library of Congress Cataloging-in-Publication Data
Lee, Raymond M., 1946–
    Unobtrusive methods in social research / Raymond M. Lee.
       p.   cm. — (Understanding social research)
    ISBN 0-335-20052-4 (hb) — ISBN 0-335-20051-6 (pbk.)
    1. Social sciences—Research—Methodology. I. Title. II. Series.
H62.L4183 2000
300′.7′2—dc21   99-056325

Typeset by Type Study, Scarborough
Printed in Great Britain by Biddles Limited, Guildford and Kings Lynn

To the memory of Donald T. Campbell

Contents

Series editor's foreword

This Understanding Social Research series is designed to help students to understand how social research is carried out and to appreciate a variety of issues in social research methodology. It is designed to address the needs of students taking degree programmes in areas such as sociology, social policy, psychology, communication studies, cultural studies, human geography, political science, criminology and organization studies and who are required to take modules in social research methods. It is also designed to meet the needs of students who need to carry out a research project as part of their degree requirements. Postgraduate research students and novice researchers will find the books equally helpful.

The series is concerned to help readers to 'understand' social research methods and issues. This will mean developing an appreciation of the pleasures and frustrations of social research, an understanding of how to implement certain techniques, and an awareness of key areas of debate. The relative emphasis on these different features will vary from book to book, but in each one the aim will be to see the method or issue from the position of a practising researcher and not simply to present a manual of 'how to' steps. In the process, the series will contain coverage of the major methods of social research and will address a variety of issues and debates. Each book in the series is written by a practising researcher who has experience of the technique or debates that he or she is addressing. Authors are encouraged to draw on their own experiences and inside knowledge.

One of my favourite books on social research methods has always been *Unobtrusive Measures: Nonreactive Research in the Social Sciences* by Eugene Webb and others. It was published originally in 1966 and is one of the most widely cited books on research methodology around. In part, it is a reaction to the unthinking use of research methods such as the interview and questionnaire, which, Webb and his associates suggested are limited by the research participant's knowledge that he or she is the focus of an investigation. Webb and his associates sought to loosen the reliance on such methods by suggesting a vast array, often resembling an inventory, of methods and sources of data which are not limited in this way. The style and tone of the book were irreverent, with the authors suggesting much greater use of the imagination than the simple and perhaps unthinking use of standard procedures. In fact, Webb and his associates were not opposed to commonly used methods like the interview; it was the over-reliance on such methods to which they objected. Also, they were keen to place their advocacy of unobtrusive methods in the context of recommending that measurement in the social sciences should not be dependent on one measurement process alone.

An updated and revised edition of the book by Webb and his associates was published in 1981, but since then there has been little further discussion of the topic, in spite of the immense popularity of the original publication. Raymond Lee's book on unobtrusive methods therefore plugs an important gap. His book is written very much in the spirit of the style Webb and his associates adopted. Lee discusses the very idea of unobtrusive methods in the context of wider debates and issues in research methodology. He examines the different types of unobtrusive methods, taking into account some of the discussions and distinctions that have been employed since 1966. He has updated the original work in at least two senses. First, he has included a huge number of new studies and slotted them into the various categories of unobtrusive method. Second, he has included new forms of unobtrusive method, which Webb and his associates could not have anticipated, most notably the Internet. Awareness of the Internet as a research tool is still in its infancy and I am sure that readers will find this discussion very timely and suggestive.

As Lee observes, there is still a massive reliance in the social sciences on data deriving from reactive methods of social research, such as the interview and questionnaire. This book will serve as a further reminder of the limitations of a dependence on such techniques, as well as offering a broader purview on alternative possibilities than Webb and his associates were able to provide in their seminal discussion.

Alan Bryman

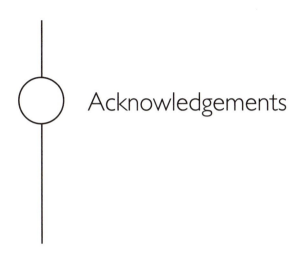

Acknowledgements

I am grateful to Nigel Fielding and Stuart Peters for comments on individual chapters. Portions of this book were written while I was a Visiting Fellow at the Centre for Interdisciplinary Studies at the University of Stellenbosch. I thank Johann Mouton, Fran Ritchie, Bernita de Wet and Lea Esterhuizen for their hospitality during my stay. For their patience I am also grateful to Alan Bryman, and at Open University Press to Justin Vaughan and Gaynor Clements.

Introduction to unobtrusive methods

Allan Kellehear has written: 'There is today, in social science circles, a simple and persistent belief that knowledge about people is available simply by asking.' He goes on, 'We ask people about themselves, and they tell us . . . the assumption is that important "truths" about people are best gained through talk – a sometimes direct, sometimes subtle, interrogation of experience, attitude and belief' (Kellehear 1993: 1). A problem with this assumption is that what we gain 'simply by asking' is often shaped by the dynamics surrounding the interaction between researcher and researched. This is so because the act of eliciting data from respondents or informants can itself affect the character of the responses obtained. One consequence of this might be a need to accomplish the 'interrogation of experience, attitude and belief' in other, less direct, ways. Webb *et al.* (1966) coined the term '**unobtrusive measures**' to refer to data gathered by means that do not involve direct elicitation of information from research subjects. Unobtrusive measures are 'non-reactive' (Webb *et al.* 1981) in the sense that they are presumed to avoid the problems caused by the researcher's presence. Specifically, Webb *et al.* advocate that social researchers should devote more attention to sources of data such as physical **traces** (the evidence people leave behind them in various ways as they traverse their physical environment), non-participant observation, and the use of documentary sources. In other words, questions about experience, attitude and belief might be addressed just as effectively by watching what people do, looking at physical evidence of various kinds, and drawing on the written as well as the spoken voice, as they are by interviews and questionnaires.

Webb *et al.*'s (1966) book *Unobtrusive Measures* became something of a minor classic. (A revised version under the title *Nonreactive Measures* was published in 1981.) Humorous in tone and sceptical in its orientation to the dominant methodological practices of its time, *Unobtrusive Measures* is a delightful compendium of offbeat methods and data sources. (The book, in fact, had its origins in an informal seminar at Northwestern University in which it became a game to come up with novel methods (Campbell 1981: 481).) Among the examples of unobtrusive measures Webb *et al.* proffer are the use of wear on the floor tiles surrounding a museum exhibit showing hatching chicks to measure visitor flows; the size of suits of armour as an indicator of changes in human stature over time; and (tongue in cheek) the relationship between psychologists' hair length and their methodological predilections. In all of this, of course, there is a serious purpose, a call to social researchers to think creatively about the sources and use of their data. Hopefully in the same spirit, the present book provides an introduction to and an overview of the use of unobtrusive methods in social research.

Why use unobtrusive methods?

One justification for the use of unobtrusive methods lies in the methodological weaknesses of interviews and questionnaires. As Webb *et al.* put it:

> Interviews and questionnaires intrude as a foreign element into the social setting they would describe, they create as well as measure attitudes, they elicit atypical role and response, they are limited to those who are accessible and who will cooperate, and the responses obtained are produced in part by dimensions of individual differences irrelevant to the topic at hand (Webb *et al.* 1966: 1).

Interviews and questionnaires create attitudes in part because respondents commonly try to manage impressions of themselves in order to maintain their standing in the eyes of an interviewer. A fairly consistent finding on surveys, for example, is that respondents will claim to have an opinion about fictitious or obscure matters (Bishop *et al.* 1980). Looking at voting behaviour, Presser and Traugott (1992) found that some of those who claim in surveys to have voted have not done so. According to Presser and Traugott, misreporting of voting behaviour correlates with factors such as education and interest in politics. Perhaps because they regard themselves as the kind of people who should vote, the better educated and politically aware feel under pressure to report having voted even when they had not done so.

Bradburn *et al.* (1979) found a tendency for survey respondents to overreport socially desirable behaviours when interviewed using less anonymous methods. Broadly, the more anonymous the method, that is, the less it involved face-to-face contact, the more likely respondents were to admit to socially undesirable behaviour. More recently, Tourganeau and Smith (1996) have also found evidence that more private methods of data collection yield gains in the reporting of sensitive behaviours. The characteristics of interviewers can under some circumstances affect the answers respondents give to particular kinds of question. In a study using both black and white interviewers, Schuman and Converse (1971) found little evidence that the race of the interviewer influenced responses to questions relating to racial discrimination, poor living conditions, or personal background. They did find, however, that black respondents were less likely to agree with statements expressing hostile attitudes towards whites when the interviewer was white than when the interviewer was black.

How one asks a question in an interview or on a questionnaire can have, sometimes subtle, sometimes substantial, effects on the responses received. Variations in wording, for example, can affect how people respond. Smith (1983) found across a variety of surveys that the word 'welfare' in questions about financial support for the disadvantaged produces lower levels of positive response than the word 'poor'. There is some evidence that respondents use the response categories attached to questionnaire items on surveys as cues to researchers' expectations about the range of particular behaviours (Schwarz and Hippler 1991). In one experiment, respondents, when asked if they suffered from headaches 'frequently', reported three times as many headaches a week as those asked whether they suffered headaches 'occasionally' (Clark and Schober 1982). It seems, moreover, that respondents dislike giving responses that seem extreme relative to the scale of responses presented to them. As Schuman and Presser (1981) point out, survey questions are never asked in isolation but as part of a flow of questions. Thus, the context or order in which questions appear can have consequences for the responses to them. Respondents, for example, sometimes adjust their response to a later question in order to make it consistent with an answer they have given previously. In various ways, responses to specific questions on a particular topic can be affected by responses to a general question on the same topic. Juxtaposing questions having an alternate form sometimes induces, it seems, a norm of reciprocity which can distort responses. Schuman and Presser argue that, although question order effects are not pervasive, neither are they rare.

The extent to which interviewing might intrude as a foreign and reactive element in the research situation can be seen in Veroff *et al.*'s (1992) longitudinal study of couples in first marriages. Compared with a control group, couples who were frequently interviewed showed more variability in reported levels of marital satisfaction during the second year of the study. By the fourth year, however, those who had been interviewed more frequently had generally more positive perceptions of their marriage than those interviewed less frequently. Veroff *et al.* speculate that the interviews might have caused couples at various points to reflect on their marriage in ways that affected the quality of the relationship. Participation in a study, in other words, can change the attitudes and behaviour of those being studied. Depth interviewing might be less subject to reactive effects than survey interviewing. Yet, even here problems can arise, at least when sensitive topics are involved. The threatening character of interviews on relatively intimate matters can be gauged, for example, from reports of interviewees lapsing into embarrassed silence (George 1983) or needing to use alcohol as a prop while being interviewed (Brannen 1988). In Maureen Padfield and Ian Procter's (1996) qualitative study of young adult women, the gender of the interviewer seemed to make little difference to what was disclosed in the interview, except in relation to one particular issue. Women volunteered information about having had an abortion to Padfield, the female interviewer, but not to Proctor. In addition, some of Proctor's respondents revealed on reinterview by Padfield that they had had an abortion. It is not clear what accounts for this pattern, but an implication might be that interviewer effects are not entirely absent in qualitative research.

As Webb *et al.* point out, respondents have to be accessible and to be willing to answer a researcher's questions for interview and questionnaire methods to be effective. There is, however, a fairly widespread perception that survey response rates have fallen in the United States, the United Kingdom and, perhaps, in some other countries as well (American Statistical Association 1974; Market Research Society Working Group 1976). Steeh (1981) examined non-response to two long-running US surveys associated with the Survey Research Center at the University of Michigan. In both, refusal rates rose steadily between 1952 and 1979. According to Groves (1989), a long-term increase in refusal rates has also been seen for a number of large-scale government surveys in the United States. Over a rather long time period, Goyder (1987) found declining response rates in both the United States and Canada for interview studies, though not for postal surveys. Those who do not respond to surveys are, of course, different in their social characteristics from those who do. Goyder suggests in a careful synthesis that, although many of the commonly assumed demographic correlates of non-response do not survive statistical controls for other factors, '[socioeconomic] status and age are key components of socio-demographic refusal bias in surveys' (Goyder 1987: 109).

Concern over **reactivity** extends beyond interview-based methods. In the 1930s, a series of experiments on the relationship between workplace conditions and levels of production attained classic status (Mayo 1933; Roethlisberger and Dickson 1939). During experiments at the Hawthorne works of the Western Electric Company into the effects of changing lighting levels, it was noticed that production went up whether levels of illumination were increased or decreased. The explanation suggested for this phenomenon was that the workers had responded not to the experimental variable – the level of lighting intensity – but to being singled out for study (Mayo 1933). Dubbed the '**Hawthorne Effect**', these experiments were an early intimation that social science measurement could be *artefactual*. In other words, simply by their presence researchers could unwittingly but systematically distort their own findings.

Research on the role of **artefacts** in social science experiments crystallized in the 1960s and early 1970s. Broadly speaking, attention was directed to three areas: (a) the role of '**demand characteristics**', (b) the effects of 'experimenter expectancies' and (c) the possible over-reliance on volunteer subjects. (For a readable, if somewhat one-sided account of the field, see Rosnow and Rosenthal (1997).) Orne (1962) suggested that the experimental situation is one that motivates participants to be 'good subjects'. Research subjects therefore try to act in ways they presume will make the experiment successful. In order to do this they look for clues to the true purpose of the experiment in the experimental situation, in their own wider knowledge and, in the case of students, in campus gossip. The sum total of such clues Orne refers to as the 'demand characteristics' of the experiment. Rosenthal (1976) presented evidence that researchers who were encouraged to believe that an experiment would yield results within a particular range produced findings in line with their expectation. Subsequently, Rosenthal and Rubin (1978) reported on a **meta-analysis** of a large number of studies dealing with experimenter expectancies. The pooled results from these studies suggested that expectancy effects are to be found in a wide range of research areas. Rosenthal and Rostow (1975) have also presented evidence to suggest that a variety of background and attitudinal variables distinguish those willing to participate in social-psychological experiments from those who are not. According to Rosenthal and Rostow, volunteering is also associated with a variety of situational factors to do with the investigation itself, the characteristics of the researcher and the incentives offered for participation.

As Campbell (1981) concedes, one can argue that an assessment of this kind is overly pessimistic. Arguments that direct elicitation methods are incorrigibly reactive have been vigorously contested, and have provoked revisionist claims. In a careful study using hierarchical multilevel modelling, Hox *et al.* (1991) point out that interviewer effects found in earlier studies might not have survived appropriate statistical controls. Alternatively, they suggest, effects found in previous studies might have come about through the cumulation of small differences between interviewers. Smith (1995) has argued that the image of free-falling survey response rates is an exaggeration. Examining non-response rates for a range of different surveys over relatively long time periods, he found varying trends in response rates, although he does concede that, 'In both the United States and elsewhere increases in both overall non-response and refusals do outnumber declines . . .' (Smith 1995:

168). Even the celebrated Hawthorne Effect has not escaped critical scrutiny. According to Parsons (1974), the workers, who were paid according to output, could see records of their output, and worked harder to increase their earnings. Kruglanski (1975) suggests that experimental studies showing the presence of demand characteristics (or subject artefacts to use his preferred term) do not stand up well to critical scrutiny since researchers have not always been clear about what produces artefacts or how exactly they affect experimental variables. Kruglanski (1975) also argues that Rosenthal and Rosnow's research on volunteer subjects shows volunteering to be associated with such a heterogeneous range of factors that it is difficult to see how volunteer bias could operate in particular studies. Reviewing a large number of studies, Barber (1976) concludes that there is some evidence for the biasing effects of experimenter expectancies. However, he also argues that, in many cases, other explanations, such as failure to follow precisely experimental protocols, can account for the results found in particular experiments. Nevertheless, one can still argue that social researchers are over-reliant on direct elicitation methods. Despite the United States and Britain's very different methodological cultures, one heavily quantitative, the other qualitative, social research in both countries still relies heavily on the direct elicitation of data from respondents. Only a little more than one-quarter (29.5 per cent) of articles appearing in major sociology journals in 1995 (n = 220) in the United States (*American Journal of Sociology, American Sociological Review* and *Social Forces*) and in the United Kingdom (*British Journal of Sociology, Sociological Review* and *Sociology*) used data sources, mainly documents, that were not collected by questionnaire or interview.

A justification for the use of unobtrusive methods sees them less as alternatives to direct elicitation methods, and rather more as complementary to those methods. In fact, having stressed the reactivity of interviews and questionnaires Webb *et al.* reserve their greatest scorn for studies using only a single method of data collection. For them, the principal objection to traditional data collection methods is typically 'that they are used alone' (Webb *et al.* 1966: 1). Webb *et al.* argue that data collection methods used singly are inferior to the use of multiple methods. They use a metaphor from geology, the idea of an 'outcropping', to point to how theory might guide the selection of data points (1966: 28). Any given theory has innumerable implications and makes innumerable predictions. The testing of theory can be done only at available outcroppings, those points where theoretical predictions and available instrumentation meet. Any one such outcropping is equivocal, but the more remote or independent such checks, the more confirmatory their agreement. The idea that data and theory meet at available outcroppings is clearly a justification for the use of multiple sources of data. The argument is that the results one gets from one's research are always to some degree an artefact of the method used to collect the data. In other words, any finding is potentially subject to a 'plausible rival hypothesis' (Webb *et al.* 1966: 5) that the findings reflect fallibilities inherent in the data collection method. However, these fallibilities are not the same across methods. In particular, the problems of reactivity that afflict direct elicitation methods are absent when data are collected unobtrusively. From this point of view, configuring different methods, each of which is fallible in a different way, gives greater purchase on the problem to hand than an over-reliance on a single method.

Another justification for the use of unobtrusive methods is related to their adaptability. My own interest in unobtrusive measures derives from an early field research experience where obtaining elicited data was extremely difficult (Lee 1995a). Studying a relatively rare and, in the context of the religious conflict there, deviant population, interreligiously married couples in Northern Ireland, a group who in addition often take care to hide themselves from the attention of the wider community, the need to supplement interview data with information from other sources soon became apparent. For example, record-based data on the geographical patterning of marital choice had to be substituted for a survey. An added attraction of unobtrusive methods over directly elicited data in conflict situations is that they reduce the potential physical hazards associated with having to venture into dangerous locales in order to carry out interviews (Lee 1995a). Another way to see this is to recognize that researching sensitive or dangerous topics encourages researchers to innovate in order to find pathways around the obstacles certain topics put in their way. Methodological innovation has its drawbacks, notably in an absorption with the technical fix, but it also requires an imaginative cast of mind. As C. Wright Mills (1959) argued, imagination forms a counter to trained incapacity. Technical competence in research skills, even of the highest quality, is leavened by imagination.

Kellehear (1993) points out that Webb *et al.*'s work predates the advent of 'post-structuralist' approaches in the social sciences. Kellehear uses the term loosely to refer to a variety of contemporary theoretical stances such as deconstructionism, discourse analysis, narrative analysis, phenomenology and **semiotics**, many of which can be collected together, Alasuutari (1995) suggests, under the rubric of 'cultural studies'. As Atkinson observes, these approaches have 'roots in diverse philosophical, theoretical and methodological inspirations' (Atkinson 1992: 38). They share, however, a hostility to the notion that the task of social science is measurement, whether unobtrusive or not, as opposed to interpretive or critical understanding of social reality. The somewhat surprising intersection of those approaches with that of Webb *et al.* lies in a rather sideways glance at traditional sources of data in social research. In the post-structuralist vision, everything in and of the world is irredeemably cultural, and therefore open to study, no matter how seemingly peripheral, insignificant or taken for granted. In addition, shaped by literary or humanistic study, such approaches have usually been less wedded to elicited data than traditional social science disciplines. Instead, they focus on the cultural meaning of products, artefacts and objects, in a sense revalorizing sources marginalized by dominant social science. In particular, textual materials, from the very grand to the very humble, products of popular culture and material culture find themselves falling under the post-structuralist gaze.

Where do unobtrusive measures come from?

Although the term is Bouchard's (1976), Webb *et al.* might easily have described *Unobtrusive Measures* as an inventory. Indeed, the core of the book, with only some injustice, can be read simply as an extended list of instances held together by little more than the non-reactivity they have in common. Formal sociologists such as Simmel and Goffman were fond of 'saturative instantiation', the piling on of examples, as a way of demonstrating the ubiquity, significance and interpenetration of social forms. (Mention of Goffman in this context is, of course, ironic. His largely undescribed methodology, whatever else it may have involved, made full use of unobtrusive methods, from disguised observation to documentary analysis (Burns 1992).) Saturating the reader with relevant instances is persuasive. The many and varied examples Webb and colleagues deploy urge the reader to recognize that the use of unobtrusive measures is both possible and desirable. Inventories have been used as a method for collecting data. Although the term 'inventory' is still sometimes used to refer to the set of items making up a psychometric scale, methods of this kind are rare today. If they survive at all, it is in the form of time budgets. Used to collect data, inventories are unwieldy and often reflect a rather atheoretical tendency towards factual accumulation. The more common use of the inventory is to list in a readily retrievable form resources of various kinds. Survey researchers, for example, can turn to published inventories (for example, Miller 1991) to locate well-validated attitude scales for inclusion in their questionnaires. The advent of the Internet, for example, produced a blizzard of inventories, in print and on line, of listservs, **newsgroups** and websites (see, for example, the resources at http//: www.sosig.ac.uk).

Creating an inventory of measures provides a database of retrievable examples. Since inventories are inclusivist in character, an inventory makes visible the range, scope and relevance of the measures contained within it. As a result, it becomes easy to identify gaps or miscellaneous elements (Bouchard 1976) within the overall framework. Inclusion also ensures that the reader is very likely to find something that catches the interest. Inventorial organization encourages browsing. Browsing in its turn encourages the 'discovery of accidents' (Glaser and Strauss 1967: 174–5). This is because the salience of each browsed item, and the basis on which it is deemed salient, tend to be assessed independently for each item. To put this another way, relevance, rather than being imposed, emerges out of browsing. The problem is that although browsing is useful, it is also quite limited. As Dabbs points out, there can be 'too many measures, some of which, quite frankly, are worthless. If one included a measure of every sign or effect of a phenomenon, the number would be endless. There are more measures than phenomena, and one must carve out a domain of measures likely to be useful and to the point' (Dabbs 1982: 34). Just as inventories are unwieldy as data collection tools without some means of data reduction, resource inventories are similarly unwieldy unless the user has a mechanism or a methodology that allows retrieval of relevant items in the database. In the original incarnation of *Unobtrusive Measures* such a methodology was conspicuous by its absence. In other words, there is little explicitly to guide a researcher seeking unelicited data relevant to a particular research problem.

Two different approaches to dealing with this problem have been taken in subsequent writing. On the one hand, some writers have adopted what might be called an *orientational* approach. This stresses the importance of the stance the researcher brings to possible and actual sources of data. The orientational approach can be contrasted with a *taxonomic* strategy, the basic aim of which is to identify particular properties of measures. From these properties, it is argued, one might be able to produce a generative taxonomy that could be used to produce on demand unobtrusive measures fitted to specific research purposes (Sechrest and Phillips 1979; Webb *et al.* 1981: 287–306).

Although implicit in much of Webb *et al*'s writing, the most clear-cut expression of the orientational approach can be found in Webb and Weick's (1983) discussion of the principles governing the use of unobtrusive measures. The first principle is that investigators should 'construct and impose multiple indices that converge' (Webb and Weick 1983: 211–12). The preference here is for capturing the complexities of social situations through the use of multiple theories, which provide potentially competing explanations needing adjudication, multiple methods of research and multiple sources of data. Second, enthusiasts for unobtrusive methods 'assume noise is rare' (Webb and Weick 1983: 212). In other words, much of what we see around us can be considered as a potential source of data. Such data should not be discarded out of hand even when at first sight they seem to be trivial, perplexing or out of the ordinary. A third principle is that 'investigators believe in amortization' (Webb and Weick 1983: 213). The assumption is that data, no matter how they are generated, can have more than one purpose and can be put to more than one use. Data obtained opportunistically should not be seen as inherently inferior to data designed for a particular purpose. Fourth, those committed to the use of unobtrusive methods 'find foolishness functional' (Webb and Weick 1983: 213). What Webb and Weick have in mind here is the importance of being able to reflect on research problems in an imaginative, playful, even fanciful, way. Such reflection serves, as they put it, to 'generate novel inputs and permit people to recognize and break the singular focus toward a problem in which they had persisted' (1983: 213). Fifth, unobtrusive measures require the researcher to 'ponder the variance rather than the mean' (1983: 214). If one measures some phenomenon, a focus on how it is distributed can be as useful as an inspection of a typical case. Webb and Weick add that the absence of variance can in some cases be theoretically significant. For example, power in an organization can be indexed by the degree to which some within it have less discretion than others. Finally, 'investigators use expectancy as a control', that is 'sophisticated and successful use of unobtrusive measures requires that investigators lay out in advance what they expect to find so that the surprise when they don't find it is visible and documented' (1983: 214–15).

There is in this a strand of what Gouldner (1973) calls 'methodological romanticism'. It is impossible here to do justice to Gouldner's complex argument about the multifaceted influence of Romanticism on the social sciences. For present purposes, what is important are his observations on how Romanticism affected the way in which social scientists think about data. First, Romanticism encouraged an 'open' conception of data. Faced with the disappearance of peasant culture under the impact of industrialization, writers in the German Romantic tradition undertook direct observation of rural life. In doing so, they extended the scope of social research to encompass those previously thought of as 'low, indecorously deviant, and worthy only either of contempt or neglect' (Gouldner 1973: 351). The idea that nothing social escapes the purview of the social scientist was fostered in this way. There are, of course, other less Romantic influences that have also encouraged an open conception of data; the application of random sampling methods to the selection of respondents is an obvious example (Marsh 1985). Romanticism, however, did not simply widen the scope of what might be studied. In true Romantic manner it encouraged a particular *sensibility* towards data. Gouldner identifies three aspects of this sensibility. First, the Romantics blessed 'the ordinary, everyday world with the pathos of the extraordinary'. Ordinary, mundane things, Gouldner goes on, 'were to be rescued by viewing them from a perspective that endowed them with new and enhanced value, rather than being routinized, ignored or thingafied' (Gouldner 1973: 331). Webb and Weick's assumption that 'noise is rare' invokes a concept – signal-to-noise ratio – from modern electronics. Nevertheless, the contention that data can be found anywhere and everywhere, even in dustbins, has a Romantic cast to it. A second aspect of methodological Romanticism is a preference for solutions to research problems which rely on imagination, insight or vision rather than standardized procedures. The slogan 'foolishness is functional' trades on just such a preference. Foolishness helps, for example, to spark and maintain interest in a research topic. More significantly, it aids the development of novel analytic perspectives and counters what Webb and Weick regard as a 'preoccupation with rational models' on the part of researchers (1983: 213). Notice how the slogan 'foolishness is functional' is premised on an incongruity. A third strand of methodological Romanticism is a fondness for the grotesque. We tend today to associate ideas of the grotesque with monstrosity. (James (1994: 80), for example, points to how popular tradition surrounding the monster in Mary Shelley's *Frankenstein* increasingly focused on his size and physicality.) More properly, the term refers to the juxtaposition of *incongruous* elements. As Gouldner notes, imagination in the social sciences is often taken to arise out of incongruity, from the analyst's ability to shift from one perspective to another or to juxtapose in a meaningful way seemingly incompatible elements. Many of Webb *et al.*'s examples provide an ingenious bridging of the commonplace and the significant. On the one hand, the populations and settings that figure in these examples are immediately recognizable. (Even those of us who have not bought jade or played baseball can identify the situations described as instances of more prototypical encounters.) On the other hand, although the measurements and instruments used have a rather humble quality, they are heavily consequential for the analytic purposes of the investigator. Moreover, to the extent that they encourage the reader to respond with 'Why didn't I think of that?', the various examples celebrate the ingenuity and imagination of those investigators.

It would be a mistake to overemphasize the Romantic elements in Webb and Weick's account. There seems to be some contradiction between an opportunistic, data are where you find them, stance and the principle of using expectancy as control, setting out what you expect so that your surprise registers when you don't find it. Moreover, although Webb and Weick stress that expectancy comes from eclecticism, they tend to restrict their examples to variability in distributions. Might not a more systematic, taxonomic strategy be a better approach to generating unobtrusive measures? The generative taxonomy proposed by Webb *et al.* (1981) takes the form of a large (7 × 13) matrix. Specific unobtrusive measures are located in relation to the two dimensions of the matrix. One of these dimensions is the characteristic the researcher wishes to investigate. Webb *et al.* suggest the following categorization. In relation to a particular characteristic a researcher is likely to want to know (i) the *probability* of its occurrence; (ii) its *capacity* to perform some task or role; (iii) its social *value*; (iv) the *sentiment* attached to it; (v) the *affective states* surrounding it; (vi) its degree of *category membership*; and (vii) its standing on some *trait* or dispositional dimension. The second dimension of the taxonomy refers to features of unobtrusive measures that provide a basis for making inferences about the characteristic of interest. Webb *et al.* suggest that 13 features of a characteristic can be measured: (i) *frequency*, how often something occurs; (ii) its *magnitude* or size; (iii) the degree of *latency*, or time taken for some subsequent action, event or consequence to take place; (iv) the degree of *resistance to change* associated with the characteristic; (v) the degree of *functional smoothness* or ability to perform skilfully associated with the characteristic; (vi) the level of *association* those who possess the characteristic have with socially similar or dissimilar others; (vii) the *acquisition* of things of value (a measure of interest); (viii) the *consumption* of valued goods (a measure of liking); (ix) the willingness to expend *effort* (a measure of interest); (x) the *inappropriateness* of responses (a measure of hidden characteristics); (xi) *bias* or the degree of divergence from expected standards; (xii) *cognitive articulation*, the ability to make more or less fine discriminations between different objects; and (xiii) the *revelatory*, the extent to which traces divulge information about characteristics.

There are some immediately obvious problems here. Although Webb *et al.* stress the importance of multiple methods, most of the categories they describe seem to involve only single measures. Webb *et al.* acknowledge that the generative taxonomy is hardly elegant; some of the categories overlap, and the dimensions they present do not have a clear logical structure. In addition, it is not clear what relationship there is, if any, between the generative taxonomy and the typology of data sources Webb *et al.* originally set forward. The characteristics Webb *et al.* (1981) list are primarily concerned with the analysis of performances, dispositions, affective states and (marginally) social relationships. It is not obvious whether these categories are relevant only to certain areas of social psychology or are meant to have general applicability. Presumably those with other disciplinary, or even subdisciplinary interests, might produce a different set of features. Sociologists, for example, might prefer to focus on acts, activities, meanings, participation, relationships and settings (Lofland 1971: 14–15). It would also seem appropriate to distinguish characteristics in relation to some level of scale. Is the characteristic to be assessed, in other words, at the individual, group, organizational, societal or some other level?

While it is relatively easy to fit examples from Webb *et al.*'s work into the taxonomy, it is not clear how much *independent* generative power the taxonomy has. In fact, the idea of a generative taxonomy sits uneasily with other aspects of Webb *et al.*'s work. It is difficult, for example, to reconcile a taxonomic approach with Webb *et al.*'s emphasis on the imaginative and opportunistic use of data. Indeed, it is instructive in this context to look at the list of exemplars of unobtrusive measures Webb *et al.* provide at the beginning of both editions of their book. Traced back to their original source, there is often little information about how the measure was generated. Some of the examples (including the famous hatching chicks) derive from anecdotal reports and, as is common in published work (Merton 1957), authors usually dwell more on their findings than on how the data were generated. In other cases, however, it is hard to avoid the conclusion that often the measures used simply reflect expedience and/or what was available to hand. It seems, then, that suitable sources of data cannot simply be 'read off' from theoretical concerns; they have to be found by means of a directed search. Another way to put this is to say that the generation of unobtrusive measures involves the use of heuristics. Heuristics are rules of thumb that help to increase the probability of solving a problem, typically by providing methods for 'eliminating unfavourable solutions, narrowing down the search space, [and] breaking complex problems into subproblems' (Lamb 1991: 102–16). A close reading of Webb *et al.*'s work suggests that underpinning their discussion of various data sources are a set of implicit heuristic strategies for finding data sources relevant to a particular research problem. This is perhaps seen more clearly if their (passive) typology of data sources is recast into a (more active) classification of modes of data acquisition. This means that, instead of focusing on physical traces, observation and documents, one should ask for a given social context what data can be *captured*, what can be *found* and what can be *retrieved*.

According to Dabbs, proponents of unobtrusive measures tend to assume that 'entities move through time and space and through social and physical encounters, all the while shedding signs that, taken cumulatively, reveal their true nature' (Dabbs 1982: 34). One important set of signs are 'ephemeral traces', as Dabbs calls them. Such traces 'make up much of the ordinary behavior of people and organizations'. However, 'unless someone or something is there to make a record, the ephemeral trace is lost' (Dabbs 1982: 34). Ephemeral traces need to be captured, in other words, if they are to be of use to the social scientist. (Used in this sense, the term 'capture' need not imply a pre-existing, external 'objective' reality; merely that if some things are not 'frozen', they disappear.) Identifying ephemeral traces relevant to a particular research problem is highly dependent on theoretical and cultural knowledge. In many cases researchers will draw directly on this knowledge. In other cases, the overwhelming 'naturalness' of such knowledge is precisely the problem. Human beings have a well-developed cultural sense. They also have a perceptual apparatus highly sensitive to interactional cues. As a result they often apprehend and understand the activity of others in ways they find difficult to articulate. The basic heuristic is therefore to ask: What features of some setting or situation can be made perceptually, normatively or culturally problematic and how? In the social sciences three strategies have generally been used to problematize social situations. These might conveniently be labelled 'perceptual shift', 'decentring' and 'disruption'. Perceptual shift involves altering the normal way in which we perceive human activity, perhaps by changing the time base for observation or the depth of focus through which some setting is viewed. This strategy often depends on shifting the capabilities of normal human perception. Decentring involves *explicitly* attending to those interactional or communicative features of settings or situations that are normally only *implicitly* apprehended. A conscious shift from focusing on the content of speech to paralinguistic features, such as pauses, pitch, intonation and the like, is an obvious example. Disruption involves altering a social situation in some way so that its underlying features are revealed.

Ephemeral traces, which need to be captured, can be distinguished from physical traces that are normally found *in situ*. The basic question in considering the generation of physical traces is as follows: 'How are the physical properties of objects inadvertently implicated in their social use?' In part, the answer Webb *et al.* give to this question is a quasi-economic one. They tend implicitly to see research problems where the use of physical traces is appropriate in terms of production, consumption, demand and supply. More specifically, a basic heuristic they employ is to ask in effect, 'What production is implicated in consumption?' It is this that triggers their interest in garbage, litter and so on. They also ask the converse question, 'What consumption is implicated in production?' However, in practice they resolve this by asking the somewhat different question of how demand is naturally calibrated. Doing so leads them to consider the frequencies to which car radios are tuned, the size of suits of armour, the abrasion of surfaces and so on. Related to all of this is a somewhat different heuristic: 'What performative opportunities do objects offer?' This allows one to consider graffiti, inscriptions and the like. Webb *et al.* distinguish between **running records**, on the one hand, and what they refer to as episodic and private records on the other. A heuristic for identifying data from running records relevant to a given research question is to ask: 'At what points and in what ways in society is information logged about social behaviour?' The same heuristic can be applied to identifying at least some kinds of **episodic records**, given their largely bureaucratic character. More generally, however, although Webb *et al.* (1981: 193–4) recommend that greater effort be put into identifying and locating potential caches of data, to use Glaser and Strauss's (1967) term, they do not suggest ways of doing so. Relevant heuristics, in other words, must be found elsewhere. In information science the growth of the World Wide Web in particular has encouraged renewed interest in how researchers 'forage' for sources of documentary data (Cronin and Hert 1995). If one takes this metaphor seriously, an appropriate heuristic might be to treat repositories as field sites, and to adapt to documentary work the sampling strategies typical of field research (Glassner and Corzine 1982; Helmericks *et al.* 1991). Drawing on procedures advocated by Helmericks *et al.*, documentary sources might be regarded as research 'sites', and their producers as 'informants'. Using personal knowledge, knowledgeable others and published guides, procedures analogous to snowball sampling can then be put in train. When no more likely sites are generated, sampling stops.

Conclusion

Although the defects of self-report methods can be exaggerated, a case can be made that social scientists rely too heavily on direct elicitation of information

from research subjects. The presence of the researcher potentially has consequences for the quality of responses, typically shaping them in socially pat-
terned ways. In addition, research based on self-report is vulnerable to the
social factors affecting both the availability of research participants and their
willingness to respond to researchers' questions.

Unobtrusive methods commend themselves as ways of producing data
complementary to direct elicitation methods, but with different weaknesses
and strengths. In their own right unobtrusive methods can also provide an
alternative where direct elicitation is, for various reasons, difficult or
dangerous. A problem is, however, that existing approaches to the generation of unobtrusive measures, whether orientational or taxonomic in character, are unsatisfactory. It might be more appropriate to develop heuristic
strategies for identifying ways of generating non-reactive data for specific
research situations.

In the preface to the 1966 edition Webb *et al.* record that *Unobtrusive
Measures* emerged only late on as a title for the book. While in preparation
it had a variety of working titles including *Oddball Research*; for a time it
was even cryptically called *The Bullfighter's Beard* (Webb *et al.* 1966: v). (It
seems that the length of a bullfighter's stubble is an unobtrusive measure of
anxiety, since his trembling hand on the morning of the bullfight ensures that
he doesn't shave too closely.) Although there is no necessary inconsistency
between humour and academic writing, humorous writing in the social sciences is sparse. Where it exists, such writing has tended towards the ironic,
sometimes with a sarcastic or satirical edge, or, perhaps less commonly, has
taken the form of parody (Jones 1980; Fine and Martin 1990; Fine 1994).
Such humour as *Unobtrusive Measures* possesses derives from its irreverent
tone. But this is irreverence with a purpose. There is in *Unobtrusive
Measures* a rather mild echo of the critique of 'abstracted empiricism'
offered by C. Wright Mills (1959). Mills challenged what he saw as the
growing dominance of a new kind of research practitioner, the survey tech-
nician, who was completely at home with the technical requirements of the
research process but who was devoid of imagination and creativity. Webb *et
al.* scarcely go very far in this direction. Nevertheless, there is a clear underlying tone in *Unobtrusive Measures* that implies that much existing work is
pedestrian, routine and lacking in imagination.

It can be argued that unobtrusive methods are valuable in themselves
because they encourage playful and creative approaches to data, under-
mining in the process the tendency to rely on particular research methods
because they are familiar or routine rather than appropriate to the problem
in hand. What this further implies is an eclectic, not to say ecumenical,
stance towards data collection. Social scientists can find useful data sources
by drawing on other methodological traditions. Physical trace data require
one to think like a forensic scientist. Data capture methods reflect the sen-
sibilities of the ethologist. Documentary research draws on the insights of

historiography and cultural studies. All of these things, Webb *et al.* contend, should be part of the normal methodological repertoire of the social scientist.

Recommended reading

Webb, E. J., Campbell, D. T., Schwartz, R. D. and Sechrest, L. (1966) *Unobtrusive Measures: Nonreactive Research in the Social Sciences.* Chicago, IL: Rand McNally. (The original, now classic, treatment of unobtrusive methods in social research. Engagingly written, and full of unusual examples.)

Webb, E. J., Campbell, D. T., Schwartz, R. D., Sechrest, L. and Grove, J. B. (1981) *Nonreactive Measures in the Social Sciences.* Dallas, TX: Houghton Mifflin. (*Unobtrusive Measures* revised, updated and retitled.)

Sechrest, L. (1979) *Unobtrusive Measurement Today.* San Francisco, CA: Jossey-Bass. (A collection of theoretically oriented articles on the generation and use of unobtrusive methods in a variety of fields and disciplines.)

Webb, E. and Weick, K. E. (1983) Unobtrusive measures in organizational theory: a reminder, in J. Van Maanen (ed.) *Qualitative Methodology.* Beverly Hills, CA: Sage. (A succinct statement of the 'orientational' approach to the generation of unobtrusive measures, with a particular focus on organizational research.)

Kellehear, A. (1993) *The Unobtrusive Researcher: A Guide to Methods.* St Leonards, NSW: Allen & Unwin. (Short, student-friendly introduction to unobtrusive methods. Good on practicalities but rather weak on analytic topics.)

2 Found data

Webb *et al.* describe a wide range of possible measures involving the use of what they call 'traces'. These are physical remnants produced by erosion of the environment or accretion to it (Webb *et al.* 1966: 36–46). Wear on floor tiles, for example, is an **erosion measure** that denotes the frequency of use of particular areas. The amount of litter left behind in a particular place is, on the other hand, an **accretion measure**. From a substantive rather than a methodological point of view, Webb *et al.* produce through their interest in traces what might be thought of as a sociology of the inadvertent. Although at first sight, perhaps, unpromising territory, close scrutiny of the things we do inadvertently has a long and distinguished history in the social sciences. Freud ([1901] 1975) explored slips of the tongue and other 'parapraxes' in *The Psychopathology of Everyday Life*. In sociology, Erving Goffman, who, as Randall Collins (1980) points out, was a student at precisely the time Freud was at his most influential in North America, catalogued the interactional dynamics of social slips, lapses and embarrassing situations (see, for example, Goffman 1956a). For both Freud and Goffman, the inadvertent is, of course, anything but. It points back to the unconscious in the case of Freud or, for Goffman, to the precariousness of the interaction order. Webb *et al.* take inspiration neither from Freud nor from Goffman. Instead they look to a fictional character – Sherlock Holmes. This is the Holmes who looks at the scratches on a pocketwatch and deduces that its owner is a drunkard, for only the unsteady hand of a drunkard would slip while winding a watch. Another way to view this is to say that, methodologically, the emphasis in Webb *et al.*'s work on traces is on the forensic. It is therefore not surprising that they also draw on the most forensic of social sciences, archaeology.

Erosion measures

If one asked people who have read Webb *et al.*'s books to give an example of an unobtrusive measure, most would probably mention floor tiles. This relates to an exhibit showing live, hatching chicks that was set up at the Chicago Museum of Science and Industry. So popular was the exhibit that the vinyl floor tiles around it needed to be replaced about every six weeks. Floor tiles in other areas of the museum lasted for years without needing to be replaced. This is a rather vivid example of an erosion measure. In a gymnasium the popularity of various pieces of apparatus might be judged from the amount of chalk consumed at each (Bird 1976). Another such example is the use of smudges, finger marks, turned-down pages and the like as an index of the popularity of library books, or sections in books (Webb *et al.* 1966: 37–8). Interested in the effects of fads of various kinds, Simón (1981) tried to measure the impact of the film *Jaws*. Released in 1975, the film deals with the hunt for a gigantic shark that terrorizes the inhabitants of a seaside resort. Counts of the date stamps on books about sharks borrowed from a public library showed a substantial increase in borrowings in the wake of the film. Simón also records that sales of marine curios such as sharks' teeth, magazine articles about sharks, and visits to museum exhibits dealing with sharks all increased following release of the film.

Although the examples are generally well known, measures based on actual physical erosion are comparatively rare in social research. Denzin comments, 'Perhaps of more sociological relevance is the analysis of the erosion and depletion of critical resources and objects in locales through which particular populations pass' (Denzin 1970: 262). Leaflets in different languages at tourist sites might be monitored to see those that are used most. In a similar way, the rates at which different kinds of postcard on a display are depleted might say something about tourist perceptions of the place they are visiting. Variations in stocks of paper handkerchiefs and cough medicine in a campus shop might be correlated with class records to see how far student attendance is being affected by epidemics of colds or flu without the need to inspect medical records. In terms of depletion, Denzin partly also has in mind pilferage. The presence in university residences of road signs, pub memorabilia and (if P. G. Woodhouse is to be believed) policemen's helmets might indicate the presence of a drink-fuelled or sports-driven student subculture. In many contexts – hotels, restaurants, workplaces and so on – small items are purloined by customers and staff alike. Bouchard (1976) suggests looking at rates of pilferage in hotels to see how they vary by the composition of groups of patrons such as conference delegates.

Ley and Cybriwsky (1974b) used an erosion measure to examine the extent to which local-level locational factors affect the commission of deviant acts. They hypothesized that deviant behaviour was more likely to occur in spaces that were not socially claimed, in other words where residents did not operate social surveillance or territorial control. As an indicator they chose the stripping of abandoned cars, since it had the advantage of 'a fixed, enduring and thereby easily recorded location' (Ley and Cybriwsky 1974b: 58). They found all the abandoned cars in one particular inner-city area, and recorded their location. Simply looked at in terms of the spatial distribution, stripped cars seemed to be more or less randomly distributed. However, there is an association between the location of vehicles and the land use around them. Stripped cars were often found on institutional land, on the 'flanks' of buildings with no overlooking doors or windows, or next to vacant buildings or open spaces. Ley and Cybriwsky comment,

> If car-stripping is one manifestation of delinquent or criminal activity, we conclude that this form of behavior does indeed make its own distinctive bid for space, and that this bid is located in zones and at points where space is otherwise weakly claimed and poorly surveilled . . . There are generic locations which encourage criminal activity. (Ley and Cybriwsky 1974b: 65)

Material objects as traces

One can also treat material objects as traces. Webb *et al.* imply that the physical properties of objects – their size, shape and mass – can yield socially relevant information. One innovative example of this is a study by Archer and Erlich (1985) looking at the relationship between press coverage of sensational crimes and sales of handguns. Archer and Erlich were not able to inspect handgun permits held by the local police force. To circumvent this problem, they asked the police to weigh permits for the three months before and after a particular sensational crime. A further innovative use of traces is found in Palmer and Maguire's (1973) study of a mental hospital. Among a very wide range of unobtrusive measures, they looked at the extent to which noticeboards were kept up to date and the volume of mail patients received. Such measures, which are indicative of factors such as morale, treatment regimes, patients' control of their own lives and their links with the wider community, were found by Palmer and Maguire to be related to outcome measures such as rates of discharge from and readmission to particular wards. In many countries needle exchange programmes have been set up to halt the spread of HIV infection among intravenous drug users. Programmes of this kind are difficult to evaluate. It is usually not possible directly to estimate, for example, the extent of needle sharing. Kaplan (1991) describes a study in New Haven, Connecticut, in which distributed syringes were given a unique code number. Users given and receiving syringes were tracked using a unique, non-identifying alias. Returned needles were chemically tested for the presence of HIV. In this way it was possible to obtain reliable estimates of needle sharing, return rates, the amount of time needles spent in circulation and rates of HIV infection.

Perhaps to the disappointment of Webb *et al.* but probably an inevitability nowadays, it seems that the popularity of museum offerings is gauged not by counting worn floor tiles but through videos. A special feature of the National Museum in Osaka is the 'Videotheque' (Omori 1995). This comprises 40 video-viewing booths connected to a control room in which video programmes are stored on optical disks. A visitor entering a viewing booth can choose from nearly 500 programmes on a variety of ethnographic topics. In choosing video programmes, visitors to the museum typically prefer exotic over more mundane topics. The most popular programme is one concerning the Netsilik Eskimo, a choice which reflects, according to Omori, a perception of racial similarities between Arctic peoples and the Japanese. Among the most popular programmes are those dealing with Europe and Oceania, both areas popular as tourist destination among the Japanese. In the case of Europe, programmes dealing with the making of whisky, wine and beer were often chosen, perhaps reflecting consumerist interests.

It is sometimes said that 'money talks'; sometimes what it says is of interest to social scientists. According to Mattera (1985), economists in the late 1960s became puzzled by the unusually high amount of currency in circulation in the United States, despite the rapid spread of financial innovations such as credit cards. A further curious feature of this situation was that a substantial amount of the currency in circulation was accounted for by large denomination bills. Subsequently, Mattera notes, it became fashionable to suggest that the use of such bills reflected in some way the extent of tax evasion, and could provide a basis for estimating the size of the 'underground economy'. Using as data what Scott calls 'circulatory devices' (1990: 13) – coins, stamps, tickets and so on – is hardly new. Interested in ecological processes within the city, pre-war Chicago school sociologists used streetcar transfers as an unobtrusive measure of physical mobility (Bulmer 1984: 153). It also seems that the discovery by archaeologists of coin hoards containing coins from widely dispersed geographical regions has encouraged medieval historians to reconsider the role of trade in medieval Europe (Geary 1986).

Over a 20-year period the archaeologist Nan Rothschild (1981) collected in a more or less haphazard way more than 1000 US pennies (1 cent coins). Being small and low in value, pennies are similar to objects often studied by archaeologists, and Rothschild sought to study them in this manner. As artefacts in themselves the pennies yielded relatively little information. The place of their manufacture could be determined directly from the coins. Wear seemed to be associated with age, with some coins also showing signs of having been used as improvised tools, for example, to open cans. Rothschild notes that the 1 cent coin underwent a change of design around 1959. Before that time the obverse of the coin showed sheaves of corn, an image subsequently replaced by a representation of the Lincoln Memorial in Washington, D.C. At the same time the words 'ONE CENT' became smaller. She speculates that such a change reflects both the declining symbolic importance of agriculture in American society and a concomitant growth in bureaucratic centralization.

The number of pennies in circulation depends on a number of factors. These include economic variables such as the price of copper, inflation, which has made 1 cent coins less useful, for example in vending machines, and the behaviour of hoarders. This last group includes those, like Rothschild herself, who routinely collect pennies without a specific purpose in mind, as well as collectors who hope to realize a profit from the future rarity of particular coins. Despite their rather casual method of collection, the pennies in Rothschild's sample mirrored quite well patterns in the actual production and distribution of pennies. For example, Rothschild's coins, collected in New York, had few pennies from the San Francisco mint. Gaps in the frequency of Denver-minted coins reflected periods when that mint was not in production. The pennies also showed an unusual peak in 1964. Because of a specific decision of the US Mint, coins minted in 1965 bore '1964' as the date. The reason for this was that coins minted in 1964 promised to be rare. They were therefore likely to be prized by collectors, and taken out of circulation. Producing '1964' coins in 1965 helped to avoid this situation. Rothschild suggests that the patterns she found do not fit entirely well with economic theories of production, distribution and consumption. They show that, under certain circumstances, coins have non-economic and in some cases ritual functions.

Quite obviously, archaeologists have learnt much from the burial sites of earlier societies. Burial places also provide data for researchers interested in contemporary societies. Dethlefsen argues that cemeteries reflect the living community that surrounds them 'with the added dimension of controlled chronological depth' (Dethlefsen 1981: 137). Among other topics, the cemetery offers insights into how people view life and death and the spiritual realm, while also indexing more mundane considerations such as status difference and the nature of kin relations. Cemeteries by their nature have a conservative character but one that remains sensitive to wider social and cultural trends. Useful data can be gleaned from the shape and material of grave markers, the pictures, inscriptions and decoration on graves, the size of markers and the layout and location of the cemetery itself. Dethlefsen studied four cemeteries in Florida, each serving areas of differing social composition. While change in rural cemeteries occurred more slowly, as one might expect, in all of these cemeteries it is possible to see discernible trends. Granite became substituted for marble, which itself had displaced slate as the dominant material for gravestones. The shape of stones has changed. The early and ubiquitous 'tablet' style of gravestone gave way early in the twentieth century to more florid styles such as obelisks and 'pulpit'-shaped markers, which in their turn were replaced by rectangular granite blocks as the century progressed. One very obvious trend has been a decline in the volubility of epitaphs. The interring of families in a shared family plot, a practice that grew up in the United States in the early industrial period, declined in the 1920s. Although the custom of burying spouses together became common, the marking of such graves changed with the use of paired gravestones giving way to shared markers. In more modern times the associational involvements of the deceased are sometimes mentioned on a gravestone and the use of non-religious symbolism decorating the grave has clearly increased. According to Dethlefsen, many of these trends are linked to wider social changes. The florid sculptural style of the early industrial cemetery, overly sentimental to modern eyes, reflected a period of 'aggressive experimentation, economic competitiveness and strong family orientation' (Dethlefsen 1981: 154). A decline in the variability of sculptural style beginning in the 1920s seems to involve a retreat from individuality towards more subtle expressions of class differentiation, although this is also a period that saw in the United States a movement towards extravagant gravestones for celebrities.

Accretion measures

One accretion measure, perhaps not for the fastidious, was employed in a public health experiment in the town of Jasper, Indiana. Electric waste disposal units were installed in households in the town. Using a before-and-after design, the volume of the local fly population, and thus indirectly the possible improvement to public health, was measured by counting the number of dead flies on the grilles of cars (Rathje and Murphy 1992: 173). In another automotive example, Webb *et al.* (1966: 39) describe a car dealer in Chicago who, when cars come in for service, has his mechanics note the station to which the car radio is tuned. He then uses this information to place radio advertising with stations popular with his customers.

Graffiti

Webb *et al.* (1981: 21) describe graffiti as the 'example *par excellence*' of accretion data. Abel and Buckley (1977: 16) make a distinction between 'public' and 'private' graffiti. The former are on external surfaces – the outer walls of buildings, fences, bridges, railway carriages and the like. Private graffiti are typically found in places such as toilet cubicles. Various aspects of graffiti can be studied (Blake 1981). Relatively understudied are the materials and techniques used to produce a graffito; has it been chiselled, scraped, written or painted? (Technically, but probably pedantically, graffiti should be considered an erosion measure when they have been scraped or gouged on a surface, but an accretion measure when drawn, painted or sprayed.) How graffiti are made has implications for their survival and for their dating. Materials and techniques might also in themselves index social and technical change, as the popularity of felt-tip markers and spray cans might suggest. A second area of interest is the various forms graffiti take: slogans, limericks, poems, solicitations, denunciations and so on. Perhaps most widely studied has been the content of messages. Blake (1981) distinguishes three different categories of content. The first he calls 'immortalizing', the inscription of names, dates, institutions, home towns and the like. Blake's second category are 'romanticizing' graffiti, 'testimonials and revelations of romantic love' (1981: 89) such as 'John loves Mary' and the like. Finally, Blake suggests one can find what he calls vulgar statements using (mostly abusive) 'sexual, scatological and phenotypical terms' (1981: 89).

Blake (1981) focused his analysis on the ethnic content of graffiti appearing in men's toilets at the University of Hawaii. For the most part such graffiti consisted of abusive slurs directed at particular groups. Typically, graffiti of this kind make invidious comparisons between different ethnic groups, often accusing the targeted group of sexual and/or mental inferiority. Nonwhite groups, according to Blake, are represented as being effeminate. Whites, on the other hand, are characterized as being 'dumb' (stupid), or are alternatively depicted as garrulous, tricky or sexually aggressive towards other groups. Blake notes that in some cases slurs directed at non-white groups are erased or have further graffiti appended to them designed to disassociate other whites from the original insult. These amendments sometimes abuse the original graffitist. Blake compared the frequency with which particular groups are mentioned in graffiti against census data. The proportions of messages mentioning whites and Japanese are broadly in line with the proportion of each group in the population. Certain groups, the Chinese and Filipinos for example, are mentioned rarely. Blake takes this to indicate that the lines of greatest racial tension in Hawaii lie between whites and Japanese Hawaiians. Graffiti typically appears on public property, in parks and playgrounds, on buses and in schools. Blake notes, however, that in Hawaii ethnic slurs appear only in the private spaces that occur within public properties, specifically toilets. He suggests that their restriction to these spaces reflects the normative unacceptability of uttering racial epithets in public in Hawaii. At this point he draws a parallel with joking behaviour. Apparently in Hawaii it is unacceptable in mixed groups for whites to make jokes at the expense of other groups. Members of other groups can, however, direct abusive remarks towards themselves in such situations, and often do so as a way of relaxing ethnic boundaries. According to Blake, 'This pattern suggests that ethnic graffiti tend to constitute a White medium for asserting ethnic messages in this land of racial aloha' (1981: 98).

Graffiti have been studied as clues to the social preoccupations of young people. Wales and Brewer (1976) examined graffiti in the toilets of four high schools in what they describe as a 'conservative Midwestern city'. Schools reflected the social and racial composition of the areas they served. Although a number of previous studies have suggested that males are more prolific writers on walls than females, Wales and Brewer found much more graffiti in women's toilets than in men's toilets. Graffiti produced by females tended to be 'romantic' in character as opposed to the sexual or scatological graffiti produced by males. However, for both males and females, sexually oriented graffiti increased as the socioeconomic level of the area served by the school rose. Only one school produced a large volume of graffiti dealing with racial matters. Interestingly, in the light of Blake's findings, at the time of the study this was the only racially mixed school.

In an interesting study, Klofas and Cutshall (1985) examined graffiti left on the walls of an abandoned correctional facility for male juveniles. One feature of this institution when it had been operational was that boys were systematically moved during their stay to rooms on different corridors. As they moved in this way, the conditions in which the boys were housed became progressively less severe. Klofas and Cutshall note that the amount of graffiti per room decreased corridor by corridor, and that the content of the graffiti changed. A high proportion of the graffiti in the initial corridor contained personal identifiers. Klofas and Cutshall suggest that this might indicate attempts by the boys to assert and maintain their identity within an institutional context that threatened to strip it away from them. They also note that the proportion of romantic messages progressively increased from the earlier to the later corridors, perhaps reflecting a way of coping with incarceration. Graffiti dealing with political issues, broadly defined, were most prevalent in the middle corridors. Perhaps, Klofas and Cutshall speculate, this was the point during their incarceration when boys were most likely to come into conflict with staff.

In Kingston, Jamaica, between 1976 and 1982, graffiti threatening dire consequences to intruders demarcated areas inhabited by different groups who were locked into fierce political faction fighting (Eyre 1984). In a similar way, street gangs in inner-city Philadelphia use graffiti to mark their territory (Ley and Cybriwsky 1974a). In general, the incidence of graffiti bearing the name of the gang increases the nearer one comes to the core of the gang's territory. The distribution of graffiti also reflects the relative strengths of particular gangs. Graffiti associated with a strong gang might appear in the territory of a weaker gang, but not vice versa. However, some territories are contested. In these places, not only are graffiti from different gangs found, but the graffiti themselves often display hostile slogans directed at rival gangs. According to Ley and Cybriwsky, there is some evidence that areas marked in this way are also sites within which clashes between gangs have taken place. Gang graffiti were uncommon in a middle-class area next to the area Ley and Cybriwsky studied. This area was targeted, however, by 'graffiti kings' not associated with a gang. Each has a distinctive signature and often their work is found on public structures such as bridges. Graffiti kings derive status from their ability to mark places that might ordinarily be considered inaccessible. Ley and Cybriwsky suggest that graffiti of this kind might represent artistic ambitions for which there is no legitimate outlet in the inner city.

Graffiti of a particular kind are a feature of what Ley and Cybriwsky call 'the defended neighbourhood'. These are relatively homogeneous areas with a clear identity that have wide informal recognition as a distinct spatial unit. Ley and Cybriwsky note that in North America the boundaries of such areas are often the focus for ethnic or racial tension. The graffiti in Fairmount, the area of Philadelphia Ley and Cybriwsky studied, displayed affirmations of local identity, such as 'Fairmount rules', coupled with racial epithets or obscenities directed at neighbouring areas. Ley and Cybriwsky found graffiti of this kind most prevalent in the 'zone of tension', the area bounding a neighbourhood of increasing black settlement. This area was a site in which newcomers were racially harassed and in which racial clashes had taken place. They suggest that graffiti might be used predictively to identify the likelihood of such behaviours.

Although territorial markings such as graffiti have generally been seen as attempts to control territorial encroachment by others, Greenbaum and Greenbaum (1981) argue that some forms of territorial marking might serve to facilitate, rather than hinder, social interaction. In a mixed method study, Greenbaum and Greenbaum focused on the ways in which householders in a Slavic-American area of Kansas City personalized the exterior of their home, for example through the use of pot plants or porch furniture or through garden maintenance or the weeding of the pavement immediately outside. Even after controlling for factors such as home ownership and long-term residence, indicators of personalization were related both to ethnic identity and to levels of neighbourhood sociability.

Hermer and Hunt have drawn attention to what they call 'official graffiti' (1996). What they have in mind is the proliferation of regulatory signs produced by official and other bodies. For them, the 'prohibition circle' is the paradigmatic emblem of official graffiti. This instantly recognizable and internationally ubiquitous icon features a red circle with a diagonal slash across it superimposed on another symbol representing the prohibited activity. Thus the graphic of a lighted cigarette surmounted by a prohibition circle denotes, of course, 'No smoking'. Hermer and Hunt distinguish five types of official graffiti: prohibitions, warnings, directions, advisories and alerts, and watches. Prohibitions include 'No smoking', 'Do not litter' and the like. Warnings include notices on packets of cigarettes pointing to the health hazards associated with smoking, or to the danger of suffocation associated with plastic bags. Directions include, for example, a sign saying 'Eight items or less' above a supermarket checkout lane. An example of an advisory would be a sign in a woodland area during hot weather indicating the level of fire danger. Watches are notices that point, for example, to the presence of video surveillance or a Neighbourhood Watch scheme. Hermer and Hunt point to the diffusion of such graffiti out of the public sphere into quasi-public and private spheres, as when advisories are increasingly found on packaging of consumer products. Drawing on Foucault's work, Hermer and Hunt argue that official graffiti represent a form of 'governance at a distance', apparently at the behest of what they call 'absent experts' (1996: 466). By seeming trivial and 'normal', official graffiti in fact represent a form of hegemony that has deeply penetrated all aspects of everyday life.

Graffiti have more overtly political functions. Bushnell (1995) notes that levels of official tolerance of the counter-culture in the Soviet Union could be gauged by the extent and spread of certain kinds of graffiti, such as those on a wall in Moscow commemorating Viktor Tsoi, a popular Soviet-era rock star who died in a car crash. The Tsoi wall, as it became known, echoed previous graffiti memorials to figures such as Mikhail Bulgakov, whose satirical masterpiece, *The Master and Margarita*, had languished unpublished for 30 years. Graffiti quoting particular characters in the novel at a site in Moscow associated with Bulgakov challenged official cultural doctrines. According to Bushnell, however, the rather banal and derivative character of the graffiti on the Tsoi wall can be taken to represent the extent to which the official popular culture of the Soviet era had effectively reached its demise.

Graffiti, the painting of kerbstones, wall murals and what Jarman calls 'quasi-murals', the use of a single painted symbol such as a flag or a slogan, are an important part of political culture in Northern Ireland (Rolston 1987; Sluka 1992; Jarman 1997). In Loyalist areas, for example, kerbstones are painted red, white and blue, whereas those in Nationalist areas receive green, white and orange paint (Jarman 1997: 209–10). (The colours are respectively those of the flags of the United Kingdom and the Irish Republic.) Graffiti and painted kerbstones often function as territorial markers. By contrast, as Jarman points out, murals are often 'hidden away in back streets' (1997: 210). They are directed, in other words, at those to whom the symbols and nuances will be readily understandable. The production, character and iconography of murals on both sides of the political divide have changed over time. The tradition, which apparently dates from the time of the First World War (Rolston 1987), was a predominantly Unionist one until the early 1980s. The fatal and fateful hunger strike begun by Republican prisoners in 1981 generated an explosion of mural painting in Nationalist areas, an activity subsequently emulated to different ends on the Loyalist side. There is some evidence that the production of mural paintings has been 'professionalized'. The work of untrained painters or those with traditional artisanal skills obtained in house or shipyard painting seems increasingly to have been displaced by painters with some degree of artistic training. On both the Republican and the Loyalist sides, shifts in mural imagery point to wider political developments. Following the period of the hunger strikes, Republican murals began to emphasize themes of armed struggle, before giving way to murals reflecting the political role of Sinn Fein and the emergence of Republican electoral politics (Sluka 1992). On the Loyalist side, according to Jarman, traditional images, such as that of the Protestant hero 'King Billy' (William, Prince of Orange, later King William III of England) mounted on a white horse, have declined somewhat whereas images associated with Loyalist paramilitary groups have become more common. Jarman sees the juxtaposition of paramilitary symbolism and traditional symbolism as representing a working-class challenge to the traditional dominance of middle-class Unionism, and a growing sense of Ulster nationalism.

Garbology

Social scientists have long recognized that 'What people have owned – and thrown away – can speak more eloquently, informatively, and truthfully about the lives they lead than they themselves ever may' (Rathje and Murphy 1992: 54). A very substantial volume of research on what people discard has been generated by the Garbage Project. The project, based at the University of Arizona and directed by William Rathje, applies archaeological techniques to the analysis of present-day household waste collected either at the kerbside or excavated from landfills. One obvious application of garbage-based research is in the study of consumer behaviour. According to Rathje and Murphy (1992), people from lower-income areas buy provisions in smaller amounts than do those in more affluent areas, presumably because of the smaller initial outlay involved. In doing so, however, they forgo the longer-term savings possible by buying in larger quantities. It also seems that regular consumption of a particular item is associated with lower levels of food waste. For example, the remains of standard-size sliced loaves of bread are rarely found in garbage. Speciality breads, on the other hand, are wasted in fairly large quantities, perhaps because they are bought for special occasions and not subsequently reused. Rathje and Murphy also record that the amount of beef discarded in household waste tripled (from 3 per cent to 9 per cent) during a period of national beef shortage in the United States. A similar pattern of increased waste was found during a sugar shortage. Rathje and Murphy hypothesize that at times of shortage people buy additional supplies, sometimes in unfamiliar forms which eventually spoil either because they are stored inappropriately or because it is not clear how they are to be used in cooking.

Using garbage as trace data can be a useful way to study sensitive topics. Between 1976 and 1984 the number of condom wrappers found in Garbage Project samples stayed at about the same annual rate. In the years following, however, the numbers found increased appreciably, a possible indication that public health messages about protection against HIV infection had been successful (Rathje and Murphy 1992: 64). Comparing garbage counts with self-reports provides one way of validating survey findings. The method might be particularly useful where it can be assumed that respondents wish to present favourable impressions of themselves to an interviewer. Survey respondents' claims about the levels of sugary and processed foods they eat relative to fresh food and more healthy alternatives are not substantiated by the contents of their garbage cans. Household members, it seems, are rather prone to under-report beer consumption compared with the number of beer cans they discard. Rabow and Neuman (1984) compared survey data on alcohol consumption as measured by the number of empty bottles appearing in garbage cans. By comparison with the direct measure of consumption derived from the garbage can study, the sample survey seriously underestimated consumption. Rabow and Neuman attribute this underestimate to a high refusal rate on their survey, together with its exclusion of teenage drinkers. Interestingly, Rathje and Murphy suggest that proxy reports by a family member on the alcohol consumption of other household members might be more accurate, as judged by bottle and can discards, than self-reports.

Reconstructing the size of a population from its material remains is a common procedure in archaeology. By combining analysis of garbage from particular households with detailed surveys, Garbage Project researchers were able to calculate a multiplier, that is an adjustment factor, that gives a population estimate when applied to the volume of a particular kind of garbage. Discarded plastic was found to provide the best level of prediction. It has also been possible to make age and sex estimates from material such as discarded toys and feminine hygiene packaging. Although it has not been used in this way because of political sensitivities, work of this kind is potentially useful in making corrections for census underenumeration (Rathje and Murphy 1992).

There are a number of problems involved in studying garbage. For example, what finds its way into the solid waste stream is affected by recycling practices. It is, however, possible to make some correction for the extent to which products are recycled. Although they are no longer used because they often ended up as litter, detachable ring-pull tabs from drink cans for a time provided one indicator of recycling (Rathje and Murphy 1992). Tabs were often not recycled along with the cans from which they came. Thus, the extent of recycling could be estimated from the number of tabs found relative to the number of cans. Tabs vary quite considerably depending on the product and where it was produced, effectively allowing estimates of different kinds of beverage consumption. Moreover, because dates for the introduction of particular designs are known, their presence in a landfill can be used to date layers of garbage in the same way that pottery shards, for example, might be used by an archaeologist to date an ancient site. Turning to operational matters, waste products can, of course, be aesthetically challenging.

More importantly, they pose obvious health risks that necessitate the use of protective clothing and appropriate inoculations. (The Garbage Project freezes its garbage. Frozen garbage smells less and breeds fewer maggots. Handled quickly, it can be sorted and counted before it thaws.) One might also need to be wary of physical hazards. A landfill, for example, will have heavy earthmoving equipment moving around it. Attention to safety is as important here as it is on any other industrial site (Kellehear 1993).

Besides such difficulties, ethical problems also arise. Garbage is what Shulman (1994) calls a 'performance vulnerability'. It can reveal aspects of someone's life they might prefer to remain hidden. The apartment building janitors interviewed by Gold (1952) collected and sorted the garbage left by tenants. Janitors often accumulated detailed, sometimes personal, information about tenants from items such as discarded letters. Shulman (1994: 224) records that the private detectives he studied regarded garbage as an important source of information: 'Credit card bills can show where someone had been when they have not been where they were supposed to be. Telephone records can reveal where a relative who has jumped bail is located.' Rabow and Neuman (1984) had a high refusal rate when they asked people whether they would permit their garbage to be sifted, and were eventually threatened with a lawsuit if they persisted with the study. Rathje and Murphy (1992) point out that in the United States examining someone else's garbage potentially constitutes an invasion of privacy given that citizens are protected against 'unreasonable search and seizure' by the Fourth Amendment. It seems, however, that, legally, when garbage is placed in a public thoroughfare to await collection it is deemed to have been abandoned. Nevertheless, the Garbage Project gives guarantees to the communities it studies that nothing of a personal nature will be examined, and that no personal details appearing on discarded items will be recorded.

Finally, Kellehear has pointed to an ethical obligation on researchers to leave some kinds of site undisturbed. Specifically, he suggests that those who study physical objects *in situ*, for example gravestones, should resist the temptation to remove items:

> This ethical issue might seem simple, obvious and needless to say but lots of people, from Egyptians to Australian Aborigines, have lost valuable objects to past researchers. Look and then leave. If you want physical reminders of the objects, photograph them! (Kellehear 1993: 113)

'Controlled' erosion and accretion

It is a small step from recording erosions and accretions naturally to the use of what Webb *et al.* refer to as 'controlled' erosion and accretion measures. In order to provide desired data, materials are deliberately placed in the environment in order to study how they are added to or eroded. One obvious strategy for assessing how far items are removed from a setting is to mark some of them to see how many marked items turn up on a subsequent count. Hayes *et al.* (1975) unobtrusively marked pieces of litter by tearing or creasing items in particular ways, or by using a small ink dot. By counting the number of marked items in collected litter they were able to evaluate the effectiveness of various litter-reduction schemes. McNees *et al.* (1976) devised a system for tagging clothes in a department store. A daily tally of tags against sales receipts revealed the number of items stolen each day. It was then possible to assess the effect of different strategies for reducing shoplifting. In another variant, Bouchard (1976) has suggested adapting for research purposes an informal advertising method much used on American college campuses. A message or solicitation appears on a single sheet of paper, one edge of which is fringed. A contact telephone number is written on each fringe so that people wanting to respond can easily tear it off. The number of missing fringes or the number of telephone calls received indicates the degree of interest in the message.

An alternative strategy is to encourage people selectively to discard items that are explicitly designed to reveal information to the researcher. In an experiment to assess how far keeping or throwing away a printed message is likely to be associated with positive or negative attitudes towards the information on it, Cialdini and Baumann (1981) placed flyers supporting different candidates on cars parked outside a polling station. They then counted the relative number of flyers discarded or kept by drivers. The number of flyers kept for a particular candidate was found to be associated with both voting preferences recorded on a survey and with voting behaviour. In a second experiment Cialdini and Baumann found that a similar method used to assess attitudes to contentious campus issues produced data less subject to social desirability effects than direct interviewing. Cialdini and Baumann (1981) suggest that littering techniques provide an easy and effective means of determining attitudes in a nonreactive way. One difficulty, however, is that people holding different attitudes might also have differing propensities to litter. Some thought might also need to be given to the physical design of the item used as an experimental stimulus. There is apparently a size factor involved in littering. Items at least 4 inches in size along at least one dimension tend to be put in bins; items smaller than this often end up as litter (Rathje and Murphy 1992: 197). In addition, researchers will presumably wish to ensure that the litter they produce is subsequently disposed of in an appropriate manner.

Found data: an assessment

Webb *et al.* contend that, 'Physical evidence data are off the main track of most psychological and sociological research' (1966: 52). Trace data, however, embody many of the virtues of unobtrusive measures (Rathje 1979). As

Rathje points out, commitment to the use of trace data tends to encourage a holistic, multi-perspectival approach to research. Traces are ubiquitous, readily available at low cost and easily quantifiable. Gathering trace data causes little or no inconvenience to research participants who are anonymous (indeed in many cases unknown). In some kinds of research – Rathje's studies of disposed garbage are a good example – many traces can be collected simultaneously. Besides these operational advantages, there are methodological benefits. Since traces record the products of actual behaviour, it is possible to avoid the problems of recall or the desire of respondents to present themselves in a socially desirable light associated with self-report methods. Frequently, traces are cumulative, permitting the collection of longitudinal data. This is not to say that trace measures are free of distortion or bias. Those they incorporate, however, are different from those produced by methods such as interviewing, which have the potential to be reactive.

There are some rather obvious disadvantages to the use of trace data. As Rathje (1979) points out, traces produce conservative estimates of behaviour because some activities leave no traces or obliterate those that already exist. Since traces are socially produced they are sensitive to changes in social practice. For example, what one can infer from studies of garbage is affected by social patterns associated with recycling practices. Denzin (1970) points out that physical trace data can take time to accumulate. The nature of physical traces means that the necessary population data that would allow one to calculate a rate for some measure are often unavailable. In addition, it might be difficult to detect the presence of response sets and patterns of selectivity in data based on trace measures. To take an example, in the case of the underground economy in the United States, Tanzi (1982) has pointed out that using the amount of large denomination notes in circulation as a measure is substantially affected by large amounts of US currency held outside the United States.

Traces are 'inferentially weak' (Bouchard 1976). This can be illustrated, according to Bouchard, with reference to a classic example of an unobtrusive measure – the use of floor wear to measure frequency of use. Differential wear can result from the location of facilities such as bathrooms or water fountains. Passage across the floor may be constrained by the arrangement of furniture. Wear is also related to the physical properties of the floor covering itself; vinyl wears out more quickly than stone. In addition, although trace data are rarely contaminated by other kinds of data, in some contexts what is eroded or deposited is not independent of other erosions or deposits. On a worn stair tread, for example, people tend to put their feet on the part of the stair that is already worn, causing it to erode at a faster rate and producing an unreliable estimate of traffic on the stairs (Webb *et al.* 1966: 44). Interestingly, Webb *et al.* (1981) record that the museum floor tiles that provided their original example were eventually replaced by tiles that resisted wear, presumably obviating their further use as a source of data. Because unobtrusive measures are inferentially weak, Webb *et al.* stress that they are best used alongside other methods. Alternatively, they may be appropriate for tracking changes in the magnitude of some activity, even if the level of the activity itself cannot be adequately measured.

Conclusion

As we go through our daily lives we inadvertently scatter remnants of our passage. Just as remnants of the past are of interest to the archaeologist, and the remnants left at crime scenes are of use to the forensic scientist, Webb *et al.* argue that physical traces of various kinds are grist to the social scientist's mill. Traces can be produced by erosion or accretion. The former implies that social scientists become aware of the social correlates of consumption or, perhaps at a more material level, the social meaning of friction. The use of accretion as a measure relies on an understanding of the ways humans are both discarding and hoarding animals. Of course, problems abound in the use of trace measures. It is difficult to draw reliable inferences from traces, and to calibrate measures based on their use. Some traces, of which garbage is the obvious example, have unpleasant or noisome properties. On the other hand, Webb *et al.* remind us that data are all around; given an imaginative cast of mind researchers can see possibilities in garbage, gravestones and the number of squashed flies on radiator grills. The cheapness, accessibility and ubiquity of trace data means that researchers might literally stumble over data more often than we think. In *The Boscombe Valley Mystery* Sherlock Holmes deduces that the murderer is tall, left-handed, walks with a limp, wears thick-soled shooting boots and a grey cloak, smokes Indian cigars through a cigar-holder and carries a blunt penknife. Explaining to Watson that he had derived the description from careful observation of the traces left on the ground around the murder scene, Holmes remarks 'You know my method. It is founded on the observation of trifles.' In the social sciences some sources of data are not so trifling as they seem.

Recommended reading

Rathje, W. and Murphy, C. (1992) *Rubbish! The Archaeology of Garbage.* New York: HarperCollins. (An interesting and informative account of The Garbage Project, and the potential analytic uses of garbage as a source of trace data.)

Gould, R. A. and Schiffer, M. B. (1981) *Modern Material Culture: The Archaeology of Us.* New York: Academic Press. (A collection of articles exploring the application of archaeological methods to the study of modern societies.)

3 Captured data

Simple observation, according to Webb *et al.*, is 'focused on situations in which the observer has no control over the behavior or sign in question, and plays an unobserved, passive and nonintrusive role in the research situation' (1966: 112). Since there is a lack of control over those in the setting, simple observation differs from observation in experimental contexts. In other words, implicitly for Webb *et al.*, simple observation is field observation. To the extent that observation, recording and coding are, as McCall (1984: 265) puts it, 'explicit, preset, and executed more or less contemporaneously', simple observation is different from approaches that depend on the post-coding of film or video records. In its systematicity it can also be distinguished from participant observation methods widely used in sociology. Weick (1968: 363–6) has presented a rather lengthy list of circumstances in which a researcher might consider the use of observational methods. Interview methods, for example, can be inappropriate in studies where research subjects, such as young children, have limited verbal ability, or where potential informants might not have a social vocabulary for answering questions about some kinds of behaviour (Riesman and Watson 1964). Some kinds of activities – sport, performances of various kinds, craftwork and the like – can engross participants in ways that would be disrupted by the intrusion of an interviewer. Settings such as bars or factories with high levels of ambient noise do not always lend themselves to interviewing. Self-report is inappropriate in some cases because analytic interest is focused not on individuals, but on the relationships or interactions between them. Observation might be the only way to capture activities that are fleeting, or where respondents are likely to react to questioning in a strongly defensive way (see, for example, Humphreys 1970).

Simple observation

Webb *et al.* organize their discussion of simple observation around five topics: (i) exterior physical signs, (ii) expressive movement, (iii) physical location, (iv) what might be called '*in situ* conversation', which involves the recording of randomly selected overheard conversations, and (v) behaviour associated with time.

Exterior physical signs

Webb *et al.* describe exterior physical signs as durable symbols that are 'inferred to be expressive of current or past behavior' (1966: 115). Hair is (in every sense of the word) an obvious example. Webb *et al.* also consider under this category such emblematic objects as tattoos, scarification and clothing styles. All of these are regarded as being relatively easy to observe and to possess considerable symbolic importance for individuals, groups and society. Sigelman *et al.* (1990) used photographs from the *Almanac of American Politics* to assess the degree of baldness exhibited by male United States legislators. They then compared their ratings with age-specific norms for pattern baldness among US males. Two-thirds of the legislators were rated as being below the 'baldness threshold' as compared with slightly less than half of the US population as a whole, a statistically significant difference. Sigelman *et al.* then asked a random sample of respondents for their responses to simulated political campaign materials. Photographs of the 'candidate' were systematically varied to show different levels of baldness. The results of this study show little systematic association between baldness and assessments of attractiveness or voting intention. Voters, in other words, do not seem to be biased against bald candidates. Yet, a good head of hair seems to be associated with attainment of elected office. Sigelman *et al.* suggest that their results might point to stereotypes of physical attractiveness among political power brokers.

Synnott (1987) notes that hair is powerfully symbolic because it combines a variety of attributes. The fact that hair is physically attached to our bodies makes it personal, its visibility in the case of head hair and facial hair makes it public, its malleability makes hair easy to shape for symbolic ends, the more so since this is usually (though not always) done voluntarily. The symbolic meaning of a particular hairstyle often takes its character from its opposite; the contrast, for example, between the short hair of men and the long(er) hair of women. Synnott observes that hair is modifiable in four ways. Its length, style and colour can be changed, and it can be added to or removed. Using pictures from the *Illustrated London News*, Robinson (1976) explored fashions in shaving and trimming the beard for the 130-year period between 1842 and 1972. The 1880s were the peak period for facial hair. Between 1880 and 1890 less than 10 per cent of men pictured in the *Illustrated London News* were clean-shaven. From a peak around 1850, sideburns declined precipitately with no appearances between 1915 and 1969, whereupon they began once again to make a limited comeback. The high point for beards was between 1860 and 1900. In this period, more than one-third of those who graced the pages of the *Illustrated London News* sported beards. Moustaches peaked between 1900 and 1925. Robinson found that once a style declined it went into a long period of dormancy. Younger men, it seems, prefer not to adopt any style that still has a hold on the older generation. Increased nutrition and other factors ensure that today physical maturity is reached earlier in human populations than previously. Moller (1987) has attempted to estimate the age of male puberty in pre-modern European societies by drawing on a range of sources – Greek vase painting, letters, diaries and paintings – that indicate the age of first beard growth. This is a useful marker, not only because it is visible, but because no shame or religious unease attaches to it.

Tattooing of the human body has a long history, perhaps even reaching back to Neolithic times (Sanders 1989). Down the ages the practice has been found in many different and diverse societies. Strictly observational study of tattooing is obviously made difficult because markings can be covered by clothing. Besides the personal preferences of the recipient, a number of factors affect the placement of tattoos. Sanders points out that tattoos are technically easier (and thus cheaper) to apply to the arm or leg, than to the torso. Tattooists also have some reluctance to tattoo on the face and hands. Sanders found gender variations in the location of tattoos. In a rather small sample, the majority of men's tattoos were applied to the arms, whereas those of women were applied to areas of the body more easily covered. Studies of incarcerated populations reveal differences in the prevalence of tattoos, their extent on the body, and their thematic content (Webb *et al.* 1966, 1981). The prevalence of tattooing among incarcerated juveniles has been seen as denoting levels of involvement in deviant activities and identification with a deviant identity (Burma 1959; Taylor 1970). Using tattoos to symbolize commitment to a particular group, lifestyle or organization seems, however, to be no longer restricted to marginal populations. Arthur (1997) describes instances where female undergraduates in the United States have had themselves tattooed with the letters designating their college sorority as a way of indicating their commitment to it. This last example suggests that the incidence and visibility of tattoos might also reflect changes in the status of tattooing as a socially organized activity. There are indications, according to Sanders, that a 'tattoo renaissance' has been under way in the latter part of the twentieth century, with younger tattooists seeking to develop and use the tattoo as an explicitly artistic medium. The tattoo renaissance seems to have been paralleled by a growing interest in 'nonmainstream body modification' (Myers 1992), involving techniques including piercing, cutting, branding and burning. Since many of these modifications, according to Myers, are directed to the genital area, modifications are often not publicly observable.

Appearance is closely linked to identity (Stone 1962). As such, clothing is often a symbolic indicator of group membership. Baizerman (1993) notes that whether Israeli men cover their heads and, if so, what they use to do so, gives an indication of their religious and political beliefs. Designs on the *kippa sruga*, a small, crocheted skull cap worn by religious Israeli men, often also provides information about their social or occupational position. Clothing styles often reflect wider social trends. According to Cort (1993), for example, the popularity of scenes from classical Japanese literature on women's outer garments in the seventeenth century reflects the value increasingly placed on female literacy at that time. Although there are clearly difficulties disentangling cause and effect, Rubinstein (1995) has put forward the provocative thesis that changes in female fashion reflect the policy agendas and political styles adopted by US presidents. Discussing a number of nineteenth- and twentieth-century presidencies, she argues that decisive shifts in fashion are more typical of strong presidents. Under weak presidents, popular sentiment rather than political sentiment defines contemporary fashion trends. Comparing the Reagan presidency with that of George Bush, Rubinstein notes that, although Ronald Reagan was a passive president, he had a very clear policy agenda. She sees the colourful and extravagant female fashions of the time as reflecting this free-market and wealth-creation agenda. Under George Bush, however, female fashion styles in various ways expressed vulnerability, reflecting domestic economic uncertainties and Bush's weak political leadership.

The clothing form that carries perhaps most symbolic weight is the uniform. As Joseph and Alex (1972) point out, uniforms have a number of functions. A uniform both differentiates the person wearing it from those out of uniform, and suppresses the individuality of the wearer. The uniform 'certifies' that its wearer has a legitimate function, and is competent to discharge it. It also implicitly enjoins the person in uniform to act in a manner appropriate to the status it denotes. Uniforms, or their lack, often reflect the symbolic meanings that professional groups attach to dress. Pratt and Rafaeli (1997) describe, for example, how the preferences that nurses in a rehabilitation unit had for wearing street clothes or 'scrubs' while working reflected differences in their status, working conditions and professional identity. The simple, modest and austere habits traditionally worn by members of Roman Catholic religious orders subordinated the wearer's identity to that of the order to which they belonged (Michelman 1997). Following reforms introduced into Roman Catholicism by the Second Vatican Council, many nuns abandoned habits in favour of secular dress. This change reflects a shift from a 'mechanistic' organization based on hierarchy, authority and vertical communication towards a more 'organic' form which places greater emphasis on collegiality, participation and horizontal social relations (Hornsby-Smith 1987; cf. Durkheim 1933).

Expressive movement

Even the smallest gestures can be interactionally significant. Webb *et al.* (1966, 1981) give the example of jade dealers who use a customer's pupil dilation to gauge their interest in a particular stone. Behaviour of this kind is, to use a (slightly stretched) chemical metaphor, 'molecular' in character (Weick 1968: 358). In sociology, anthropology and some strands of social psychology, however, much of what is observed is 'molar' in character. That is, the observer is concerned with fairly large, visible, ongoing streams of behaviour or action. Behaviours that signal deference and demeanour are important molar behaviours. In a study in London Norris *et al.* (1992) systematically recorded information on the demeanour of both police officer(s) and citizen(s) in situations where a citizen had been stopped by the police. During an encounter blacks and whites were equally likely to present a calm and civil demeanour towards the police. There were also few differences in police demeanour and action towards the two groups. Norris *et al.* note that their findings do not support competing claims that the police are overtly hostile towards blacks, or that blacks display disrespectful attitudes towards authority as represented by the police. They point out, however, that their observations show blacks to be more than two-and-a-half times more likely to be stopped than whites, with an even greater differential in the case of young males. They conclude, '. . . overall perceptions of police behaviour will remain unfavourable because Blacks feel, for understandable reasons, that they are subject to excessive levels of police surveillance' (Norris *et al.* 1992: 223).

Ridgeway *et al.* (1985) have explored the role nonverbal cues play in the status processes in face-to-face groups. They conceptualize nonverbal behaviours such as eye gaze, touching and verbal latency (the length of time before someone speaks after someone else has finished speaking) as 'task cues' that give information about a group member's actual or potential performance. They link task cues to differences in external status characteristics such as gender, arguing that such differences set up different expectations about the task performance of group members. To the extent that these expectations are confirmed they reproduce the external status differences that first produced them. Manipulating such expectations experimentally, Ridgeway *et al.* found that patterns of eye gaze and verbal latency tend to reflect external status differentials.

Judith Hall (1996) studied intentional non-mutual touching at academic conferences. There was no strong evidence that, as might be expected, higher-status individuals touched lower-status individuals more than vice versa. Neither was there much evidence of gender asymmetry in touching behaviour. Compared with low-status individuals, however, high-status individuals used different kinds of touch such as pats and handshakes, perhaps representing a symbolic bestowal of charisma. In less public settings, the social ambiguities associated with touching can require rather careful interactional management. Heath (1988) observed doctor–patient interaction during medical examinations. While being examined patients typically adopt a 'middle distance orientation', according to Heath. As an examination begins, the patient turns somewhat to the side, slightly lowers the eyelids and looks into the middle distance, apparently not focusing on any particular object. Heath argues that, by turning slightly, patients both make their bodies available to the doctor for examination and allow themselves to monitor what the doctor does with their peripheral vision. The lack of eye contact this produces minimizes self-consciousness and embarrassment.

In a long, complex and subtle article, Katz (1966) explores how laughter is produced. The site of his study was a funhall containing distorting mirrors in a Paris amusement park. Attracting a relatively heterogeneous population, the fixed position of the mirrors which forced people to stop in front of them and participants' ready acceptance of spectators made the funhall ideal for Katz to observe how people interacted with the mirrors. Laughter in the funhall emerges out of a sequence of actions. The person looking in the mirror frequently calls to someone else, often a family member, who can both see the image for themselves and appreciate the first person's interpretation of it. Those viewing the distorted image contrast it in various ways with the presumed normal identity of the person depicted. It is the recognized juxtaposition of image and identity that produces laughter. Katz notes that an initial laugh is sometimes succeeded by a further laugh – what he calls being 'done by humour' – which involves some level of bodily engrossment and is different from the first. This second laugh is not so much at the occasion of the first laugh but rather celebrates 'the achievement of presumptively shared experience' (Katz 1996: 1198). Katz also makes the point that people will change the character of their laugh as they shift their attention from one person to another. In so doing, they take their leave, as it were, of one interaction in order to initiate another.

The meaning of particular expressive movements varies across cultures. Similar gestures have radically different meanings in different countries. For example, the 'thumbs up' gesture that means 'OK' in North America, Britain and Ireland apparently signifies 'money' in Japan, and has obscene connotations in Ethiopia and Brazil (Archer 1997). Waxer (1985) notes that studying nonverbal behaviour in a naturalistic way across cultures can be difficult, if only because of the costs involved in travel. He points to the potential of live television coverage as an alternative source of data on gestures. Waxer examined the nonverbal behaviour of contestants in US and Canadian game shows. (Some shows had to be excluded from consideration because contestants were coached in how they should react to winning and losing.) Despite the many cultural similarities between Americans and Canadians, Waxer judged US contestants to be more emotionally expressive than Canadian participants, and to use different gestural systems to display their feelings.

Physical location

Proxemics is the study of how human beings organize and use space for the purposes of social interaction. What we see, what we hear, what we smell, how we touch and what we feel on our skin, all vary depending on the distance we are from someone else (Hall 1966). Moreover, particular combinations of sensation coalesce at particular distances. At least for the middle-class Americans Hall studied, four distinct zones of distance were distinguishable: intimate distance, personal distance, social distance and public distance. Hall notes that these patterns are not necessarily reproduced in other societies and cultures. He gives the example (Hall 1959) of an American, talking with someone from another country, backing along a corridor, trying to maintain a suitable conversational distance from the other person who kept trying to decrease the distance to one the second person regarded as culturally appropriate.

How people maintain distance from one another and resist intrusion into their own space seem often to have socially significant correlates. Ruback and Snow (1993) observed people drinking at a water fountain in a shopping mall. They looked at situations in which one person stood nearby waiting to drink while someone else was already using the water fountain. Drinkers who were intruded on in this way took longer to drink than those who were not intruded on. Ruback and Snow also found that there was no difference overall in the time blacks and whites took to drink following an intrusion. However, when the race of the intruder was taken into account, a different pattern emerged. Cross-race intruders took significantly longer to intrude than did same-race intruders, with the effect being stronger for whites than for blacks. Following a cross-race intrusion, drinkers stayed significantly longer than they did following a same-race intrusion.

Faced with a disappointingly low response rate on a survey of the effects of living in urban areas, Davis (1975) realized that the problem she was having in fact provided an unobtrusive measure of what she wanted to study. She compared the response rates for two different areas. Each had been built at the same time, had clearly defined boundaries and were broadly matched in terms of socioeconomic status, ethnicity and length of residence. The two areas were quite different, however, in terms of population density; one containing high-rise dwellings, the other single-family detached houses. Interviewers, all of whom were smartly dressed, white, male college students, rated responses in terms of how far respondents maintained physical or social distance from them. Although the differences found were not statistically significant, Davis reports that householders in the high-density area were more likely than those in the low-density area to maintain physical and social distance from the interviewers.

Much influenced by the work of Erving Goffman, naturalistic observational studies suggest that behaviour in public places is underpinned by social processes that serve to maintain an underlying social order. Lyn Lofland (1973) observed people in the waiting rooms of public facilities such as bus stations and airports. She notes that there are clear patterns in the way individuals enter such settings. Very often prior to making an entrance people check their appearance, often smoothing or patting their hair, for example. On entering, they 'take a reading' by sweeping their eyes about the setting, often pausing very briefly to do so. Where entrants did not take a reading in this manner, they tended to enter head down, ignoring everything but possible obstacles on the floor ahead. Those who have taken a reading will either make directly for some point such as a free seat (the 'beeline tactic') or will move towards some visible object in order then to take another 'fix' on where they want to go. Once settled in the setting, Lofland notes, a set of rules typically comes into play which allows the individual to maintain a stance of privacy and social distance. Broadly speaking, facial expressiveness, body contact and eye contact are all minimized, as are intrusions into the space of another. When settings are disrupted, by an untoward incident, say, two further strategies come into play. Either the setting is abandoned altogether or strenuous efforts are made to convey by means of one's demeanour that nothing out of the ordinary is happening.

Wolfinger (1995) notes that considerable skill is required to be a pedestrian. Often when we walk, for example, we manoeuvre quite adroitly to avoid obstacles without breaking stride or concentration. According to Wolfinger, successful pedestrian behaviour depends on being able to trust that others will know and use implicit rules for behaving like a competent pedestrian. Wolfinger collected his data in a novel manner. He commuted to and from his university by rollerskating, dictating fieldnotes about his experiences when he arrived at his destination. Because of the speed, silence and manoeuvrability of rollerskates relative to walkers, Wolfinger often encountered situations where the rules surrounding pedestrian behaviour became problematic, allowing him to explore the role of trust in pedestrian behaviour. Specifically, he analyses the conditions under which he felt the need to offer an apology to a passing pedestrian or where someone else apologized to him. He also explored how people were made to feel uneasy by his presence, for example when he rollerskated behind them. Wolfinger notes that in a small number of cases, contests emerged between him and other pedestrians. In these instances, others indicated by their body language or actions that they wanted to use the space Wolfinger sought to occupy. In each case matters were resolved by one participant having to yield with some small loss of face to the other.

What Hall (1966) calls 'fixed-feature space' – how a particular setting is spatially organized – has important consequences for the nature of the interaction taking place. Sherri Cavan (1966) undertook an observational study of bars in San Francisco. She notes that both the ratio of seats at the bar to those elsewhere and how the seating is configured affect the nature of the interaction of the patrons. In this context, Cavan explores how bar patrons initiate, maintain and terminate encounters with other customers. It was unusual for an encounter to occur when more than three bar stools separated patrons. Once an encounter was initiated, the distance between participants was usually reduced by one person moving to a bar stool that was closer to, though not adjacent to the other. If one patron bought another a drink, however, there was an obligation for the treated person to move to an adjacent stool. In all of this, males moved but females did not. In addition, someone who moved to be adjacent to someone else temporarily relinquished their control over the termination of the encounter. In the 'marketplace bars' studied by Cloyd (1976), men and women used the space differently. Females usually entered the bar in small groups and made directly for a table. They would look around only after they were seated. Men, on the other hand, typically walked around the bar noting where groups of females were sitting, before finding a vantage point from which they could look out over the setting.

In situ conversation

Webb *et al.* (1966) describe early studies of public opinion in which researchers, by locating themselves in public places or thoroughfares (and sometimes more private settings), unobtrusively obtained samples of conversation. Although not altogether lacking in methodological awareness, it is easy to see how such relatively haphazard methods would offer little competition to the use of survey research methods as sources of information about people's opinions and interests. Nowadays, as Chapter 6 intimates, a researcher who wanted to emulate these early studies would probably turn to the Internet rather than the high street as a fruitful, convenient and less ethically fraught source of language behaviour. Gumperz (1972) records that by the 1970s a renewed interest in syntax and semantics had presaged a shift in linguistics away from formal interviews with specially selected informants towards a more naturalistic style of collecting data on language. Labov commended the use of 'rapid and anonymous' data collection (Labov 1972: 210) as a method for studying the public use of language in everyday life. For example, Labov hypothesized that whether New Yorkers sounded the 'r' in words such as 'car' or 'four' was related to their social position. He went sequentially to three department stores which differed in their location, price and clientele. In each he asked a sales clerk to tell him of the location of a department he knew was on the fourth floor. He then privately recorded whether the reply 'Fourth floor' was pronounced with or without the 'r' after the vowel, together with other relevant observational data. The stores showed clear variations in the speech of their staff that were clearly in line with his hypothesis.

Pinch and Clark (1986) undertook a detailed study of 'pitchers'. These are market traders who sell their goods by means of a sales 'spiel'. Pitchers use rhetorical strategies in order to present their goods as bargains. Central to the spiel is a listing process in which the claimed worth of the goods offered is increased incrementally while the price is at the same time decreased incrementally. The aim is to reach a final point of maximum contrast between the two at which the sale can finally be made. (Pinch and Clark suggest that the use of 'rhetorical contrast formulations' is also frequently found in speeches by politicians.) The market pitcher's spiel is only one part of their selling activity. The pitcher must be adept at building a crowd and engaging them in the selling process. Potential customers are encouraged, for example, to come close to the stall. This creates an impression of interest and can make it difficult for people to move away, although the seemingly reluctant might be harangued in various ways to encourage them to leave. According to Pinch and Clark, pitchers have various devices for increasing the likelihood of a sale. Pitchers will sometimes prolong the handing over of goods so that other potential customers can see that sales are being made. Alternatively, they might try to create a sense of urgency or of scarcity by implying that goods must be bought immediately, or that only a small number of people will actually be allowed to buy what is on offer. In some cases, accomplices are used to express interest or to come forward to buy goods as a way of encouraging others to do likewise.

Time-related behaviour

Time is something of a neglected variable in social research. Much existing research on uses of time is based on time budgets, detailed diaries in which respondents keep a record of their daily activities. Time durations, behaviour related to perceptions of time and the patterning of activities over time, are all amenable to observational study. Zerubavel (1987) gives many examples of how time durations serve to indicate the relative importance of activities or the relative status of individuals. The amount of time devoted in the school curriculum to particular subjects reflects social judgements about their value. People of high status typically afford less time to those of lower status, and can make them wait. Being 'always available' to meet the needs of a specific individual is usually indicative of kinship or intimacy. Nash (1990) notes that, before writing, people who use a word processor often engage in computer-related tasks. These might range from reorganizing and tidying files and folders on the hard disk to customizing software (and, one might add, checking one's email). Nash refers to these tasks as 'computer fritters'. Although they can often be justified as 'necessary' or 'urgent', they are in many cases socially legitimated tactics for procrastination. Deadline effects appear in many different contexts. The volume of applications for graduate study, trading on the New York Stock Exchange and the tempo of play in American football games, all rise the closer one gets to the point at which the time allowed expires (Webb and Weick 1983).

For Juliet, the few hours before she can set in train her elopement with Romeo are 'twenty years till then' (*Romeo and Juliet*, Act II, Scene 2). In saying this she expresses the common awareness that subjectively experienced time can be very different from its objective, measured passing. Using newspaper and other accounts in which people talked of time dragging for them, Flaherty (1987) explored 'temporal anomalies', episodes in which the everyday experience of time was made problematic in some way. A variety of situations seem to produce such situations: the threat of violence, suffering or intense emotional experiences, boredom, periods of intense concentration, novel experiences or altered psychological states. Flaherty suggests that experiences of this kind constitute severe departures from daily routine which encourage a recognition that there has been a shift in the nature of social reality. People who experience anomalies tend therefore to intensify the appreciation of time duration, often accompanied by an attempt to translate an experienced duration into clock time. Of the states described by Flaherty, boredom is perhaps the most amenable to external observation, as manifested by the checking of watches, visually inspecting one's surroundings, fidgeting or doodling (Conrad 1997). Additional contextual knowledge might be needed, however, about the absence of alternative involvements (what Conrad calls understimulation) or the thwarting of some goal such as getting to the airport on time.

Social activities vary across the daily cycle. Melbin (1978) makes the intriguing suggestion that there are strong similarities between the characteristics of the night-time hours in the contemporary United States and those of the Western Frontier during the nineteenth century. Despite their reputation for violence and lawlessness, frontier communities were also notable for their hospitality and cooperation. Melbin used a series of **field experiments** to test how far cooperative behaviour could be found during the night hours of a large US city, Boston. The experiments Melbin used were 'modest situations, not emergencies to which one has to respond under stress, but part of the common stream of social events' (Melbin 1978: 13): asking for directions, requesting a brief interview, returning a lost key, or being sociable in an all-night supermarket. Except for the most anonymous condition, returning a lost key, higher levels of friendliness and cooperation were found at night than during the day-time hours.

Sampling in observational research

McCall makes the point that 'observation is always selective and purposive' (1984: 270). The researcher must decide not only what is to be studied, but where and when the observation is to take place. Decisions also need to be made about what the observer should notice and record during the observation, and what can safely be ignored. Put briefly, observation involves sampling. However, as Weick notes, although naturalistic settings are valued as research sites, paradoxically, 'observers are surprisingly careless when they chose a setting' (Weick 1968: 366). Researchers are prone to assume either that the setting they have studied can stand for all such settings, or that it is so unique that generalization is precluded. Matters are further compounded by the problems involved in identifying suitable sampling frames for observational studies, and the lack of procedures for determining how many periods of observation are needed and how long each should be (McCall 1984: 270).

A number of procedures have been developed for sampling the elements to be viewed during an observation. Although their work draws mainly on field studies of animal behaviour, Martin and Bateson (1993) provide a clear and succinct summary of the major procedures for sampling the elements to be viewed during an observation, 'within-episode' sampling as McCall (1984: 271) terms it. According to Martin and Bateson, it is important to make a distinction between sampling rules and recording rules. The former govern which subjects are to be observed, whereas the latter specify how behaviours observed are to be recorded. (The reason for keeping the two distinct is that, as will be seen, recording can involve **time sampling**. Confusion arises if the sampling of time and the sampling of behaviour are conflated.) Martin and Bateson distinguish four kinds of sampling: (a) *ad libitum* **sampling,** (b) **focal sampling,** (c) **scan sampling** and (d) **behaviour sampling**. In *ad libitum* (L = as desired) sampling systematic procedures are not followed. Rather the observer notes down what is visible and potentially relevant. There is thus a tendency to focus on more visible and discernible behaviours. Transitory or subtle behaviours might well be missed. Focal sampling involves observing one sample 'unit' for a specified time, and recording during that time all instances of a number of different categories of behaviour. A unit is often an individual, but does not have to be; it could be, for example, a pair or group of individuals. Focal sampling can be difficult under field conditions because the focal unit can leave the setting or otherwise be out of sight of the observer. Since behaviour out of sight might well be different from that which is readily observable, focal sampling, potentially produces a bias towards the recording of public behaviour. Scan sampling, as the name implies, involves scanning a group of subjects at regular intervals. At a particular moment the behaviour of each individual in the setting is recorded. Typically in these circumstances it is practicable to record only one or two categories of behaviour. Again, individuals or kinds of behaviour that are conspicuous in some way are more likely to be noticed and therefore over-represented. Croll (1986) notes that coding categories need to be fairly simple with this procedure. Otherwise, an observer might not be able to decide what is to be recorded at the appropriate instant. With behaviour sampling some group or setting is observed in its entirety. Each time a particular behaviour occurs, its occurrence is recorded along with a note of which individual was involved. Here, as Croll points out, patterns normally have to be discerned during analysis rather than being immediately obvious to the observer.

Martin and Bateson identify two methods for recording behavioural data: continuous (or 'all occurrences') recording and time sampling. An intensive and thorough procedure, **continuous recording** aims to produce a precise and faithful record of how often and for how long particular behaviours occur, with accurate recording of start and stop times. The method allows the frequency and duration of behaviours to be measured precisely, and it does not involve the loss of information inevitably associated with sampling. Continuous recording methods are therefore particularly important when sequences of behaviour are of analytic interest. On the negative side, because of the demands continuous recording makes on the researcher, it is a burdensome activity. Continuous recording is also limited by the fact that, typically, it is possible when using the method to attend to only a relatively few categories of behaviour.

Time sampling, as the term implies, requires that observations be recorded periodically rather than continuously. The sample points, those instances during which data are recorded, are selected randomly. Time sampling has some advantages over continuous recording. Because observation is carried out only intermittently, the burden of work on the observer is reduced. This in turn allows more categories to be measured and more of the subjects present in the setting to be studied. Where observation is less demanding, it is more likely to be reliable. Martin and Bateson make the sensible point that in some contexts continuous recording can be combined with time sampling used for a different purpose. There are two types of time sampling (Martin and Bateson 1993: 90–8): instantaneous sampling and **one-zero sampling**. In instantaneous sampling (also known as point sampling) the period of observation is divided into short sample intervals. At the instant each sample point is reached, the observer records whether the behaviour of interest is occurring or not. Martin and Bateson point out that the accuracy of instantaneous sampling is related to several factors. Specifically, sample intervals should be short, whereas, relative to the interval, the duration of the behaviour studied should be, on average, long, as should the average time between successive bouts of behaviour. Instantaneous sampling is appropriate where one wishes to record data on behavioural states that can be said to be occurring or not at any given instant. Examples might be the proximity of individuals to one another, postures or the use of gestures. Rare events or those of relatively short duration are not well captured by instantaneous sampling. There is some tendency when using instantaneous sampling for observers to record conspicuous behaviour, potentially biasing results towards visible or obvious behaviours at the expense of those that are more subtle.

When one-zero sampling is used, the observer records at each sample point whether the behaviour of interest occurred or did not occur during the preceding sample interval. Unfortunately, the method introduces systematic bias. Behaviour is recorded no matter how often it appears or for how long it occurs; a behaviour that occurs only briefly is treated as if it had lasted for the whole sample interval. The number of individual bouts of behaviour, on the other hand, are underestimated, since behaviours are counted only as having occurred or not occurred. In addition, events clustered at particular times tend to be undercounted relative to those spaced evenly across the whole period of observation (Croll 1986: 71). Martin and Bateson point out that because of the bias it introduces, one-zero sampling is controversial, and some researchers have counselled against using it at all. They suggest, however, that although care might need to be taken in using one-zero sampling, it can be appropriate in some contexts. In particular, they argue, it is useful in studies of intermittent behaviour where brief periods of activity occur that repeatedly start and stop. Behaviours of this kind are difficult to capture with either continuous recording or instantaneous sampling.

In behavioural sampling there is a need to balance the accuracy of measurement against its reliability and the ease with which measures can be obtained. The former implies short sample intervals, the latter long ones. There is no automatic way of determining how long or how short a sample interval should be. In many cases, Martin and Bateson suggest, choosing an interval will be a matter of trial and error and/or judgement. If a pilot observation is possible, data collected by continuous recording can be retrospectively sampled using different sample intervals. An interval can then be selected which gives a good approximation of continuous recording without introducing too great a level of inaccuracy. Of course, time sampling is most often needed where continuous recording is impractical. In many cases, then, the procedure just outlined will not be possible.

The role of the observer

The role of the observer in systematic observation is essentially a passive one. However, this passivity might be hard to sustain. Weick (1968: 370) makes the point that in many settings passive involvement is suspect; it can actually make the observer conspicuous and subject to challenge. Participants also sometimes try to elicit the observer's involvement. The possibility of this seems greatest where small pre-existing groups are observed. Long ago Simmel (1902) noted that when a third person is added to an existing two-person group, the new member risks being drawn into coalitions and collusive relationships of various kinds, or of being used as a source of information by one of the existing parties about the other.

Reactivity, the extent to which the presence of an observer affects the behaviour of those observed, seems to be a 'common but far from universal' feature of observational studies (McCall 1984: 273). Some kinds of observed behaviour might typically exhibit relatively low levels of reactivity. Reviewing a number of large-scale, methodologically sophisticated British studies, Croll (1986) contends that there is little evidence for gross reactivity effects in observational studies of classroom behaviour. Teachers debriefed after a period of classroom observation typically report few changes in the behaviour of pupils while the observer was present. Although there is less firm evidence about the effect of observation on teacher behaviour, observation does not seem, according to Croll, to have major effects on how teachers operate in the classroom. One obvious factor affecting levels of reactivity is the relationship between the observer and observed. McCall (1984) suggests that the procedures and rules established to guide the observation provide a set of role expectations that govern the actions of both researchers and setting members. Thus, Croll links the absence of reactive effects in the studies he examined to the way in which researchers had developed good working relationships with teachers. McCall (1984) argues that focusing on the role expectations surrounding systematic observation allows researchers to draw on the more extensive literature concerned with participant observation. It also has the advantage of forcing attention towards the social organization of the observational situation. Where multiple observers are used, an understanding of such situations can be fed into training. Rather than simply assuming that the observer will be able to maintain a passive stance, training procedures can be developed that recognize the cross-pressures likely to be operating on observers, and can focus on the possible range and limits of the observer's discretion.

Reactivity is also affected by 'engrossment', the extent to which people are caught up in what they are doing, and by 'habituation', the extent to which they have become accustomed to the presence of the observer. Some writers have suggested that the situational demands facing participants in some contexts are sufficiently engrossing to override a subject's awareness that an observer is present. On the other hand, maintaining a pattern of activity designed to present to the observer a sanitized view of what goes on in a setting requires considerable effort on the part of those observed. In many cases the effort becomes too great after a time or those observed simply forget about the presence of the researcher. One of the observers working for Reiss (1971) noticed that the police officers he observed initially were careful not to use profane language. As the observation went on, however, levels of profanity increased, something he took to be an (unobtrusive) measure of the degree to which they had become used to his presence. Gittelsohn *et al.* (1997), in their study of rural Nepalese childcare and feeding practices, found that in relative terms, levels of reactivity as measured by a variety of indicators decreased over a seven-day observation period. It was also clearly the case that the first day of observation was the most reactive. The effects of engrossment and habituation on research subjects' awareness of being studied can also be seen in Schaeffer's (1995) study which involved installing video cameras in people's homes to record patterns of interaction. For ethical reasons, Schaeffer engaged in a lengthy process of recruiting research participants, informing consent for the project, familiarizing families with the equipment and so on. The camera equipment itself, while unobtrusive, was clearly visible. In short, there was in this study considerable potential for reactivity. However, by the end of the study period, according to Schaeffer, most participants had come to regard the equipment as 'part of the furniture' (1995: 263). In addition, the longer people were in sight of the camera or the more involved they were in what they were doing, the less they were aware of the camera. Schaeffer adds, however, that 'A major secondary factor affecting camera awareness was formal education in, or perhaps more simply contemplation concerning the behavioural sciences – call it sophistication. The more sophisticated the participant the greater was his [*sic*] camera awareness' (Schaeffer 1995: 262).

All of this indicates that it is important, as Reiss (1971) suggests, to assess the reliability of one's observation. In the study of police–citizen interaction he directed, multiple observers from different backgrounds were used. Observers were asked to collect some kinds of data in two forms: one on a checklist, the other as a narrative account. Each source of data was then used as a check on the other. In addition, the social backgrounds of the observer and self-reports of the level of rapport between the observer and the police officers were analysed to see whether there were correlations with the observed data. Observers were also asked to assess the degree to which they thought subjects were acting in an 'unnatural' manner. The observers in Gittelsohn *et al.*'s (1997) study of childcare and feeding practices in rural Nepal rated the overall level of reactivity at the end of the observation. They systematically recorded how far household members interacted with them, and how often they seemed to be shielding what they were doing from view. Where observers judged that there had been a major change in behaviour due to the observation, they attempted to corroborate their judgement with the person concerned after the observation had ceased.

A number of different aspects of reliability can be distinguished. First, is intra-observer reliability high? That is, are individual researchers consistent in their practice (Martin and Bateson 1993: 117), or are they subject to drift (McCall 1984: 273)? The basis for assessment in this context is to judge how far the same observer presented with the same behaviour on different occasions (say on videotape) codes it in the same way. Second, are levels of inter-observer agreement high? Do different observers produce similar results when they observe the same behaviour on the same occasions (Martin and Bateson 1993: 117)? In some settings, notably in education where one might want to compare individual teachers or classrooms, an issue arises related to the stability of observations (Croll 1986). If observations are stable there should be less variation within the observations made of a particular individual, say, than between the observations of all individuals who have been observed. Systematically assessing the effects of observers, settings, situations and observational categories (Medley and Mitzel 1963), it is possible using analysis of variance techniques to assess the ratio of within-individual (or observer) variation to between-individual (or setting) variation.

Field experiments

In natural settings, in contrast to experimental settings, people are usually preoccupied with everyday events and typically assimilate things that happen into their routine (Weick 1968). Thus, it is often possible without too much disruption to introduce into a setting some event whose consequences can be observed. 'Provocation', as Weick calls it, is typically appropriate where the investigator has a prior hypothesis to be tested, rather than where the aim is an entirely naturalistic study. (In these contexts, though, naturally occurring 'provocations' such as accidental disruptions to the setting often yield valuable information.) Massive interventions are also to be avoided since they change the setting in an 'unnatural' way. Instead, the aim should be what Weick calls 'tempered naturalness', making 'subtle changes in natural settings which increase clarity but do not destroy the setting' (Weick 1968: 361). There are a number of reasons why it can be useful to proceed in this way. Some behaviours are relatively rare and might need many hours of observation in an unmodified setting for a large enough number of instances to be recorded. One might also need, as Weick points out, to influence the range of behavioural variation observed or the magnitude of an outcome, to evoke some kind of novel behaviour or to amplify an incipient response.

Weick suggests that one can slightly modify many everyday activities to yield opportunities for observation. For example, Mooney *et al.* (1992) told students either that they would be carrying out an interview with someone who would be an AIDS patient, a homosexual, a cancer patient or another student. Students were then asked to arrange two chairs for the interview. The distance between the chairs was measured. When students thought they would be interviewing an AIDS patient the chairs were placed significantly further apart than was the case for any of the other types of anticipated respondents. In social psychology, there are by now recognizable 'observational genres' that have grown up, for example, around activities such as driving behaviour, help-seeking, the return of lost objects and the provision of goods and services. For example, because it is a rule-bound and goal-directed activity, driving behaviour lends itself to studies of norm violation, frustration, aggression and social distance. One well-known example of naturalistic intervention is the 'lost-letter technique' (Milgram *et al.* 1965). According to Webb *et al.* (1981), the method originated in the 1940s with an experiment to test levels of public honesty: small sums of money were put into envelopes dropped in public places to see how often they would be returned. Perhaps the classic example of the technique, however, is Milgram *et al.*'s attempt to gauge political attitudes in an unobtrusive way using lost letters. Milgram and his colleagues left pre-addressed, stamped letters (*n* = 400) at a variety of locations in New Haven, Connecticut. The addresses on the letters were identical but there were four different addressees: 'Friends of the Communist Party', 'Friends of the Nazi Party', 'Medical Research Associates' and 'Mr. Walter Carnap'. While, overall, nearly three-quarters of the letters addressed to 'Medical Research Associates' and 'Mr. Walter Carnap' were picked up and posted, only a quarter of letters to 'Friends of the Communist Party' or 'Friends of the Nazi Party' were returned. Milgram *et al.* suggest that the method is unobtrusive, naturalistic and convenient. Bernard comments, 'The lost-letter technique has sampling problems and validity problems galore associated with it', adding, 'But you can see just how intuitively powerful the results can be' (Bernard 1994: 353).

More dramatic interventions are also possible. Following a horrific incident in New York City when a young woman was murdered in full view of a large number of witnesses, none of whom apparently intervened to save her, a number of research studies appeared that looked at factors affecting bystanders' willingness to intervene in an emergency. Early laboratory studies (Darley and Latané 1968; Latané and Darley 1968) suggested that, paradoxically, intervention was less likely the more bystanders were (thought to be) present. These findings are consistent with a 'diffusion of responsibility effect', in which individuals feel that their own responsibility for coping with an emergency is diminished by the availability of others to deal with the matter. Piliavin *et al.* (1969) conducted a field experiment to test this hypothesis, while also assessing how far the characteristics of the victim affect helping behaviour. Each trial of the experiment consisted of a team of students boarding an underground train. At a particular point, a student playing the role of victim staggered forward and collapsed. While the 'victim' was dressed identically on each occasion, in a number of trials he seemed to be drunk, and in another trial he carried a walking stick (implying that he had an illness). The race of the 'victim' was also varied. In some trials, a team member offered limited help after a short period to see if this would induce others to do likewise. Other members of the team observed passengers' reactions to the 'incident'. Piliavin *et al.* found little support for the diffusion of responsibility hypothesis. They also found that an apparently ill person was more likely to be helped than one who seemed drunk, that men were more likely to help than women, and that there was a tendency towards same-race helping. This last tendency was more marked in the drunk as opposed to the ill condition. Piliavin *et al.* develop a model for explaining these patterns based on the social costs involved in helping versus non-helping.

As Weick points out, provocation can be used to 'amplify' a response. In other words, one might choose to observe in some settings or situations rather than others because they provide better opportunities to observe the behaviour of interest. Amplification also helps to avoid the problems associated with what Bochner refers to as the 'bird watching model' – 'standing around hoping that some rare creature will perform some unusual act' (Bochner 1979: 42). Bochner (1979) describes a study he carried out to examine racial variations in social distance in Australia. He asked two women, one white, one Aboriginal, to walk a dog in a public park. The number of smiles, nods and greetings addressed to each was recorded. The white dog-walker received almost three times the number of such responses as did her black counterpart. Most important in the present context is that Bochner's use of a dog was explicitly intended to amplify the response. In his judgement, the presence of the dog had two effects. First, it increased the visibility of the walker. In addition, however, 'Dogs also seem to act as social facilitators, so that people are more likely to be approached by strangers if they are in the company of a dog than if they are by themselves' (Bochner 1979: 42). Weick (1968: 377–8) speculates that responses might be amplified by scarcity or constraint. The argument here is that removing props, resources or personnel from a setting might throw some kinds of behaviour into sharp relief as people struggle to overcome the deficiencies that confront them.

Recording techniques

Many variations exist in the structure of recording instruments, their complexity and mode of operation. What are called here 'descriptive records' involve the concrete depiction of a setting or situations. This kind of description aims to record what was observed in extensive detail with an avoidance of evaluative language. Recording is done contemporaneously either by writing notes directly or by dictating into a tape recorder. A common alternative and rather simple format for recording an observation is a checksheet. This is simply an arrangement of rows and columns to form a grid. Each column represents a behaviour to be observed. Each row represents the time at which the observation occurred. Marks are made on the grid depending on what is observed and whether continuous recording, instantaneous or one-zero sampling is being used. More complex systems use pre-formatted forms or notational representation. One does not have to construct an observational system from scratch. A number of existing systems have been collected into anthologies (see, for example, Simon and Boyer 1974). Recording can also be done remotely. For example, to assess how far anxieties about low levels of physical activity by children are justified, Biddle and Armstrong (1992) used a miniaturized heart monitor to capture data on the heart and lung function of a sample of boys and girls aged 11–12 years over the course of a normal school day.

Over the years a variety of more or less ingenious mechanical and electronic devices have been constructed to facilitate the observational process. Currently, software packages exist to aid the observing, coding and analysis of observational data. Martin and Bateson (1993) offer a useful overview of the advantages and disadvantages of computerized tools for systematic observation. Computer methods offer better precision and reduced levels of error than paper and pencil methods, especially where rapidly occurring streams of data are being observed. Larger volumes of data can be collected, using more categories which themselves might be more complex. Against this, Martin and Bateson make the important point that use of computer methods can involve a greater level of sophistication than is required: 'There is no point in using a complex and expensive piece of equipment if paper and pencil would do just as well. As a general rule, it is wise to chose the simplest recording technique that will do the job' (1993: 109). Especially under field conditions, hardware can be less mechanically reliable than simpler approaches. Customizing hardware and software can in some cases be difficult. Although computers potentially encourage the collection of large amounts of data, this might simply disguise a lack of clarity in the questions being asked by the researcher.

Video methods

There are many instances where it is appropriate to use videotape as a recording medium in observational studies. Video seems particularly useful in observing thoroughfares. Katz (1996) recorded the patrons of the Parisian funhouse described earlier as they made their way past its distorting mirrors. Shrum and Kilburn (1996) videotaped the somewhat risqué ritual exchanges associated with Mardi Gras in New Orleans in streets so crammed with tourists that other research methods were probably impossible and on a more mundane note, Zube (1979) used time-lapse filming to examine the effects of high wind speeds on pedestrian behaviour.

Dabbs (1982: 40) observes that:

... people think flies are fast and snails are slow. Presumably flies and snails think their speeds are just right. There is no intrinsic advantage to the point of view of any of the three. The human observer would have a better understanding of the others after watching a film that slowed down the fly and speeded up the snail.

The underlying point Dabbs is making here is that we view the world from the standpoint of a particular kind of organism: upright, bipedal, between 1.5 and 1.8 metres tall, with binocular vision and an ambulatory gait. As a result, social processes involving very large or very small spans of time or space might need to be manipulated in ways that allow our sensory apparatus fully to apprehend them. Prost (1995), who has made extensive use of high-speed filming to record human locomotion, argues, for example, that the subtleties of some forms of human behaviour can be discerned only at film speeds at or above 64 frames per second. Taking the opposite tack, Dabbs (1982), like Zube (1979), has experimented with time-lapse and time-sample photography as a way of studying the use of public spaces. Time-lapse photography has been widely used to study, for example, the movement of cloud formations or the growth of plants. Focused on a social space, time-lapse recordings can be used to register the ebb and flow of social interaction. Time-sampling, by contrast, involves filming at normal speeds in bursts of a few seconds at a time with relatively long periods in between. Because, when filming does occur, it happens in real time, sound can also be captured. It should be clear that time-sampling provides for a rather more episodic perspective on what is being observed than does time-lapse. Dabbs (1982) suggests that it is advisable, when using time-lapse or time-sampling methods, to begin with a wide-angle view and to film over a long time period. Only later should the angle of focus or the time-span be narrowed to record particular instances of interest. As Dabbs comments, this shift from a wide to a narrow focus 'might parallel a progression from exploratory to confirmatory, hypothesis generation to hypothesis testing, or qualitative to quantitative research' (Dabbs 1982: 43).

One advantage of video is that it captures, and retains for analysis, a great deal of detail. Sometimes, however, detail is a hindrance. A case in point relates to the study of expressive movement. Researchers interested in studying human movement have traditionally used point-light displays. Small lights or reflective patches are attached to the major joints of research subjects. Research subjects are then filmed in a darkened room. The patterns of light that result from this procedure allow movement to be analysed very precisely, free from the distorting effects of physical appearances and from possible reactive effects. Video technology provides an alternative to the point-light display method. A technique called 'quantizing' produces a mosaic-like display of rectangular pixels. The procedure degrades the image in a way that removes identifying information but still allows data to be gathered about movement. A further advantage is that the procedure can be applied to existing videotapes (Berry *et al.* 1991).

Still photography

Harper comments that, 'Many sociological categories are based on observable phenomena, and indeed many of these can be understood better if frozen in a photographic image than they can if written about in a field memo' (1989: 88). For example, Harper notes, drawing on his own ethnographic work, that tramps categorize one another on the basis of how they look and what they carry; information more easily documented in a photograph than in words. (Research uses of 'found' photographs will be examined elsewhere. Nor will any attention be paid here to the use of photographs as an aid to interviewing (see, for example, Harper 1986; Schratz and Steiner-Löffler 1998).) Cultural anthropologists have used photographs to document people's material possessions. Collier and Collier (1986) suggest that 'cultural inventories' of this kind often contain clues to the diffusion of valued objects and cultural practices. Photographs often also index levels of social engagement. Israeli immigrants in the United States have relatively high levels of education, can usually speak English, and are familiar with Western urban culture. Although Gold (1994) accepts that such immigrants are often ambivalent about their presence in the United States, he argues that they are, nevertheless, heavily involved in a wide range of community activities. Photographs of these activities taken by Gold tend to undermine competing accounts depicting immigrants as being isolated from mainstream US culture, and from the American Jewish Diaspora.

Margolis (1990) describes the use of maps and computer graphics to monitor the spread of HIV in San Francisco. This research was paralleled by ethnographic work that documented various features of the local social structure, including the activities of CHOWs (Community Health Outreach Workers). The photographs Margolis presents show CHOWs as they go about their work in the San Francisco Tenderloin, providing bleach for sterilizing needles, giving condoms to prostitutes, passing on health education messages and referring those in need to appropriate agencies. For Margolis, the importance of photographs in this context is perhaps less that they provide 'data', and more that they convey on a human scale the tragedy of the AIDS epidemic, and elicit the human bond the viewer shares with those being studied.

Collier and Collier (1986) point out that photographs can be used as a tool for mapping. Aerial photographs or even panoramic photographs from high vantage points can show patterns of land use and how they change. Harper (1997) took photographs of dairy farms in upper New York State from a small aeroplane and used the results to amplify, supplement and contextualize non-visual data from interviews and statistical research. Because photography freezes a particular instant in time, it is possible to track social change by rephotographing a scene previously photographed. Malcolm Collier took photographs over an 18-year period from the same high point overlooking a valley in New Mexico. These photographs show shifts in the distribution of residential and farming land, shifts that are related to long-term patterns of population movement (Collier and Collier 1986). It is possible to take this principle further, or, perhaps one should say, higher. Although a variety of technical problems exist, satellite images are potentially useful for estimating urban population size in rapidly urbanizing countries where reliable census data are not always available (Webster 1996). Satellite imagery has also proved invaluable in exploring the depletion of natural resources. Much of the work in this area has involved interdisciplinary efforts by ethnographers, geographers, life scientists and space scientists. Detailed ethnographic study of the social organization of crop and/or animal husbandry can be linked to broader patterns of habitat change obtained from satellites (Behrens *et al.* 1994; Brodisio *et al.* 1994; Stoffle *et al.* 1994; Sussman *et al.* 1994).

Prosser comments: '. . . visual sociology lacks an overarching cohesive, theoretical and methodological framework' (1998: 102). There are few detailed guides to research methods in visual sociology (Suchar 1997). Collier and Collier (1986) present a four-stage model of analysis for visual data. (Although they regard the model as being widely applicable, they acknowledge that it might need to be modified somewhat in individual circumstances.) In the first stage, the analyst should try in effect to obtain a holistic overview of the material, asking questions of the data while taking care to note down impressions and feelings. All of these initial responses to the data should prompt a set of orienting questions that provide a context for the later stages of the analysis. In the second stage, an inventory or log of the material is created, but one organized around the analytic categories emerging from the first stage. The third stage involves structured analysis, perhaps some of it quantitative or based on the identification of formal properties that transcend specific recorded situations. Finally, the data are re-examined in an overall manner, to help the analyst re-establish a wider context for the data.

Suchar describes a set of methodological procedures based on what he calls the 'interrogatory principle of documentary photography'. This refers to 'an interactive process whereby photographs are used as a way of answering or expanding on questions about a particular subject' (Suchar 1997: 36). Suchar suggests that one can combine the use of 'shooting scripts' with the analytic procedures of **grounded theory** (Glaser and Strauss 1967) to provide a rigorous and systematic way of collecting and analysing photographic data. Although he does not make the comparison explicit, shooting scripts seem to be analogous to the use of an *aide-mémoire* in depth interviewing. The script is made up of a series of questions that suggest what kind of things should be photographed. Shooting scripts are not meant to be rigid templates but are capable of being elaborated and modified as analysis progresses. The researcher takes photographs to provide responses to questions listed on the shooting script. A descriptive narrative is then written around the resulting photographs. It is possible to code this narrative using, for example, the procedures associated with grounded theory. The aim is to 'provide a means by which photography can be grounded in a strategic and focused exploration of answers to particular theoretically-generated questions' (Suchar 1997: 34). Using this approach, Suchar developed an 'iconography of gentrification' in a study of neighbourhood change in the Lincoln Park district of Chicago. Period renovations, the use of statuary and artwork, and the construction of walls, gates and fences in particular styles all suggested the development of an 'urban romantic' aesthetic. Suchar argues that this allowed residents to see their neighbourhood as combining elements of *Gemeinschaft* and *Gesellschaft*. Theory emerging out of the photographic data collection can subsequently be tested using interview data.

How people respond to being photographed depends on how they define the photographer or the act of taking a photograph. In some cases, the presence of a camera can cue those being photographed to pose in conventional or parodic ways. In others, the photographer is assimilated to some pre-existing social category. Shanklin (1979) records that many of the photographs she took early on during her fieldwork in a rural Irish community show puzzled housewives thrusting hens in her direction. Local people thought she was a recently appointed poultry inspector. Cameras can sometimes be unwelcome. Collier encountered hostility while trying to photograph Amish farmers in Pennsylvania (Collier and Collier 1986). Because it involves making a graven image, the Amish regard taking photographs of humans to be sinful. After discussing the matter with the local Amish bishop, Collier found that the hostility towards him subsided, and he was able to photograph inanimate objects. The Amish, however, turned their backs on him whenever he raised his camera. Researchers might need to be careful about the use of cameras in conflict situations. In these kinds of contexts photography can sometimes open researchers to the threat of assault (Lee 1995a).

Collier and Collier (1986) suggest that photographic technique is less important than the researcher's eye. In particular, the framing of shots is important. For example, a wide-angle view is often preferable to provide context to what is being photographed, although some kinds of activity require close-ups. Although there are a variety of camera formats, 35 mm seems to have become standard, offering a combination of convenience and technical quality. Film sensitivities now reach levels where photography under a wide variety of light conditions is feasible. Because differentials in processing costs have shrunk, there has been a move away from black-and-white prints and colour slides towards colour prints. Collier and Collier stress the need for efficient filing of negatives, contact sheets and photographs. In particular, they suggest that contact sheets always be preserved intact to allow each image to be viewed in the context of those that preceded and followed it. A duplicate can be produced which can then be cut up to allow sifting and sorting in the analytic process.

It is likely that researchers will increasingly make use of digital photography. Slides and prints can be digitized either commercially or by using a scanner. Having material in digital form might increase analytic capabilities. Digitized media allow the use of image databases which permit rapid indexing, searching and retrieval of images. It is not clear yet what the implications of this are. Digital cameras are becoming increasingly common. Still rather expensive, they can be bulky and need frequent recharging of batteries. At present, the quality of digital images lags behind that obtainable by traditional photographic methods. Portions of the image can be washed out, with shadows underdeveloped and highlights overexposed. On the other hand, digital images do not need processing and can be downloaded from the camera directly on to a computer while in the field.

The ethics of unobtrusive observation

Observational studies minimize the problems of reactivity that occur in research based on self-report. Put simply, people who do not know they are being studied do not change their behaviour. Studying people without their permission, however, violates some important ethical principles. It is generally considered ethically proper to respect the personal autonomy of those being studied. This implies that those participating in a research study do so voluntarily and on the basis of adequate information about the proposed inquiry. It also implies that their privacy should be protected. Researchers, moreover, should do no harm to those they study. Indeed, where possible they should maximize the possible benefits from their research while minimizing possible harms. Particular vigilance is required where researchers deal with research subjects who are actually or potentially vulnerable in some way.

Observational studies potentially negate the principle of informed consent. The obtaining of prior written consent, or even the debriefing of research subjects after the event, are rarely feasible in public settings. As a result, those studied cannot refuse their involvement. Some kinds of observational study involve at least a measure of deception, and where videotaping is used, for example, there is a risk of invading people's privacy. In fact, unobtrusive observation carried out in public settings has frequently been regarded, even by ethicists from widely different philosophical positions, as much less problematic than, for example, covert participant observation or the deception of subjects in social science experiments (Capron 1982; Dworkin 1982; Kelman 1982; Macklin 1982). This is because of the nature of the social expectations that govern behaviour in public places. Even if we do not explicitly expect the presence of an observing social scientist, when we act in public we do expect that our behaviour will be observable and subject to scrutiny by others. From this point of view, 'the researchers' observations differ neither in kind nor in intensity from those we can normally expect other people to take' (Capron 1982: 225). In addition, as Capron goes on to point out, people can freely leave or otherwise circumvent the observation if they do become aware of it. Although, conceivably, people might be annoyed to learn of the presence of a researcher, direct harm to those studied rarely occurs as a result of unobtrusive observation in public. Those observed in public places are almost always complete strangers and, as a result, data are anonymous at the point of collection. Moreover, as Dworkin (1982) points out, an intention to harm is absent from research observation, something that distinguishes it from a situation where, for example, a pickpocket observes a crowd in order to pick a 'mark'. Nevertheless, difficulties are still possible in systematic observation studies. One problem is that the boundary between public space and private space is not always as clear as some commentators have assumed. A second problematic area is that of field experiments involving the use of deception, such as investigations of bystander intervention in emergencies. Third, because they potentially compromise the anonymity of research participants, the use of video or photographic data can present ethical problems.

Without disclosing he was doing so, Roger Homan observed the liturgical practices of old-time pentecostalists (Homan and Bulmer 1982). Homan learnt what behaviour patterns within the group signified allegiance and 'I purposively practised them'; however, he did not 'profess to beliefs which I did not hold' (Homan and Bulmer 1983: 113). According to Homan, the meaning of privacy in the context of a religious service is a contentious one. The service had a sign outside saying 'All welcome'. This implies that, just as in a football match, outsiders are free to attend on their own terms. Homan decided to conduct a covert study because an overt one would have been intrusive. Pentecostal worship is uninhibited in the sense that free expression of joy in the heart and praise for God are encouraged. Homan makes the point that, in this context, a right to privacy is in part the right to be free of interruption and inhibition. He also makes the point that much of the literature produced by the group he studied was intended for private consumption, yet no ethical strictures are seen to attach themselves to the **content analysis** of such material. There might have been something like a partial consent in the case of Homan's study, since he did apparently discuss the research with pentecostal pastors, who confirmed that open observation was likely to be disruptive. A difficulty remains because the bounded character of the setting probably obviates the kind of tacit or implicit consent (Dworkin 1982) that would derive in a more public setting from the expectation that people's actions are freely observable. The covert nature of Homan's study derives directly from the unwillingness of those present to be studied. Some social scientists are rightly concerned that the requirement to obtain informed consent does not produce a situation that systematically excludes certain kinds of group from scrutiny. (For a summary of the arguments, see Lee 1993, Chapter 8.) Homan seems to come close to saying, however, that the wishes of people can always be overridden for the purposes of research.

In the case of bystander intervention studies the problem is one of possible harm to research participants. There exist, for example, some 'hypothetical, but far-fetched, possibilities of physical injury' (Kelman 1982: 73). Diener and Crandall (1978) suggest, for example, that someone might be injured in a rush to help the apparent victim, or have a (real) heart attack brought on by the incident. They also contend that minor psychological harm to unwitting research subjects is also a possibility in such experiments. People might be shocked by what they see or suffer a loss of self-esteem brought on by the recognition that they had not acted when perhaps they could have or should have. Although the likelihood of such effects being severe or long term is small indeed, a major difficulty is that participants cannot give informed consent because they are not aware that an experiment is being conducted. Nor can they easily be debriefed after the event. One longer-term consequence of all of this might be a breakdown of public trust. In time, failures to intervene of the kind uncovered by bystander intervention studies might conceivably reflect people's concern that they are being confronted by a bystander intervention experiment.

The legal status of bystander intervention studies is not clear. Silverman (1975) asked three legal experts, one of them a criminal court judge, to assess the legal risks attached to common field experiments involving, for example, lost letters, requests for help, surreptitious filming and the staging of emergencies. Two of the experts argued that the intent and purpose of the experiment were likely to be weighed in a court case against the annoyance or harm to members of the public in ways that would be favourable to the researcher. The remaining lawyer, perhaps not coincidentally a specialist in medical malpractice suits, argued that the misrepresentations involved and the intent to evoke a response that might be unwelcome to research participants could produce a basis for liability. Reiss (1971) makes the additional point that organizations can be fearful about being exposed to litigation or insurance claims if something untoward should happen during the course of the observation. It is also possible for observers to become privy to confidential information or to be witnesses to illegal or legally contested events. In these situations, observers have little protection against, for example, attempts to subpoena their data (Reiss 1971; Lee 1993).

Photographs present ethical difficulties not associated with other methods. During the course of his fieldwork in a refugee community Gold (1989) photographed a wedding. Not only were individuals identifiable from the photographs, but problems of possible collective jeopardy also arose. Some of the photographs Gold took showed people in possession of expensive consumer durables. These items had usually been purchased collectively. Their appearance in photographs, however, might encourage those hostile to refugees to assume that consumption had taken place at the taxpayer's expense. Clark recounts using photographs to document mothers' care-giving practices at home (Clark and Werner 1997). One of the mothers who was in hiding from an abusive husband refused to co-operate, fearful that a published photograph might lead him to her and her child. Another mother, misunderstanding a reference to academic publication, was worried that photographs of her and her baby would appear in a newspaper. Increasingly, there might be some technical solutions to problems of this kind. Clark and Werner describe a number of experiments made by Werner to explore how best photographs could be anonymized. One technique involved converting the photograph into a digital form and then using image manipulation software to change parts of the photograph that might produce identification. Using a mosaic pattern, rather like that sometimes used in television programmes to obscure identifying detail, effectively anonymized those in the photographs. However, subsequently shown the photographs, research subjects were upset by the use of mosaics, precisely because they associated such devices with criminality. Werner has subsequently experimented with converting digital photographs to line drawings using photo-manipulation software. During the process, which is not a difficult one, details can be changed or removed to protect participants. Werner and Clark note, however, that manipulation in this way raises ethical issues to do with data accuracy and fidelity. It is not at all clear when and how such techniques stray over the boundary into misrepresentation of data.

Conclusion

McCall (1984) notes that, although widely used in areas of applied psychology relating to child development and to assessing organizational performance by teachers and others, non-participant observation methods were relatively little used in social research until the 1970s. The re-emergence of the methods was linked to a number of factors. As evidenced by the work of Webb *et al.* (1966) and Rosenthal and Rostow (1975), both the growing reliance on interview and survey methods and the conduct of social psychological experiments came under critical scrutiny. At the same time, some clinical researchers were showing increasing interest in the use of explicitly behavioural approaches to assessment and treatment. Meanwhile, strongly influenced by the work of Erving Goffman and by newer developments such as ethnomethodology, micro-level studies of social interaction became popular in sociology.

What we do and say during the daily passage of our lives, how we move through time and space, and the social meanings associated with posture, position, demeanour and display, are all amenable to simple observation. Moreover, with some ingenuity researchers can contrive situations that enhance the observational potentialities in a given research setting. Although simple observation assumes that the presence of the observer in the setting is unobtrusive, the absence of reactivity cannot simply be taken for granted. The implications of the observer's role in the setting needs always to be assessed. Sampling and data recording are often problematic aspects of observational studies. It is also in observational studies, perhaps more than with other kinds of unobtrusive methods, that ethical issues are most troublesome. This is perhaps especially true where recording hardware is used, or where particular populations such as children are observed. Observation often provides 'content-limited data' (Webb *et al.* 1966: 140), since the researcher is necessarily restricted to the information contained within what is visible, the import of which might not be obvious without access to other more potentially reactive forms of data.

Writers such as Reiss (1971) and McCall (1984) bemoan the absence of a strong tradition of field-based non-participant observation. The methodological problems posed by observational studies are, in their view, no more nor no less debilitating than those affecting other approaches. Moreover, the ability of observational methods to garner precise and reliable information about naturally occurring events and episodes, often unobtainable by other means, should not be discounted.

Recommended reading

McCall, G. J. (1984) Systematic field observation, *Annual Review of Sociology*, 10: 263–82. (A good overview of the topic, arguing the case for a greater use of non-participant observation methods in sociology.)

Martin, P. and Bateson, P. (1993) *Measuring Behaviour: An Introductory Guide.* Cambridge: Cambridge University Press. (Although this book is focused primarily on animal behaviour, it provides an excellent overview of technical issues in the collection and analysis of observational data.)

Croll, P. (1986) *Systematic Classroom Observation.* Lewes: Falmer. (A primer on observational methods in the classroom, but sufficiently general to make it useful for researchers in other fields.)

Collier, J., Jr. and Collier, M. (1986) *Visual Anthropology: Photography as a Research Method.* Albuquerque, NM: University of New Mexico Press. (The second edition of a classic text on uses of photography in anthropology.)

Prosser, J. (1998) *Image-based Research: A Sourcebook for Qualitative Researchers.* London: Falmer. (This collection of articles on the use of visual methods in the social sciences covers a range of disciplines and applications. It reproduces a number of classic articles but is sometimes tendentious in its treatment of the history of social research.)

4 Retrieved data: running records

Webb *et al.* make a rather arbitrary distinction between the 'ongoing continuing records of a society', which they refer to as 'running records', and
'episodic and private records' which are archival materials having a discontinuous form. Material contained within the running record is usually factual in character. It is often rather restricted in terms of its content and the
population to which it refers. In many instances, running records cover
lengthy time periods, and generate considerable volumes of material. In
some respects, Webb *et al.*'s separation of running records from other forms
of archival data reflects a sensibility much more like that of the secondary
analyst than the historian or historical sociologist. Running records are
valued for their ubiquity, their low cost and their convenience, as well as for
their utility in studying topics not readily amenable to self-report. Above all,
Webb *et al.* value running records because they permit longitudinal analysis
and record linkage. Precisely because they do extend over long periods, running records allow trends to be established, permit the exploration of temporal patterns and provide opportunities for quasi-experimentation. In
addition, associations, continuities and discontinuities between different sets
of records yield information, sometimes of a kind impossible to obtain by
other means. The price of all this, however, is a need for constant vigilance
over the constraints, restrictions and hidden fallibilities of data collected at
the hands of others.

The growth and diversity of personal records, paper and electronic, held in bureaucratic repositories both reflects and is an unobtrusive measure of the bureaucratic surveillance that is an increasing feature of modern societies. Only rudimentary systems existed for the registering and recording of populations until the eighteenth century (Starr 1987). Partly driven by and in response to reformist concerns, the nineteenth century saw the emergence of a more professionalized and bureaucratized system for the routine production of statistical information. As Starr points out, by the latter part of the twentieth century, most developed countries have come to depend on complex systems of statistical indicators to estimate and monitor a wide variety of social and economic conditions. Statistical monitoring systems span ever wider segments of social life and penetrate more deeply into the workings of society. The statistical series produced by governments and other official bodies are thus an important source of running records.

Webb *et al.* describe the mass media as the 'most easily available and massive sources of continuing secondary data' (1981: 118). News stories are perhaps the most obvious element of the mass media to command the attention of social researchers. News, however, does not exhaust the content of the print media in particular. Features, photographs, advertising and even items such as obituaries and wedding announcements can all have research uses. Nowadays, anonymized records, aggregate statistics and newspapers are often obtainable in digital form via the Internet or on CD-ROM. For example, one Internet site, <http: //odwin.ucsd.edu/idata/>, makes available more than 400 data sets suitable for social science research purposes. Directories and almanacs can be found on-line in the Reference Collection at the Internet Public Library <http: //www.ipl.org/ref/RR/static/ref0000.html>. A comprehensive site containing links to many legislative and governmental bodies is <http: //www.psr.keele.ac.uk>. Links to newspaper websites worldwide can be found at < http: //library.uncg.edu/news/>.

As Scott (1990) points out, virtually no subject area is without specialist reference works that can be of use to social scientists. He gives as an example books on horse-racing form. Although these might be thought to be of interest only to connoisseurs of the turf, they provide a good deal of insight into the structure and organization of the horse-racing industry. Scott identifies three genres of published reference books: directories, almanacs and yearbooks. Directories list people by geographical area or on the basis of their membership of a group, profession, organization or trade. Almanacs provide a calendar of dates with information relating to those dates. Yearbooks, as the name implies, are annual publications that give up to date information relating to a particular area of interest. Most widely used in social research are commercial directories, specialist trade directories and genealogical directories. The last category, which would include for example, *Debrett's Peerage* in the UK, or the *Social Register* in the USA are particularly useful for the study of elites.

What might be called 'records of proceedings', the documentation of discussions and decisions that take place within formally constituted bodies, are a further source of running records. Many bodies, deliberative assemblies such as legislatures, courts and tribunals of various kinds, business meetings and so on, reach decisions or render judgments on the basis of defined procedures that often include voting or position taking. That the procedures involved have a formal, open, public character is important to their legitimacy, as is the fact that they are recorded. In such contexts, individual decisions, outcomes or determinations are often interesting in themselves. As Webb *et al.* (1981) point out, however, trends and patterns in such matters potentially reveal much about the predispositions of those involved, their interests and their susceptibility to the opinions of others.

The uses of running records

Actuarial records, the tallies of births, marriages and deaths collected by the state (and often by religious bodies), are perhaps the most obvious example of running records. Demographers have long been interested in the seasonality of conceptions and births. Thang and Swenson (1996) found, for example, that births in Vietnam are more likely to occur in years deemed auspicious according to Vietnamese and Chinese astrological calendars than in years that were considered undesirable. In the United States, there is a rather obvious and consistent pattern of seasonality in births. September is the peak month for live births, suggesting December as the peak month for conceptions. Parnell and Rodgers (1998) found a peak for abortions in North Carolina in February, a pattern consistent with the rise in conceptions in December. However, for unmarried women aged 18 and younger, there is an additional abortion peak in August. Parnell and Rodgers suggest that, in this case, conceptions are lined to celebrations surrounding the end of the school year.

In addition to information about the social attributes of those registered, actuarial records contain a further, often overlooked, source of data; the first names of those to whom they refer. Although they can imply religious, national or ethnic identity, first names in British or American society are usually regarded as having personal rather than social significance. Differences in naming patterns by gender, by class or race, suggest otherwise. Alice Rossi (1965) found that boys in the middle-class families she studied were likely to be named after kin, whereas girls were not. She took this to indicate a subtle process of gender differentiation in which male family members symbolically carried 'the temporal continuity of the family' (1965: 503). Lieberson and his associates have used data on children's names to explore processes associated with cultural innovation. They note that innovations in the realm of culture are difficult to study independent of organizational or institutional influence. Naming practices, however, should be relatively free of such influences, and thus provide a basis for examining how existing cultural practices constrain creativity and imagination. Lieberson and Bell (1992) looked at popular boys' and girls' names in a random sample of all names given to white and black children born in New York State between 1973 and 1985. Although boys were typically given names that were part of the 'standard repertoire' of American male first names, girls were more likely to be given 'non-standard' names. These might be invented names, names that were derivatives or diminutives of other names, or names not previously much used. Shifts in the popularity of names apparently occur more slowly for boys' names than for girls' names. Gender differences even extend to the origins of names. Girls are given names of French origin more often than boys. Lieberson and Bell suggest that these patterns reflect the subtle influence of longstanding stereotypical roles. Girls' names are seen as more decorative and open to fashion, while boys' names 'are approached in terms of historical continuity and stability' (1992: 548). According to Lieberson and Bell, there is some evidence to suggest that these patterns are more prevalent for lower-class groups. There is also a suggestion of class-based diffusion in Lieberson and Bell's data. Names initially popular with upper-class parents subsequently gain popularity in other classes. Lieberson and Bell note, however, that this diffusion is very rapid, and the mechanisms involved are not clear. In a separate study Lieberson and Mikelson (1995) note that African Americans often give their children distinctive or unique names not found in the standard repertoire of American first names. (For their purposes, a unique name is defined as one given to only one child in a given year.) Between 1916 and the early 1960s the proportion of unique names remained relatively constant in Lieberson and Mikelson's data set derived from birth records in Illinois, with African American children always being more likely to receive a unique name. Beginning in the 1960s, the proportion of African American girls receiving unique names rose sharply, matched by only a slight rise in the proportion of uniquely named white girls. For boys the pattern is rather similar though somewhat less dramatic. Lieberson and Mikelson link this shift to broader social and political changes, although they note that even before the 1960s in Illinois names popular with African American parents tended not to overlap with those popular with white parents. On the basis of a small-scale experiment, Lieberson and Mikelson found that people could generally correctly guess whether a unique name had been given to a boy or a girl. Lieberson and Mikelson suggest that unique names often have linguistic features, such as ending in 'a' or in 'n', that marked them out as female or male. Lieberson and Mikelson recognize the influence of African and Muslim names on African American naming practices. They note, however, that such names are usually adapted to mainstream linguistic gender conventions, so that, for example, African boys' names ending in 'a' are used as girls' names in the United States. Lieberson and Mikelson conlude that even in a situation where there are no formal rules, as in the naming of children, subtle but powerful processes constrain cultural innovation.

Married couples who differ in their social characteristics are often held to be at greater risk of marital instability than those who are socially similar. In a study by Bumpass and Sweet (1972) religiously intermarried couples had a greater likelihood of divorce than religious homogeneous couples. Burchinall and Chancellor (1963) found survival rates for intermarriages in Iowa to be only somewhat lower than for marriages where both partners were of the same religion. When controls were introduced for age of wife and status level of husband, the survival rate differences were reduced even further. In a similar study in Indiana, Christensen and Barber (1967) were able to link together marriage, birth and divorce records. Here, divorce was only very slightly more likely to have been an outcome in cases where the marriage had been religiously mixed than was so for religiously homogeneous marriages, although divorce rates did vary considerably by the particular combination of religious identification recorded by couples. It should be noted, of course, that self-recorded religious preference is not necessarily a good indication of religious belief or practice. In addition, Vernon (1960) observes that if one focuses on survival rather than dissolution rates the vast majority of marriages at the time of study remained intact whatever their religious composition.

Personal advertisements are a useful source of information about individuals' interests and choices (Hatala *et al.* 1998). By their very nature, they are unobtrusive and self-disclosing. Because personal advertisements need to be concise, they presumably reflect rather sharply the conceptions of self and others held by those who place them. Advertisements lend themselves to study over time, so it is relatively easy to track in a reliable way trends for a variety of subpopulations. Using an advertisement to seek a partner is not a new phenomenon; Jagger notes that newspaper advertisements seeking 'mail order brides' were a feature of the Western Frontier of the United States during the nineteenth century. Although the practice largely fell into disuse in the early part of the twentieth century, there has been more recently a dramatic increase in the use of advertising as a way of meeting a potential partner. Across the four British newspapers Jagger studied, the number of dating advertisements rose from virtually negligible numbers in the 1970s to a total of almost 500 a week in 1995. Earlier studies of lonely hearts advertisements typically show men offering financial and occupational attributes and seeking physical attractiveness in a partner, while women offer physical attractiveness and seek financial and status resources. In contrast to these studies, men in the advertisements studied by Jagger offered potential partners lifestyle attributes such as interests and activities rather than occupational or financial resources. Women, on the other hand, offered 'masculine' attributes to do, for example, with ambition and assertiveness, while seeking men with 'feminine' attributes such as empathy or nurturance. In terms of physical attributes women marketed 'attractive-ness' while men marketed height, but almost three-quarters of advertisers presented themselves as 'slim', with little difference in the proportions of men and women doing so. Jagger (1998) suggests that these patterns might point to shifts in traditional gender conceptions in postmodern consumer societies.

Personal advertisements provide a window on to partner choice in situ-ations that might otherwise be difficult to study. Yancey and Yancey (1998) note that theories of interracial marriage often assume a compensatory logic. Whites are assumed to trade their racial status for attributes such as physical attractiveness or financial security. Minority group members, on the other hand, are assumed to trade such attributes for higher racial status. Despite their emphasis on choice processes, existing studies are typically based on established relationships. Looking at personal advertisements might better allow such theories to be evaluated. Yancey and Yancey found in a sample of advertisements that race made little difference to whether advertisers sought or offered physical attractiveness or financial security. They argue that increased availability of other-race partners better explains than exchange theories why individuals enter interracial relationships. Hatala *et al.* (1998) analysed personal advertisements appearing in three San Francisco newspapers placed by homosexual men who disclosed their HIV status. They found that HIV-negative men requested only HIV-negative men and that HIV-positive men sought only other HIV-positive men. HIV-nega-tive men were more likely to seek attractiveness in a partner, to seek a seri-ous relationship, to be older and to write longer advertisements. HIV-positive men were more likely to include health-related information in their advertisements, and specifically to indicate that they were healthy or health-conscious. Hatala *et al.* suggest that, at least for those seeking part-ners through personal advertisement, viral diagnosis constitutes a significant social barrier to the formation of personal relationships.

Moving from partner choice to marriage itself, Blumberg and Paul (1976) studied marriage announcements in the society pages of the Sunday *New York Times*. Most of these upper-class marriages were traditional in form with attendant trappings and rituals. Most weddings were conducted under Protestant, mostly Episcopalian, auspices. Only one-fifth were celebrated in a Roman Catholic church, and in only a handful of cases was a civil cere-mony involved. (Jewish weddings are underrepresented in the Sunday *New York Times*. Many take place on Sundays to avoid the Sabbath, and are more usually reported in the *New York Times* on Mondays.) Overwhelm-ingly, the fathers of brides and grooms were businessmen or professionals. Both grooms and brides were likely to have attended elite private schools and prestigious colleges and universities. Grooms were predominantly found in professional occupations. Only a minority of brides listed an occu-pation. Where they did, however, they either held professional jobs or were in traditionally female occupations such as teaching, social work or nursing. Comparing their findings with a similar study conducted just after the Second World War (Hatch and Hatch 1947), Blumberg and Paul conclude that, despite massive social change, the American upper class has remained remarkably intact. They do note, though, that over time the upper-class marriage market in the United States is taking on an increasingly national, rather than local, character, and that its boundaries have become somewhat more open than had formerly been the case.

The end of life is also often marked in the running record. When Mao Zedong died, Chai (1977) analysed obituaries in the Chinese press in order to gauge the strength of various political factions within the country. A content analysis of obituaries in two US newspapers suggests that women are accorded an obituary less often than men (Maybury 1996). Moreover, when obituaries do appear they are significantly shorter than men's, and the longest women's obituaries are reserved for the wives of famous men. Cameron *et al.* (1994) used obituaries to examine the impact of the AIDS epidemic. They compared nearly 7000 obituaries from papers catering primarily to homosexuals with two newspapers targeted at a general audience. The median age of death recorded in the general press agreed closely with US averages for longevity. The median age of death recorded in the homosexual press was much lower; only 9 per cent were recorded as having lived to old age. For those who died of AIDS, the median age of death was 39. Both male homosexuals and lesbians were more often recorded as having violent deaths than was the case for men and women in general.

The etiquette surrounding problematic events, whether momentous or mundane, provides important clues to the factors shaping social conduct. Since the early part of the century the period of time set aside for mourning a family member has declined considerably. Funerals have become much shorter, with fewer mourners and fewer of the traditional accompaniments, such as viewing the body. Drawing on etiquette guides, business regulations, and reports from government, business organizations and consumer groups, Pratt (1981) charted a shift in the norms relating to time off work following bereavement. Pratt found that firms in the United States increasingly have formal policies for providing paid leave for workers when a family member dies. Between 1943 and 1973, the proportion of firms specifying a fixed period of paid leave (usually three days) rose to more than 80 per cent. Pratt notes that this practice has a variety of ramifications. Such changes mean that bereavement practices in effect take on the temporal norms of business. In this way, 'bereavement has come to reflect and reinforce a view of the social order as efficient, under control, and based on businesslike management of time' (Pratt 1981: 331).

Many newspapers and magazines contain columns from which readers can obtain advice of various kinds. Garner *et al.* (1998) looked at the advice columns in women's magazines directed at young teenagers and at older teenagers and women in their early 20s. They note that, although the magazines in their design and use of photographs convey an image of being up to date and fashionable, advice given on sexual matters has changed little over the years. As they put it, the 'rhetorical vision presented in teen magazines . . . is one of containment, in which women fit themselves into a subordinate, male-defined sexual role' (Garner *et al.* 1998: 74). As Evans (1996) points out, another form of advice, astrology, has become a staple element of the popular media. He analysed horoscopes offered in magazines in the United States targeted at working-class and middle-class women. The social class of the magazine's readership proved to be a better predictor of the advice offered than zodiac sign. Horoscopes in working-class magazines were less likely than those in middle-class magazines to advise travel, spending money or to predict career advancement. Those in middle-class magazines did, however, encourage readers to expect more autonomy than was the case with the astrological advice given to readers in magazines targeted at a working-class audience. Chalfen (1992, 1998) used advice columns to investigate what he calls the 'pictorial home mode of communication'; the use within the household of photographs, snapshots, home movies and videotapes. As he points out, it is difficult to observe the actual production of home mode pictorial communication in a systematic manner. The presence of the researcher is unlikely at an opportune moment, and in any case is likely to be reactive. Chalfen turned to newspaper etiquette columns to explore questions concerning who and what can be photographed and displayed and about appropriate locations and occasions for display. Both questions and responses give clues to the normative context within which home photography takes place.

Print media materials that appear in a regular form are a useful source for the exploration of long-term trends. Melbin (1978) argues that modern societies increasingly operate on a round-the-clock basis. One measure of this is the growth of 24-hour radio and television stations, since night-time programming presumably implies the presence of a wakeful audience. Melbin was able to demonstrate this rise of 24-hour programming for one US city, Boston, over a 25-year period using a readily available data source, programme listings in local newspapers. (Related to this, Webb *et al.* (1981: 112) suggest that utility records could be consulted to determine when people are likely to retire for the night. Presumably, as the proportion of people asleep increases one would expect to find slumps in electricity demand and rises in water pressure.)

Beniger investigated the extent to which the spread of television in the United States encouraged the development of a shared symbolic environment, that is one in which a relatively large proportion of the population can identify abstract symbolic representations of various kinds. The focus of Beniger's study is the editorial cartoon, those cartoons that appear on the editorial pages of newspapers and often offer commentary on issues of the day. If television did have an effect on the symbolic environment, Beniger hypothesized that it might lead to a decline in the extent to which cartoonists explicitly attached labels to persons or objects appearing in the cartoons. On the basis of an examination of five leading metropolitan newspapers between 1948 and 1980, Beniger concluded that there had been a decline in labelling beginning in the 1950s, the period during which television diffused rapidly in the USA. Alternative explanations, such as a change in stylistic fashions in cartooning, the generational replacement of older cartoonists, or shifts in the educational level of newspaper readers, appear not to account for the trends Beniger found.

Caudill *et al.* (1987) examined job advertisements in a trade magazine for journalists in order to assess the frequent claim that journalism is becoming increasingly professionalized. They reasoned that if this were the case one would expect to find job advertisements specifying as requirements attributes such as formal training, specialization or a theoretical orientation to work, associated in other contexts with a professional orientation. Over a rather long period, 1920–1980, they found few changes in the content of advertisements. These tended still to look for 'traditional' requirements such as experience, or for personal attributes such as tenacity. Baker and Faulkner (1991) also used trade publications to assess the effect of 'blockbuster' movies on the Hollywood film industry. Combining data on financial returns derived from ticket sales with information in publications such as *Variety*, they argue that patterns of professional specialization and segmentation changed as a result of the technical and organizational challenges induced by blockbusters.

A number of researchers have used data on book production to track trends in social attitudes and values. It is often assumed, for example, that modern societies are more secular in their orientation than traditional societies. It has been difficult, though, to find longitudinal, cross-national data that might track changes in religious commitment at the societal level. Wuthnow (1977) has suggested that figures produced annually by UNESCO on the number of books published by country might provide one suitable source of data. The data seem to be fairly reliable in that in almost all countries there is a centralized procedure for counting books published. Moreover, books are classified on publication according to the Universal Decimal Classification system, which makes it possible to distinguish books on religious topics from those dealing with other subjects. Wuthnow notes that the ability to identify detailed trends is hampered by missing data and rather wide fluctuations in the annual number of books published in some smaller countries. Nevertheless, at least for modern Western countries, data on religious book publishing correlate reasonably well with other measures of religiosity and with national data on changes in religious belief and practice.

Mullins and Kopelman (1984) sought evidence for the assertion that American culture has become increasingly preoccupied with the self, as seen, for example, in the growth of interest in psychotherapies. Arguing that any trend towards 'societal narcissism' should be apparent in the content of best-sellers, Mullins and Kopelman used a variety of sources to compile lists of bestselling non-fiction books over a 30-year period. Books were categorized according to the Dewey Decimal Classification system, with individual titles being inspected where necessary. In line with their expectation, the proportion of bestselling non-fiction books dealing with topics such as personal psychology, sexuality, dieting, self-help and so on, rose decade by decade between 1950 and 1979. Kiser and Drass (1987) argue that in periods of economic turmoil issues relating to the efficiency and fairness of economic systems come to the fore. Often such issues are addressed as imaginative alternatives. Using data from a comprehensive bibliography of Utopian literature, and statistics on annual book production from trade publications, Kiser and Drass found that for the period 1883–1975 production of Utopian novels seems to be related to economic contraction in both Britain and the United States.

Interested in changes in the control of large firms, Fligstein (1987) looked at the organizational origin of presidents or chief executive officers in large firms in the US between 1919 and 1979. The firms studied were selected from lists of the 100 largest non-financial corporations regularly listed in *Fortune* magazine. Information on senior officers was derived from reference works such as *Moody's Manual of Industrials*, *Who's Who in America* and *Who's Who in Business*. Fligstein found that in the early part of the century large firms were dominated by entrepreneurs or manufacturing personnel. By the 1930s dominance had passed to sales and marketing personnel. This pattern had changed by the 1960s. In parallel with the growth of large conglomerates, the leaders of large firms were being drawn increasingly from those who had a background in financial management. In another study using data from directories, White has explored in detail what he calls the 'regenerative nature of opportunity' (1970: 1). White's focus is on 'vacancy chains'. Such chains are created when (under certain restrictive labour market conditions) someone moves into a job position that has been vacated by the move of someone else to another job. White chose three US denominations, the Episcopal Church, the Methodist Church and the Presbyterian Church. Clergy in each church move between pastorates. Information about who is incumbent, where, when and for how long, is publicly available and easily retrievable from published directories. White suggests that vacancy chain models have wide applicability, not just in the study of job mobility, but in relation to housing moves and patterns of organizational succession.

Running records can sometimes be used to explore issues difficult to tap using other methods. It is often argued that piecework stimulates unsafe working behaviour as workers attempt to maximize output. Wrench and Lee (1982) note, however, that it is difficult to demonstrate a statistical relationship between piecework and accidents. Usually, official accident reports do not give information on payment systems. Examining accident rates before and after the introduction of piecework is also problematic. Such changes are often accompanied by changes to organization, production and so on, the effects of which are usually difficult to disentangle. Wrench and Lee argue that pieceworkers are likely to speed up their work rate the nearer they get to pay day. As a result, one would expect to see accidents increase towards the end of the working week. Using accident data from a number of firms, Wrench and Lee found that, compared with day workers, accidents experienced by pieceworkers increased the closer they came to the day when wages were calculated. Archer and Erlich-Erfer (1991) were interested in exploring the social effects of a series of gruesome murders that occurred over a fairly short period of time in a small city in California. As they point out, 'fear is methodologically elusive' (Archer and Erlich-Erfer 1991: 342). However, they were able to detect some consequences of the events by examining several types of running record. Receipts of the local bus company rose sharply during the period of the murders in comparison with the corresponding period in the previous and subsequent year, a pattern they attributed to a decline in hitchhiking by students at the local university. Archer and Erlich-Erfer also examined the volume of handgun purchases in the local county. Compared with both a neighbouring county and a remote county, purchases of handguns showed a sharp increase during the period in which the murders were taking place.

In a variety of fields researchers have used running records to estimate the size of populations ordinarily hidden in some way from direct observation. Estimates of this kind tend to rely on 'implicative methods' (Lee 1993) involving the use of 'multipliers', or alternatively the size of discrepancies occurring between different data sources. Multiplier methods depend on the assumption that the portion of a population that can be measured stands in a fixed ratio to that which cannot. For example, it seems that those having the surname Cohen form a relatively constant proportion of the Jewish population (Waterman and Kosmin 1986). This constant can be derived empirically by noting the proportion of Cohens recorded in birth and death notices in Jewish newspapers. Waterman and Kosmin were able to estimate the size of the Jewish population in London by counting the number of Cohens found in telephone directories and on the electoral register and applying the relevant multiplier. Multiplier techniques have also been used in the study of drug misuse (Hartnoll *et al.* 1985). It has been assumed that there is a direct relationship between the number of drug-related deaths and the prevalence of drug misuse. If the death rate for users is known or can be reliably estimated, the number of deaths in a given year multiplied by the annual mortality rate can be used to give an annual period prevalence. This particular method has a number of obvious shortcomings. There may be difficulties in reliably identifying user deaths from mortality data. It is plausible to suggest that rates of mortality are different for known addicts and for those who have hidden their drug use. Changes in the way drugs are used, for example, a shift from injection of the drug to smoking, can also affect mortality rates, as can variations in purity.

In theory, estimates of the size of a population derived from different measures should coincide. Where they do not, the discrepancy between two measures can be used as an estimate for some portion of a population that is hidden. Walsh (1970), for example, estimated the extent of religious inter-marriage in the Republic of Ireland by assuming that such marriages accounted for discrepancies between rates of marriage performed under the auspices of various denominations and the proportion of members of those denominations recorded as ever-married in the Census. Dilnot and Morris (1981) used a discrepancy method to estimate the extent of tax evasion and social security abuse in Britain using data from the 1977 Family Expenditure Survey. They inspected (anonymized) data for households in the FES where expenditure exceeded reported income, but where the income-expenditure discrepancy could not be explained by factors such as the run-down of existing wealth. A difficulty with discrepancy measures is that one is always dealing with an 'unexplained residual' (Frey and Pommerehne 1982), that which is assumed to be left over when all other factors have been taken into account. As Frey and Pommerehne point out, in cases where direct measurement is impossible use of the residual might well be reasonable. But in many cases its size is likely to be affected by a variety of factors, not all of them obvious or directly measurable. To be confident that the unexplained residual contains only what one is interested in requires both good data and a sound underlying theoretical model. Research on the size of the hidden economy is perhaps a good example of a field where both have been lacking (Lee 1993). Jim Thomas (1990) has criticized much of the work in the area for being based on 'measurement without theory'. Neither has the calibre of the data used been impressive, for, if sociologists can be accused of being too sceptical of official statistics (Bulmer 1980a), economists can be chided for caring little about the basic quality of their data (Morgenstern 1963; Reuter 1982: 182; Jacob 1984; Thomas 1988, 1990).

As a further example of the use of running records, one can note that survey researchers have on occasion used them as a source of validation data. This is only possible, of course, for activities of the kind for which records are kept (Bateson 1984). Even if data exist at an individual level suitable for validation purposes, it might not be possible to gain access to them because of concerns over data protection. (The direct matching of interview reports against written records is not possible for methods which produce anonymized reports. It is possible, though, to estimate *levels* of agreement.) Sudman and Bradburn (1982) recommend that, even where individual level data are not available, it is wise to compare self-reports against aggregated data. Even here, though, there are difficulties. As Bateson (1984) points out, data can be aggregated in different ways. As a result, although marginal frequencies might seem similar, there is no guarantee that bivariate and multivariate relationships remain unaffected. In addition, there can be a considerable lag between the origination of the written record and the survey self-report. The records themselves can be in error, while matching procedures are sometimes open to question. A study by Miller and Groves (1985), in which survey data were matched with written records using a variety of manual and computer procedures, found wide variations in the number of matches found. Again, there is no reason to suppose that levels of agreement between survey data and official records will necessarily be high. Bateson argues that, since written records often depend on the report of an original respondent, invalidities found in the self-report data can also be found in the written record. In some cases, though, written records can be more reliable than the respondent's account. Cannell and Kahn (1968) note, for example, that patients often lack detailed knowledge of the surgical procedures performed on them. In these cases, one would expect hospital records to be more reliable. In a similar vein, Midanik (1982) remarks that alcoholics might not recall events surrounding their hospitalization as a result of having been too drunk or too confused at the time it occurred. Consumption figures derived from sales data are sometimes compared with self-reports in studies of drinking behaviour. Midanik (1982), however, points to some of the difficulties inherent in this procedure. Principally, purchasing and consumption are not the same. Sales data will not include alcohol which was home made, or purchased from a duty free shop and therefore untaxed. Problems also arise because of alcohol used in cooking, bottle breakage and stockpiling. There might also be some difficulty in making meaningful comparisons between estimates based on widely different units of measurement.

The availability of running records

Webb *et al.* observe that, 'Archives are ubiquitous and numerous, and we all appear in them, usually in many of them' (1981: 84). While one ostensible advantage of running records is their availability, the extent to which data can readily be found depends on a number of factors. Scott (1990) notes that published reference works are often produced in large quantities. However, because they are treated as ephemeral publications, they are often not preserved, potentially making difficult the later retrieval of trend data. There can sometimes be cost barriers to availability. In the case of official statistics governments make decisions about availability, pricing, marketing and the nature of the links between data producers and users (Starr 1987). According to Starr and Corson (1987), the development since the 1980s of a statistical services industry has potentially serious implications for the availability of statistical information. Commercial organizations increasingly collect, collate, package, repackage and disseminate for profit large volumes of statistical data, some of it originally collected at public expense. Much of this material is inaccessible to researchers because of cost.

As noted earlier, running records are increasingly available in digital form. While this undoubtedly widens access to relevant material, Ray Thomas (1996) has questioned the use of terms such as the 'information explosion' in relation to available statistical sources. In general, he argues, information technology does not of itself provide new information. Instead, by making existing materials available in digital form it transforms the analytic possibilities open to researchers. Thomas, however, notes that researchers need to be aware of the systematic bias in the availability of data sources introduced by new technologies. The spread of digitization is uneven. Some sources, newspapers for example, became readily available in digital form because their underlying production processes are already computerized. Contemporaneous material is more likely to be available in digital form than older material, and there can be a lack of comparability between digital and pre-digital series. Making a similar point, Scott (1990) points out that reference materials are increasingly being converted to machine readable form. As the material is updated older information is overwritten, a circumstance that might in the future have serious implications for the understanding of trends.

More generally, the availability of statistical material derives in part from the varying degrees of 'recordability' (Scott 1990) that surround different areas of social life. To take one example, the extensive literature on estimating the size of the underground economy partly reflects the fact that the scale and scope of economic measurement is extensive relative to other areas of social life (Miles and Irvine 1979). On the other hand most societies have statistical blindspots, to use Starr's (1987) phrase. Information of one sort or another that could in theory be collected routinely is not produced because it is thought politically inconvenient, culturally inappropriate or too technically difficult to do so. In the United States, for example, official data on religious affiliation are lacking. This is not only because of constitutional constraints but the result of worries of, among others, Jewish groups, who, with the Nazi experience in mind, dislike the official recording of religious identification.

How activities are socially organized provides opportunities for concealment or disclosure (Best and Luckenbill 1980) which in turn reflect their reportability. Some kinds of deviant behaviour, for example, are multifaceted in ways that leave multiple traces. Thus, levels of drug misuse can be tracked to some extent through rates of notification of viral hepatitis, drug seizure statistics and so on (Hartnoll *et al.* 1985). On the other hand, activities that take place in secret might come to light only rarely, if at all. The sexual abuse of children is an obvious example. One might add that in some contexts the use of running records is actually a substitute for obtaining information directly or for information that exists but is deliberately restricted in its circulation. Shlapentokh (1987) records, for example, that in the absence of opinion poll data, sociologists in the former Soviet Union analysed publications in certain literary magazines as a way of monitoring trends in political opinion. Of course, restricted information is sometimes inadvertently disclosed or materializes from an unexpected source. For example, figures for the yearly incidence of Catholic–Protestant inter-marriage in Northern Ireland withheld from social scientists emerged as a by-product of research by a geneticist (Masterson 1970) on cousin marriage in Ireland (Lee 1981).

Running records: an evaluation

As Hakim (1983) points out, records originally produced for another pur-pose cannot be assembled to the researcher's specification; it is usually neces-sary to design a study around the records as they exist. In this context, as Hakim suggests, one should not assume that such records can be used 'off the shelf'; it is usually advisable, where possible, to consult those who pro-duced them. One reason that this is important is that the amount and detail of information collected by bureaucracies is affected by the primary admin-istrative purposes served by the records. If, for example, as Hakim points out, minimum standards or requirements are set down, the fact that those standards have or have not been met is likely to be recorded, but details of how a particular situation has exceeded existing standards are unlikely to find their way into the record. Where rules are applied in a universalistic manner, not only is more detail likely to be collected, but information will tend to be recorded consistently and systematically across cases. On the other hand, administrative records generated as an adjunct to the service delivery functions of an organization are likely to be closely tailored to the task itself, potentially limiting their wider applicability.

Hakim (1983) suggests that records vary depending on the nature of the processes involved in recording them. Routine records are essential to the work of an administrative body and are generated in the course of day-to-day work. Regular records encompass additional information not needed for the job itself to be done, but which administrative staff are obliged to col-lect. Special records are the result of *ad hoc* and usually one-off exercises where information, beyond what is strictly speaking administratively neces-sary, is collected for monitoring, management or statistical purposes. Hakim suggests that, as the range of information collected increases, the quality of the information will decline. Putting this another way, the closer infor-mation is to the work needs of the person collecting or using it, the better its quality is likely to be. Routine records are less likely to be error-full and more likely to be comprehensive, consistent and reliable than regular records. It is more difficult to assess the likely extent of error in special records. 'Although one-off exercises can attract interest, and hence greater care in the recording, they are usually carried out at the same time as (and in addition to) existing work, so that there is often less time available for special care, notwithstanding the interest' (Hakim 1983: 493). Since in a given context information is likely to be collected in a variety of forms, administrative records can be rather heterogeneous. One implication of this is that the quality of the data might have to be assessed separately for different types of data.

Webb *et al.* comment that, 'There must be a careful evaluation of the way in which the records were produced, for the risk is high that one is getting a cut-rate version of another's errors' (1981: 140–1). Cain and Treiman (1981), reviewing the usefulness of the *Dictionary of Occupational Titles* produced by the United States Department of Labor, caution against its use for estimating temporal changes in the American occupational structure. Some researchers have used changes in successive editions of the dictionary to argue that the content of jobs in the US economy is changing. However, much of the information on jobs is carried over from one edition to the next, and procedures for incorporating new kinds of jobs are not well developed. Thus, Cain and Treiman starkly conclude, the *Dictionary of Occupational Titles* simply cannot be used to study how jobs in the US economy are changing over time. One problem that arises is that of reactivity at the point when data were collected. Macintyre (1978) found, for example, that nurses and midwives in the antenatal clinic she studied were embarrassed to ask pregnant women questions about nervous or genetic disorders. They therefore phrased questions about these topics in vague or leading ways, which tended to produce socially acceptable answers. Yet the responses to these questions formed the basis for official medical records. In a similar vein, Cook and Campbell (1979: 212) describe an unpublished study in which data on accidents were collected from hospitals in order to assess the effects of a campaign on lawnmower safety. Data from one hospital suggested that the campaign had actually produced a rise in the number of accidents. Investigation revealed that administrators at that hospital were aware of the study and had been especially diligent in identifying cases possibly involving lawnmowers. However, as with other forms of secondary analysis, response biases arising from reactivity might be less serious when running records are used for something other than their original purpose. The analytic intentions of secondary analysts are less likely to be transparent to those who supplied the data than those of the original data collector (Bulmer 1980a).

Apparent trends found in running records can reflect external factors. To take a classic example (Morgenstern 1963), the agricultural censuses held in Bulgaria in 1910 and 1920 apparently showed a doubling in the number of pigs over the course of the decade. This apparent change came about because after the First World War Bulgaria adopted the Gregorian calendar.

Religious feast days, however, were still calculated according to the old Julian calendar. Pigs are normally slaughtered before Christmas, but in 1920 because of the calendar change the feast was celebrated after 1 January, the census date. The vast majority of the country's pigs had therefore not yet met their fate. How records are compiled can also change as policies and organizational priorities change. In 1960 the City of Chicago appointed Orlando Wilson, a distinguished criminologist, as its new Police Commissioner, and gave him the task of rooting out graft and corruption in the city's police force. Campbell (1969) records that Professor Wilson's appointment was followed by an apparent crime wave. In less than a year the number of petty larcenies in the city almost tripled. This rise reflects, of course, the improved record-keeping procedures that Wilson instituted as part of his reorganization of the force.

Selectivity is often a problem with running records. In the case of directories, for example, editorial policies concerning inclusion and exclusion vary. Nor is it always clear how entries are collected, checked or collated. Particularly where those listed directly contribute information about themselves, mistakes and sometimes fabrications can creep into the record. Records purporting to represent levels of crime illustrate the effects of selectivity processes very clearly. A number of factors serve to inhibit the reporting of crime. An offence might not be reported because it is perceived not to be serious. The difficulty or inconvenience of making a report sometimes outweighs an individual's inclination to do so. In some instances, instead of reporting the matter to the appropriate authorities, an aggrieved party might make an informal response to a particular act. A formal complaint might not be made because to do so is potentially to risk embarrassment, intimidation or publicity. Computer fraud apparently goes undisclosed because financial institutions affected by it fear the embarrassment of admitting they have been defrauded. In a similar way, a very different crime, child sexual abuse, often remains unreported because it is accompanied by threats which seek to forestall discovery. Victims can also experience feelings of fear or guilt which inhibit disclosure (Taylor 1989; La Fontaine 1990).

Even when crimes are reported they are not always recorded. The law is enforced in a discretionary way; what is recorded as crime reflects the policies and priorities of local forces. The police might record only the most serious of a number of related offences. Although crimes can be reported, they may not be solved, nor the perpetrator(s) apprehended. Even if an apparent lawbreaker can be found, the case can be disposed of in a variety of ways which do not show up in the statistics, for example, by caution or through acquittal (Box 1981; Downes and Rock 1988). La Fontaine (1990) has described some of the difficulties that arise when judicial statistics are used to estimate the extent of child sexual abuse. In England and Wales, she points out, statistics are given for offences and convictions, but not for offenders. One cannot tell from this, therefore, the number of individuals who have committed sexual offences against children. Particular individuals may have been counted more than once by virtue of having been charged with multiple offences, while charges can relate to the same or a number of different victims. Furthermore, in cases of child sexual abuse obtaining convictions can be difficult. The nature of the crime means that some kinds of evidence, for example testimony from very young children, might be inadmissible, and corroborative evidence might also be lacking. In addition, La Fontaine points to the possibility of plea bargaining taking place. This will, of course, increase the apparent number of less serious offences while underestimating more serious crimes.

What Moore (1983) calls 'invisible crime', crimes without victims, white-collar crime, and crimes of victimization in which complaints by the victim are repressed in various ways, often receive a specialist response. If the issue has been medicalized this can involve the intervention of specialized diagnostic or treatment agencies. Alternatively, activities might be targeted by specialist units involved in proactive policing (Marx 1980; Braithwaite *et al.* 1987). As with official statistics, reliance on figures based on the case records of particular agencies can be hazardous. Figures for the number of cases referred to specialist agencies represent those which have become known to professionals and exclude those which remain hidden. Agency cases are usually therefore unrepresentative, making difficult not only estimation but also bivariate analysis (La Fontaine 1990). Those cases that do come to light often reflect the character of the referral process. To the extent that specialist surveillance units are used to police certain kinds of crime, their procedures will affect the estimates derived. Every year the US Internal Revenue Service intensively examines a random sample of tax returns on about 50,000 individuals. Despite these efforts the ability of IRS investigators to uncover evidence of non-compliance partly depends on the resources available to them. As Mattera puts it: 'This measurement technique thus has the peculiarity that its efficacy is a function of IRS budgetary decisions' (Mattera 1985: 52). Moreover, the detection of fraud depends on the existence of a paper trail capable of being followed by an IRS investigator; 'income which is entirely off the books – unreported by both the payer and the recipient – will escape detection' (Mattera 1985: 52).

In the eyes of some writers official statistics reflect the organizational contingencies embedded in their production more clearly than they do the behaviours they are alleged to measure. Or, as Kitsuse and Cicourel (1963: 137) put it, the rates presented in statistical tables can be viewed as indices of organizational processes rather than as indices of certain forms of behaviour. Like Kitsuse and Cicourel, Webb *et al.* are sceptical about the *unproblematic* use of official statistics. This scepticism is tempered, however, by a radical empiricism. The use of statistical series might be warranted for particular purposes where one has sufficient knowledge of how the figures were produced, where one can assess patterns against the 'normal' behaviour of series or where information is available from other sources of data (cf. Campbell 1969; Bulmer 1980a).

The confidentiality of records

Under some circumstances it might be possible to deduce the identity of individuals from published tables or data from running records that have been made available for secondary analysis. (To state this as a possibility is not, of course, to imply that it has happened.) In particular, special care needs to be taken to avoid 'deductive disclosure' where one is dealing with what Campbell *et al.* (1977) call 'public variables'. These are variables for which identifying information can be found elsewhere, for example, in data on occupational and professional groups or organizations which appear in registers of various kinds. The availability of such records might be greater than it at first seems. As Webb *et al.* (1981: 84) point out, even such apparently innocuous records as driving licence applications and commercial registration records contain quite large amounts of personal information. In these situations the relevant variables may simply have to be deleted from the released data.

The likelihood of deductive disclosure from record-based data can be minimized by using a variety of strategies for introducing indeterminacy into the data. These include: 'broad banding', releasing results on only random subsamples of the data, microaggregation, error inoculation, and mutually insulated file linkage. (For a more detailed review than is possible here, see Campbell *et al.* 1977.) As might be expected, because these strategies use imprecision to cloak identity, their use involves certain penalties since the reliability of the data is degraded. It is also, ironically, the case that data that have been treated in these ways might fall foul of data protection laws in some countries which insist that only accurate data be held (Akeroyd 1991).

Data that are broad banded are categorized into crude rather than finely detailed report categories, so reducing the visibility of specific data entries. In surveys of employers, for example, the identity of a particular firm can often be deduced from information such as its size and industrial classification (Hedges 1987: 282). Care must therefore be taken in reporting such data to ensure that the report categories used are crude enough to preclude the identification of individual firms. Inevitably, of course, broad banding means a loss of information. Boruch and Cecil (1979: 212–13) point out that if one has a large number of cases, the possibility of disclosure can be forestalled by reporting, or releasing for secondary analysis, not the complete data set but only a random sample of cases. In this way there is no guarantee that a given individual is actually present in the data. Even here, though, it might be possible to identify some distinctive individual if the information refers to a small or relatively closed population, such as a prison, and a number of sufficiently detailed analyses are carried out. In this situation it may become necessary to go so far as to construct different tables based on independently generated random subsamples of the data. This is done so that any given individual who appears in one table will not necessarily appear in another.

To preserve confidentiality, data are often aggregated to higher-level naturally occurring units. For example, census data for enumeration districts might be aggregated to ward level or beyond. The principle here is that the less sharp the 'resolution' of the data, the more difficult it is to identify individual responses. The technique known as 'microaggregation' works in a slightly different way by merging data for similar individuals to produce synthetic rather than 'natural' aggregates. The strategy was originally proposed by Feige and Watt (1970) to permit the secondary analysis of data in cases where even anonymized individual records cannot be released. Synthetic cases are constructed, composed of small, carefully designed clusters of individual sample units. Provided these composite cases are generated properly, useful analyses can be carried out without compromising the identity of individual cases. Sample size is, of course, reduced when microaggregation is used and there is a loss of statistical efficiency, although, according to Feige and Watt, the estimates obtained are not necessarily biased. Campbell *et al.* (1977) point out that microaggregation procedures need to be carefully thought out in relation to the data concerned. In particular, the variables used as the basis for aggregation need to be selected so as to be independent of sampling variation.

Sometimes it is useful to link archival records from two different sources without compromising confidentiality. One common way to do this is to use a procedure known as 'mutually insulated file linkage' (Campbell *et al.* 1977). In brief, the procedure works in the following way. Lists of individuals are grouped according to some statistical criterion, say socioeconomic level. Each sublist formed in this way is randomly allocated a code name, and the lists are sent to someone else. There, records on the individuals named on each sublist are consulted and summary statistics are computed for the sublist as a whole. (In some cases, to introduce further indeterminacy, one individual might be deleted at random from each sublist.) The summary data for each sublist are then returned to the originator who reassembles the data according to the original scheme for grouping the sublists. Using this procedure, confidentiality is preserved since neither party has access to information held by the other on identifiable individuals.

It was noted earlier that procedures for maintaining confidentiality often depend on creating imprecision in the data. By their nature these procedures also make difficult assessments of the reliability of the underlying data. This is a major disadvantage of the techniques described above, although, as Boruch and Cecil (1979: 99–100, 115–16) point out, the problem is not an entirely insurmountable one. The data collected can at least be inspected for internal consistency. In approaches that use the link file method of preserving confidentiality, there is a brief period when identifiable data are held and which might provide an opportunity for carrying out reliability checks. A further disadvantage of many of these procedures is that they bring with them increases in the cost of research, and in the time taken to complete data collection and analysis. In general, the more care that is taken to prevent deductive disclosure, the more cumbersome the procedures which have to be adopted. Demands on time and resources are, in consequence, pushed even further. Furthermore, many of techniques for maintaining confidentiality have had only limited field testing. As a result, there is a limit to the extent to which they can be used 'off the shelf' without time spent in careful pre-testing or in the absence of specialized training or statistical assistance (Caplan 1982). (This is something, incidentally, which probably inhibits the wider diffusion of the methods.)

Index numbers

Relatively little is said in Webb *et al.*'s work about what should be done with unelicited data once they have been found, captured or retrieved. What discussion there is proceeds by and large from an assumption that unobtrusive measures typically yield data in the form of simple scores or counts. For physical trace data, from which complex measures are rarely produced, this assumption is for the most part a reasonable one. Running records, too, often yield simple frequency counts, although obviously in this case time adds an element of complexity.

Where the use of unobtrusive methods produces data in a quantitative form, questions arise about how measures are to be expressed, how they might be combined and how changes over time are to be handled. Putting this another way, and more technically, problems arise to do with transformation, aggregation and time series analysis. Saying that data take a simple form is not to say that their meaning is unproblematic. On the contrary, for Webb *et al.*, any individual piece of data is inherently ambiguous. The value of a given unobtrusive measure is merely a hypothesis. 'In each case there are rival hypotheses which account for the score, and rivals are more or less plausible depending on a number of factors' (Webb *et al.* 1981: 73–4). Employing the metaphor of the researcher as detective, Webb *et al.* suggest that attention needs to be given to what might be called the procedural contexts within which a particular measure was generated; for example was there sloppiness, error or rule evasion in collecting the data? In addition, one should try to rule out the possibility that a particular piece of evidence was produced by processes or factors that might weaken the hypothesized link between it and what it is taken to measure. An important 'clue' here is the extent to which the information gained from the measure is consistent with information from other sources. More directly, 'auxiliary intelligence', as Webb *et al.* call it, can be used to adjust frequency data for the effects of other relevant factors. To take Webb *et al.*'s example, suppose one was assessing the popularity of a museum exhibit by measuring the wear on the floor tiles around it. The frequencies obtained are affected, among other factors, by seasonal and diurnal variations in visitor numbers. A number of simple mathematical transformations suggest themselves to deal with such variations. Frequencies might be expressed, for example, in a standardized way, perhaps per thousand visitors, or the counts at a particular (relatively inactive) time could be converted into a base figure with which subsequent counts could be compared.

As they acknowledge, Webb *et al.*'s thinking in all of this is strongly influenced by a long (but not uncontroversial) tradition in economics and demography concerned with the construction and use of index numbers. Technical and conceptual issues abound in this field, only a few of which will be lightly touched on here. In the first place, the information needed to make transformations has to be available, appropriate and accurate (Jacob 1984). Population is often used to standardize a particular measure. However, accurate figures are not generally available for the years between decennial censuses. In certain circumstances, therefore, one might have to estimate annual rates of population change for intervening years (Jacob 1984). It can sometimes also be difficult to find data appropriate to the spatial level of the analysis. A generally unremarked feature of studies using unobtrusive measures is their often localized character. Population data are often not available for very small social units, although the relevant information can, of course, often be generated, at some effort, directly by the researcher.

It is important to use appropriate transformations. As Webb *et al.* point out, it makes sense to express vehicle accidents per thousand registered vehicles but not per thousand telephones. Live births per thousand females aged 15–44 gives a more realistic sense of fertility behaviour than live births per thousand women or, even more clearly, live births per thousand population. Data used for standardization purposes also need to be checked to ensure freedom from error. Despite fairly heroic efforts by national statistical agencies, errors do sometimes creep into published statistics. As Kruskal (1981) points out, even cursory perusal of published sources can turn up examples such as census reports recording teenage girls with, biologically speaking, implausibly large numbers of children, instances where columns of data are transposed with one another, and sudden shifts in data series that on the presented information defy explanation. Further problems arise when one wants to combine several measures into a composite index. The easiest procedure is to give equal weight to each item in such an index. Often, however, this does not make theoretical sense. It is usually more appropriate to combine items in ways that reflect their relative importance. The weighting of individual items in a composite index contains in itself an implicit theoretical model that might require explication and justification (Carley 1981). Furthermore, at every stage, as the index becomes more complex problems to do with the availability, appropriateness and accuracy of the data are multiplied.

Conclusion

Catherine Hakim makes the point that methodological discussion in social science research is oriented to the collection of new data as opposed to the use of existing materials. Moreover, where such discussion focuses on documentary sources, it is primarily directed towards the interpretation of what she calls 'single-unique documents and records' (Hakim 1983: 489). Relatively little attention is devoted to the issues involved in using running records or the information organizations generate as a byproduct of their administrative functions. This is unfortunate. The use of running records can be methodologically problematic. Running records are socially situated products. They emerge out of particular social and organizational processes that reflect a variety of usually bureaucratic contexts and contingencies. Some researchers have recognized in this circumstance a mandate to focus precisely on such processes in ways agnostic or sceptical to the use of running records as indicators (see, for example, Kitsuse and Cicourel 1963). Webb *et al.*'s point, by contrast, is that an understanding of how records are produced alerts us to their forensic implications (as, for example, when the contingencies surrounding the production of different series allow comparisons that point to information otherwise hidden from the researcher).

The ubiquity of running records is striking. The average library bulges with directories, statistical series and newspapers. The rites of passage surrounding birth, marriage (less often divorce) and death are usually marked, if not comprehensively then at least routinely, in the running record. Pointers to trends in production and consumption, social custom and practice, and even organizational structure and function can also be found relatively easily. Running records permit the inspection of trends over time. Dominant social science methods, both quantitative and qualitative, tend to take a single slice through time. Often the result of theoretical blindness, snapshot views have the merit of convenience. Adding time as a dimension in social research has inevitable resource implications. Running records often provide a cheap, if indicative rather than definitive, window on to social and historical trends. In addition, the use of running records seems to pose few ethical problems except where record linkage makes deductive disclosure possible. Even here, prophylactic measures, if sometimes complex, are generally available. Ironically, the rather prosaic character of running records can sometimes be a disincentive to their use. As Webb *et al.* comment, it requires imagination to see data 'where associates only see "someone else's" records'

(1981: 142). They go on, 'Imagination cannot, of course, provide data if none are there. Our thesis is solely that the content limitations of archival records are not as great as the social scientist bound by orthodoxy thinks.'

Recommended reading

Jacob, H. (1984) *Using Published Data*. Beverly Hills, CA: Sage. (A succinct but informative guide to the opportunities and pitfalls associated with the use of data from published sources.)

Morgenstern, O. (1963) *On the Accuracy of Economic Observations*. Princeton, NJ: Princeton University Press. (A classic text exploring the fallibilities of data production, and their analytic consequences.)

Alonso, W. and Starr, P. (1987) *The Politics of Numbers*. New York: Russell Sage Foundation. (Although somewhat narrowly focused on the United States, this book gives an insight into the social production and organization of statistical systems.)

5 Retrieved data: personal and episodic records

It is clear that in recent years the use of documentary sources by researchers outside disciplines like history has grown appreciably. Rather than attempt an exhaustive coverage, this chapter will focus on three distinct areas, each of which has seen a good deal of recent work. These are the study of **personal documents**, visual images in the mass media, and documents produced through 'institutional discovery' procedures.

Personal documents

Often part of the 'archaeological record of a household' (Scott 1990: 173), personal documents encompass items such as letters, diaries, household accounts, memoirs and so on. The use of personal documents as a data source was a significant element in the transformation of US sociology in the early part of the twentieth century, away from 'armchair theorizing' and towards empirical social inquiry. Personal documents provided a window on to subjective experience at a time when there was still some distrust of the interview on theoretical grounds (Bulmer 1984: 54). Thomas and Znaniecki's (1918) *The Polish Peasant in Europe and America* incorporated what was for its time an innovative use of empirical materials. Among many other kinds of documentary evidence, Thomas and Znaniecki drew on letters to and from Polish emigrants in the United States to explore how migration affected the structure and organization of family life. The use of personal documents subsequently declined in sociology, although recent years have seen something of a revival of interest. This should not be seen simply as the rediscovery of 'lost' methods (Stanley 1993). Rather, it reflects a variety of interrelated trends in contemporary social science. These include a growing interest in discursive and textual practice, a desire to incorporate elements of personal experience into the research process, and a commitment to give voice to those, such as women and members of minority groups, that social science has traditionally excluded, silenced or marginalized (Denzin 1989; Stanley 1993; Atkinson 1999).

Quite obviously, as Scott (1990) points out, literacy is a precondition of the production of personal documents; their volume increased as literacy spread. Maynes (1989) shows how the appearance of working-class auto-biographies followed the diffusion of literacy. They appeared earlier in Germany than in France, and earlier for men than for women. Maynes also points to how the production of working-class autobiographies was linked to the development of political and trade union organizations. The extent to which such autobiographies were produced by women reflected their presence or absence within such movements. Letter writing also depends on a mechanism of distribution, the postal service. It is not clear how the substitution of other means of distribution such as the telephone, and latterly email, affects the propensity to write letters (Scott 1990). Letters come to be available to researchers by a variety of routes. In some cases, the correspondence of (usually powerful and/or prominent) people is assiduously collected or preserved for (auto)biographical or memorializing purposes. Relatively little used in disciplines such as sociology, collections of this kind are conventionally understood as providing clues to the character, activities and purposes of their producer(s). For Bytheway (1993), by contrast, collected letters are useful as a repository of more-or-less unselfconscious reflection on a familiar and universal process: ageing. Bytheway notes that much sociological writing on the ageing process is based on retrospective interviewing. As a result relatively little attention has been directed towards how people experience ageing as they themselves age. This is something gleaned more clearly, Bytheway suggests, from letters and diaries than from interviews. Bytheway examined self-perceptions of ageing in the published selected letters of Bernard and Mary Berenson. (Berenson was a noted art historian.) Bytheway identifies a series of models of the ageing process implicit in their correspondence. Sometimes ageing is seen as a process of stages, sometimes as the sudden onset of decline and loss. At different times it is seen as the product of adversity or contingency, even sometimes as not involving change at all. Those who compiled the published collections of letters were not explicit about the selection criteria used. There is no reason to suppose, however, that letters dealing with ageing were differentially likely to have been included or excluded.

An alternative route to obtaining letters for study is to solicit them directly, as Thomas and Znaniecki (1918) did. Advertising in Polish language newspapers in Chicago, they paid a relatively small amount for each letter. In this way they accumulated an extensive collection of so-called 'bowing' letters (as in phrases such as, 'I bow to you my father and my mother' conventional in such letters). Thomas and Znaniecki distinguish various subtypes of the bowing letter according to its apparent function. Ceremonial letters celebrated occasions such as weddings at which the distant family member would normally have been expected to attend. Informing letters narrated what had happened to the sender. Sentimental letters aimed at reviving feelings alienated by separation. Literary letters incorporated poetry or sentimental verse, and business letters dealt with topics such as finance, inheritance or farming matters. In some cases letters unsolicited by their recipient can be studied. In 1963 Bishop John Robinson published a controversial bestselling religious book called *Honest to God*. He received as a result more than 4000 letters that were made available to Robert Towler (1984). The letters are not representative of any wider population; internal evidence suggests, for example, that young, working-class males are underrepresented. Towler argues that the letters provide an insight into the causes, character and consequences of existential doubt and anxiety, elements of the personal sphere not well captured with conventional methodologies. From a content analysis of the corpus of letters followed by a more detailed analysis of letters on particular themes, Towler produced a typology identifying varying forms of what he describes as 'conventional religion'. Each of these forms, he suggests, seeks in a different way to reduce the sense of disorder induced by religious doubt. Social scientists have sometimes used as source material letters sent directly to them. One example, the tongue-in-cheek 'Poems by chairpersons and their agents' which excerpts a series of rejection letters sent to a candidate seeking academic employment, satirizes the shrinking academic job market of the 1970s (Ledger and Roth 1977). More seriously, Gill Valentine (1998), a British geographer, has examined a stream of malicious phone calls and viciously homophobic letters she began to receive in 1997. Valentine analyses the negative imagery that the letters contain, and uses the experience of her own harassment to reflect on the nature of space and its relationship to personal security, as well as on the nature of personal and professional social networks.

Hannah Cullwick was a Victorian maidservant who secretly married her employer Arthur Munby, a poet and author who was also clerk to the Ecclesiastical Commissioners (the body dealing with the property assets of the Church of England). Between 1873 and 1877, and at Munby's behest, Hannah Cullwick kept a record of her daily life (Stanley 1984). The Hannah Cullwick diaries in themselves, and in conjunction with Munby's, shed considerable light on the lives of working-class women in Victorian Britain, the material and symbolic structuring of gender and class relations, and the social shaping of fantasy and desire (Davidoff 1979; Stanley 1992). In addition they have sparked theoretical, methodological and epistemological debate on (auto)biographical writing (Swindells 1989). Stanley (1992) presents a layered picture of the relationship between the pair by juxtaposing Cullwick's diary with Munby's (the manuscript version of which contains material not found in the published version), and drawing on letters that refer to a serious, but unexplained, rupture in their relationship. Stanley shows Hannah's understanding of, and resistance to, the gender and class relationships that confronted her. She also explores how Munby's relationship with Hannah and other working-class women was articulated through an apparently obsessive symbolic conflation of dirt, darkness and disfigurement.

Berman (1995) notes that the diary or daily journal is a form particularly suited to dealing with feelings of ambivalence. He analyses the journal of Claire Philip (1995). A Cleveland social worker, Philip was diagnosed with cancer just before her forty-fifth birthday. Philip's journal was begun three years after her diagnosis and continued over six years. According to Berman, the diary articulates a series of tensions to do with the withholding or disclosure of feelings, with the problem of having no future and with how her illness affected her relationships with friends and colleagues. Wyatt-Brown (1995), from a different perspective, notes the location of Philip's work within a genre of personal 'disaster-writing', but stresses its positive character. Within Philip's journal she finds a developing creativity, partly expressed through a series of poems interspersed with the journal entries. Wyatt-Brown also notes the function of the journal in sustaining Philip's relationship with her family and friends.

White (1998) used published autobiographies to explore the different social positions and social worlds children and adults inhabit in households. She charts the sense of bewilderment, marginalization and exclusion associated with childhood in the autobiographies she studied. Against this, White notes that autobiographies also provide insight into how children develop and express a sense of their own autonomy and agency. Van den Hoonaard (1997) points out that the literature on widowhood pays little attention to the emotional experience of losing a spouse. As a source for such experiences, van den Hoonaard looked at 10 published autobiographical accounts of widowhood. Common themes appearing in these accounts include feelings of lost identity, transformations in the character of friendship after the death of a spouse, and the taking on of new and unfamiliar responsibilities. In contrast to the social science literature, widowhood appears in these accounts as a transformation rather than as a process of adjustment or recovery. Although published autobiographies do provide insight into the experience of widowhood, van den Hoonaard concludes that, given the nature of the genre, systematic comparison between the accounts is difficult. As she observes, the availability of autobiographies in part reflects the contemporary popularity of self-help books. The influence of the market on biographical accounts is not, however, a new phenomenon. According to Maynes (1989) working-class biographies that appeared in the nineteenth century exhibited a variety of narrative forms. The author's life might be cast, for example, as a series of adventures, embedded within the telling of a family history, as a picaresque self-portrait, or as a story stressing the successful overcoming of humble beginnings. Maynes notes that some of these forms reflect the oral tradition. However, a more complex relationship exists between working-class autobiographies and the narrative forms typical of literary autobiography. This relationship, influenced by the growing market for working-class autobiography, was shaped by expectations about the 'authenticity' of such accounts, and the perceived need to draw a contrast between middle-class and working-class lifestyles.

Peggy Giordano has analysed some 7000 inscriptions appearing in US high school yearbooks for what they reveal about the nature of adolescent friendship (Giordano 1995). Although the resulting sample is representative neither of yearbooks, nor of students, Giordano tried to ensure a degree of variability in terms of year, geographical spread and socioeconomic status of the school's student body. Giordano observes that there are three implicit social rules for inscribing messages in high school yearbooks: say something nice about the recipient of the message, say something about your relationship with the recipient of the message, and offer advice, words of wisdom or good wishes. While these rules tended very broadly to be followed, Giordano notes that there are systematic differences in the content of the message depending on the social distance between inscriber and recipient. As compared with close friends, classmates in what Giordano refers to as the 'wider circle' were more frank in their comments, pointed to the recipient's level of social desirability, and gave some indication of how the recipient fitted into the wider social milieu of the school. Drawing on Simmel's work, Giordano suggests that these more distant and ostensibly objective views provide an alternative basis for the socialization of adolescents during the transition to adulthood.

Once a rarity, according to Miller and Morgan (1993), the curriculum vitae is now a ubiquitous feature of British academic life, as institutions adopt more explicit management practices and face pressures towards greater public accountability. Based on their own experiences, as well as on the CVs of colleagues and university guidelines governing the production of CVs, Miller and Morgan analyse the presentational strategies used to produce a satisfactory curriculum vitae. Drawing on Goffman's (1956a) analysis of interactional performance, Miller and Morgan suggest that the CV must artfully convey sincerity, seriousness and the status of its own evidentiary character. At the same time it must avoid lapsing into obfuscatory detail, triviality, misrepresentation or an underselling of the self. Miller and Morgan conclude that the CV increasingly articulates a set of contradictions surrounding the relationship between individual and occupational identity in academic life.

While the curriculum vitae is a summation of the life lived thus far, the leaving of life also has its documentary traces. Douglas (1967) analysed the diary, originally obtained by Ruth Schonle Cavan (1928), of a young woman, Marion, who eventually murdered her lover before killing herself. Douglas traces the breakdown of Marion's life, her growing thoughts of murder and suicide, and her conviction that the lovers would be reunited after death. Jacobs (1967) studied the notes left by 112 individuals designated as suicides by the Los Angeles Coroner's Office. Although there were variations in content, Jacobs contends that the notes have a common form in which the suicide recognizes suicide as a form of trust violation, but one that cannot be avoided. Typically in the notes, suicides define the situation as not of their own making, as being unresolved despite efforts to do so, and in consequence capable of resolution only through death. In line with other studies, O'Donnell *et al.* (1993), in a study of deaths on the London Underground, found few differences in the characteristics of those who left notes compared with those who did not. Notes were more commonly found for successful suicides than for attempted suicides probably because police procedures following a fatal suicide are likely to ensure that notes are recovered. O'Donnell *et al.* make the point that since most published studies are based on determinations by coroners, where the leaving of a note is often an important factor in rendering a verdict of suicide, estimates appearing in the literature of the proportion of suicides who leave notes are likely to be inflated.

Bryant and Snizek comment that the last will and testament 'appears to be the single most neglected document in sociological research' (1975: 219). Yet, wills are socially significant because death potentially disrupts the patterns of obligation and expectation inhering in property relations. Wills are potentially useful from Bryant and Snizek's point of view because they potentially shed light on the self-conceptions of those making a will, their understandings of social relationships, and patterns of sociometric preference. There is an inherent bias in will-making since a relatively large proportion of the population dies intestate. However, wills are usually readily accessible through the probate process. A will typically contains a large amount of generally accurate information about the person who made it. Schwartz's (1993) study of wills filed in the Providence (Rhode Island) Probate Court suggested that disinheritance was relatively rare. There was also little evidence that testators were affected by legal or tax developments; most were not wealthy enough to take advantage of such considerations.

The issue of representativeness refers to the relationship between the set of documents studied and the wider universe of potentially relevant documents that exist or have existed. Representativeness is affected by patterns of differential survival and variations in the availability of documents for inspection (Scott 1990). Documents are fragile. They can be deliberately or accidentally destroyed, or be lost. There are well-known instances of personal documents being destroyed following the death of the person who produced them. The poet Lord Byron entrusted his memoirs to his friend, the Irish poet Thomas Moore. After Byron's death Moore allowed the memoirs, which apparently contained graphic details of Byron's sexual entanglements, to be burnt. Isobel Burton, the wife of Sir Richard Burton, the Victorian adventurer and sexologist, destroyed his diaries after his death apparently in an attempt to present to posterity a positive view of Burton's life. In the case of partial loss, it might be possible to assess how different the resulting analysis would have been had the missing material been available. About one-third of the material W. I. Thomas had originally secured for his study of the Polish peasantry was lost when the First World War broke out. Thomas judged, for example, that the incorporation of the lost material would not have changed substantially the conclusions he and Znaniecki reached in *The Polish Peasant in Europe and America.*

As Scott points out, the availability of personal records usually depends on their finding their way into public archives. This means that, in general, records produced by the wealthy are more likely to be preserved than those of the poor. However, the process of 'sedimentation' (Hill 1993) by which personal documents come to be available to the researcher can be a somewhat haphazard one. Hill distinguishes three phases of sedimentation. Primary sedimentation occurs through the largely unreflexive processes by which people acquire, maintain, discard or dispose of written materials. Sedimentation will be affected by what someone thinks is worth keeping and why, and by patterns of personal organization and orderliness. Hill gives the hypothetical example of an academic scholar who keeps for sentimental reasons school report cards but discards rejection letters from publishers to avoid being reminded of an earlier, less successful career phase. Secondary sedimentation is the process by which material finds its way into an archive. Unless precise arrangements have been made for ensuring that matters proceed smoothly, say by appointing a literary executor, the process is likely to be somewhat haphazard. Material can be lost, damaged, destroyed or scattered. When documents do arrive at an archive, a third process of sedimentation occurs. Material will be sorted, organized, classified and indexed according to the needs, concerns, priorities and resources of archivists. These might not correspond well to the needs, concerns and priorities of a researcher interested in the material. Access to repositories of documentary sources often has to be negotiated with the archivist responsible for the materials. Hill (1993: 41–4) usefully discusses some of the situational and interpersonal contingencies that surround such negotiations.

Documents are socially situated products (Scott 1990). As Scott points out, neither the recovery of a document's intended meaning, nor of the meaning received by its recipient(s) or audience(s), is unproblematic. A detailed documentary analysis requires an appreciation of genre and stylistics, and an understanding of the context of production in terms of authenticity, credibility and representativeness. For Scott, the authenticity of personal documents is an important issue, 'perhaps more so than in any other type of document' (1990: 175). Platt (1981) notes, however, that in practice sociologists, unlike historians, rarely encounter problems of authenticity. The kinds of documents they typically use are usually unproblematic in their provenance, or offer little incentive for forgery. The potential for reactivity present when data are elicited face to face is, of course, absent in the case of personal documents. It would be wrong, though, to assume that documents are free from pressures towards positive self-presentation. Material produced with an eye to eventual publication or in rather contentious circumstances might well have a self-serving character. On the other hand, some kinds of personal document might be rather frank. Scott gives the instance of diaries kept for religious reasons during the seventeenth and eighteenth centuries. Here the behaviour of the writer was the focus for keeping a diary; the accounts of failings and misdemeanours recorded were used to provide a basis for improving future conduct. Scott speculates that the kinds of people who keep diaries are different from those who don't. They might, for example, be more methodical and introspective. Moreover, the motivation for keeping a diary might change over time. 'As the project of keeping a diary becomes incorporated in a person's self-perception, so the diary may become more of a self-justificatory autobiography rather than a daily record of events: the construction of the diary becomes a central element in his or her moral career and self-definition' (Scott 1990: 177). The diary, in other words, becomes constructed in the diarist's own self-image.

The photographs typical of what Chalfen (1998) calls the 'home mode of communication' can be thought of in an important sense as personal documents. As Chalfen points out; the advent of mass consumer cameras enabled people to document their lives in ways previously accessible only to elites. 'Ordinary people have never had so many images of themselves' (1998: 214). Family photograph albums provide a useful source of data on family communication practices. Typically in family albums, certain types of events are privileged over others; the new over the old, the first over the last, beginnings over endings (Musello 1979; Chalfen 1992). One sees the new born not the newly dead, the wedding not the divorce. Although sometimes satirized by being shown in embarrassing poses, family members are most often depicted in ways that present them in an idealized and positive light. The family photograph collection is, thus, 'a highly select, fragmented, and yet regularized sampling of everyday life', as Musello (1979: 116) puts it.

Family photograph albums are organized in ways that document relationships and developmental change in the family, allowing both the depiction and (re)enactment of family bonds in the process. Despite this commonality, Chalfen suggests that there are social class differences in the composition of photograph albums. Those of working-class families predominantly show family members looking and smiling directly at the camera. By contrast, the albums of middle-class families have a greater degree of variability both in terms of who is represented and the range and variety of expressions and poses shown (Chalfen 1992: 230; see also Firth *et al.* 1970). Interestingly, Chalfen (1992, 1998) found noticeable discrepancies between the actual practice of home photographers and the instructions contained in manuals and guides on home photography and the making of home videos and movies. While the latter tend to stress preparation, the careful framing of shots and technical proficiency, the former show quite the opposite tendency. Chalfen suggests that home photography has personal, social and cultural functions at variance with the professional norms and values informing the manuals.

In subsequent, largely interview-based work, Chalfen has explored differences between the United States and Japan in the use of family photographs. He notes that the duplication and sharing of photographs with those depicted in them seems to be more common in Japan than in the United States. Except for photographs of recently deceased family members or formal ancestor portraits, photographs of family members tend not to be displayed in Japanese homes. Chalfen notes the custom of carrying pictures of dead relatives on journeys to places they were familiar with or might have enjoyed visiting. Photographing and sharing photographs from work-related social events seems to be common in Japan, but, compared with the United States, photographs of family members are rarely displayed in the workplace. Personal photographs carried in wallets and the like seem to be rare, too, and where carried are done so unobtrusively. Chalfen suggests these patterns are related to wider cultural concerns surrounding privacy and modesty, the desire for assimilation into work-related social networks, and animistic religious beliefs.

Visual images in the mass media

A fairly obvious contrast exists between the home mode and mass mode of communication. Sketched out here are areas of the mass media that provide potentially useful sources of data. The emphasis is on visual sources. Briefly discussed are: advertisements, news photographs, 'how-to-do-it' manuals and textbooks, and ephemeral sources such as postcards and product packaging.

A number of writers have explored how advertisers depict women and minorities. Sullivan and O'Connell (1988) analysed the content of advertisements appearing in eight US general interest periodicals in 1983, and compared their findings with similar studies from the 1950s and 1970s. They found, over time, an increased tendency to depict women as employed, and in business and professional roles rather than in stereotypical family roles. However, when men and women were shown together in work settings, advertisements tended not to show women interacting with men. Sullivan and O'Connell comment that 'the use of alluring female models to sell masculine products to male audiences is now quite rare' (1988: 188). On the other hand, Dilevko and Harris (1997) found that in advertisements for technology products in fields such as business or computing men are often portrayed as forward-thinking, while women are used to convey an image of the product as easy to use. Goldman (1992) has used an interesting source, advertisements in the trade press, to show how advertisers have tried to co-opt feminist themes into their advertising. Goldman found that advertisements for leading women's magazines actively present images that try to capitalize on the marketing potential of the 'emancipated woman'.

The proportion of advertisements showing blacks in US mass circulation magazines has apparently risen over the years (Colfax and Frankel 1972; Humphrey and Schuman 1984; Bowen and Schmid 1997). Bowen and Schmid point out, however, that blacks remain underrepresented in relation to their numbers in the population, and that members of other minority ethnic groups are rarely portrayed at all. Although, over time, advertisements portraying blacks in lower-status occupations has declined, Bowen and Schmid found some tendency in recent times to portray blacks stereotypically as musicians or sports people. Echoing earlier work and the research on women in advertising (Humphrey and Schuman 1984), Bowen and Schmid note that where blacks and whites do appear together in advertisements, they are rarely shown directly interacting with one another. Advertisers, they conclude, add blacks to advertisements to forestall criticism, but do so in ways that scarcely challenge charges of latent racism.

Van Zoonen (1994) attributes the 'optimistic' character of studies showing declining levels of stereotypical depictions to a methodological preference for studying the *manifest* content of advertisements. An alternative tradition in the study of advertising communication, deriving from semiotics, seeks to uncover how the articulations within an image convey latent ideological messages. Drawing on the work of Althusser, Lacan and Barthes, Judith Williamson (1978) has provided a detailed analysis of the ideological encodings and decodings that operate in advertising images. For Williamson, an advertisement works by encouraging the reader to make a connection between the product and some referent. That connection might be made in various ways, through the spatial juxtaposition of pictorial elements, or linguistically, for example, through punning. Thus, putting together in an advertisement a picture of a bottle of perfume and the face of a famous film star imputes to the perfume qualities of sophistication, beauty and glamour (qualities that the perfume itself cannot possess). Referents exist within a wider system of pre-existing meanings. How those meanings are read on to a particular advertisement has a variety of implications. Williamson argues that as a consumer the reader is induced into a complicit identification with the social attributes implied by the advertisement. Purchasing the product seems like a natural consequence of that identification. As a result, the act of reading the advertisement becomes a site for an alienated relationship to consumption, and the reproduction of class and gender ideologies.

A different, and rather formal, analysis of gender depiction in advertisements is found in Erving Goffman's singular book, *Gender Advertisements* (1976). Slightly more than 500 black-and-white, still photographs are reproduced in the book. The vast majority of them are commercial advertisements, together with a handful of news photographs and line drawings. (A few footnoted family portraits from the turn of the nineteenth century are also used for contrastive effect in the section showing portrayals of families.) The images are arranged in columns and are designed to be read from top to bottom, and column to column across the page in the manner of a newspaper. Photographs are grouped according to the principle Goffman wishes to demonstrate; the postures associated with the 'ritualization of subordination', for instance, or 'licensed withdrawal'. Although the behavioural styles associated with masculinity and femininity operate in almost every social situation, attempts to observe the 'idiom of posture, position and glances' in everyday life can be thwarted by the fluid and transitory character of much socially situated activity (Goffman 1976: 21). However, it is precisely this idiom that advertisers must draw on (indeed cannot avoid) if their images are to be interpretable at a glance by any culturally competent reader. Moreover, to the extent that they must do so in ways that are clearly visible and relatively unambiguous, the task of the analyst is made easier.

In some respects *Gender Advertisements* is neither about gender, nor about advertisements. It is instead an exercise in observation-by-proxy, a catalogue of the interactional forms through which human beings display deference, demeanour and social approbation. Despite their apparent spontaneity, the images found in newspaper photographs also depend on highly conventionalized representations of particular topics. Hagaman (1993) has systematically examined processes of photographic conventionalization by examining entries to a prestigious annual contest for newspaper journalists and photographers. Since contestants are likely to submit pictures they think are likely to embody professional values, such entries provide a good source for the study of conventionalization. Focusing on sports photographs, Hagaman notes, for example, how gesture is used to convey an image of winning or losing. In pictures showing winners, the direction of movement, of the head or of the arms, is typically upwards. Conversely, the direction of movement in photographs showing losers is typically downwards. Photographs often aim to capture admirable character traits associated with sporting prowess, such as bravery or endurance, by focusing on facial expressions such as grimaces, or else make use of water, either being drunk or poured over the head, to convey athletic fortitude. Hagaman comments that sports journalism is somewhat unusual since, at least for the localized American media, explicit partisanship is acceptable. Even in more apparently 'neutral' contexts, the use of implicit story-lines, gestures and compositional elements can convey partiality. According to Edge (1999), news stories about sectarian murders in Northern Ireland often incorporate family photographs of the deceased. The practice, she argues, implicitly conveys a view that violence in Northern Ireland is to be understood in an emotive and individualistic way. Edge draws a contrast with photographs accompanying news stories involving murdered policemen. These typically focus on official symbols such as flags or wreaths present at funerals. For Edge, these photographs contribute to an inclusivist discourse that contrasts with, in her view, the hiding of an important dimension to the conflict, the prevalence of sectarian murder directed at a particular segment of the community.

There has been little attempt to assess what impact newspaper photographs have on those who view them. Walter *et al.* (1995) notice a growing trend in the United Kingdom for press reports of tragic death to focus on the grief of survivors, often through the use of photographs showing family or friends in a distressed, tearful state. They hypothesize that, in effect, such photographs socialize readers into appropriate grieving behaviour in a situation where the privatization of death has removed cultural guidance on suitable ways to display grief. The point Walter *et al.* make might be put more generally. In modern societies, characterized as they are by both complexity and compartmentalization, didactic materials of all sorts sit on the boundary between public and private. This is perhaps particularly true in relation to health education and promotion. Jewitt (1997) studied images of male sexuality in leaflets and posters on sexual health produced by health promotion agencies. She suggests that the composition of images together with the symbolic attributes attached to the actions and actors portrayed in them reinforce traditional gender roles. Men are implicitly seen in the leaflets as promiscuous, competitive and predatory, while women are represented as victims or as guardians of sexual morality. Dingwall *et al.* (1991) compared books published in Britain and Japan dealing with pregnancy and birth. Men are largely absent from images in Japanese health promotion material. Such materials tend also to imply a degree of ignorance on the part of readers. Information is presented in a didactic fashion that suggests knowledge is the province of professionals. Commercial parenthood books in Japan also tend towards a didactic tone, although fathers have more prominence in the images portrayed than they do in health promotion materials. British material by contrast presents images of parental choice and joint decision-making. Couples are presented in essence as informed and active consumers. Newer commercial texts in particular assume both a multicultural social environment and the involvement of the father, and depict the birth process itself in a realistic manner. This is in contrast to Japanese materials, where birth is presented in a stylized and heavily edited manner. In formal education some areas of the curriculum are heavily dependent on visual images. Lawrence and Bendixen (1992) looked at how for the better part of a century medical student textbooks have presented male and female anatomy. They conclude that modern anatomy texts perpetuate a longstanding anatomical tradition that takes male anatomy as a standard against which female anatomy is compared. This process is accomplished by a number of illustrative strategies: male illustrations are used for non-sex-specific features, female structures are compared to male structures rather than the other way round, and readers are directed to visualize female regions as altered male regions. Lawrence and Bendixen conclude that anatomy textbooks, by their use of illustrations and language, make it difficult to learn female anatomy without first learning male anatomy.

Visual images are available from a wide range of sometimes rather emphemeral sources. Edwards (1996) points out, for example, that the very ubiquity and ephemerality of tourist postcards has led to their neglect as a source of data. According to Edwards, tourist postcards showing 'ethnographic' subject matter tend to emphasize aspects of other cultures that can be construed either as 'exotic' or 'authentic'. A third strand, which is sometimes found, Edwards identifies as 'family of man' imagery. Often based on portraits of social types, these images permit a degree of identification between the tourist and local people. In practice, the various types of image can be juxtaposed or combined, and they might even be ironized. Edwards suggests, however, that they reflect two important motivational structures that fuel tourism as a mass industry: the desire, on the one hand, for out-of-the-ordinary experience, and, on the other, for authentic experience. Graham Dann (1996) has sought to understand how the predispositions and motives of tourists are created and moulded by 'cultural brokers of tourism' such as travel companies. Dann analysed a sample of tourist brochures aimed at the British holiday market. He shows that the presence or absence of tourists and locals in brochure photographs is related to how different kinds of 'paradise' are presented for tourist consumption. The potential for privacy and seclusion is signalled in brochure photographs by an absence of people, and familiarity is shown by pictures with groups of tourists. Locals are most prominent in photographs showing what Dann calls 'paradise controlled', most often appearing in brochure pictures but as servants, entertainers, guides or vendors. In some cases, females might appear in a seductive guise. Photographs in this context might even try to convey a sense that tourists can transform themselves into locals through consumption of the local culture.

In another exploration of tourist themes, Gottschalk (1995) notes that Las Vegas has frequently been seen as a strategic site for exploring postmodern logic, aesthetics and subjectivities. He presents a series of photographs which are used not as straightforward illustration, but rather impressionistically as counterpoints to his own subjective, biographically mediated, response to the city. What almost seems like a meditation is organized around a number of themes. One is the superlatism of Las Vegas, its incessant championing of 'the biggest', 'the best' and so on. A second is the surface appeal of instant unearned wealth with the invisibility of the poorly paid workforce that keeps the illusion going, 'the spectacular flaunting of infinite economic possibilities and the systemic enforcement of violent poverty on designated Others' (Gottschalk 1995: 205). A third theme is the relentlessly recycled refraction of events through their media representations. Casinos built to form fantastic simulacra of remote civilizations such as Ancient Egypt or Medieval England, creating an illusion of authenticity to disguise their underlying similarity as sites of frenzied consumption. At one point in Gottschalk's article the images of Las Vegas are juxtaposed with a photograph of Holocaust victims lying in a huge mass grave, evoking for him childhood memories of a long-held ambivalence towards the liberative and oppressive sides of American culture.

Mooney *et al.* (1993) compared birthday cards for women with those intended for men, and cards intended for children with those intended for adults. Randomly selecting cards from retail outlets, they coded them in terms of the categories used by Goffman in *Gender Advertisements*. Although their results were somewhat mixed, they found in general that images on the cards tended to reflect the subordinate position within society of women relative to men, and of children relative to adults. Although ubiquitous, product packaging is often discarded with little further thought. Packaging, however, carries social messages. Rebecca Ginsburg (1996) examined the packaging of feminine hygiene products. Uniformly, the packaging of such products is plain, uses staid or sterile colours like white, light blue and pink, and avoids reference to the objects inside or to their use. Ginsburg argues that packaging the products in this way contributes to an ideology of concealment that surrounds menstruation in Western societies. This ideology, in her view, resonates with dominant expectations informing what is permitted to be brought and not brought under the male gaze.

Investigative methods

Some writers have argued that research is powerfully shaped by the structured inequalities in society. Gary Marx (1984) has reviewed a number of documentary-based investigative techniques by which researchers can circumvent the control of information by powerful others. According to Marx, hidden information is yielded up in a variety of ways. Of particular interest here are: (a) 'institutionalized discovery practices', (b) data put into the public domain by 'whistleblowers', and (c) information resulting from 'uncontrollable contingencies' (Marx 1984). Institutionalized discovery practices result in individuals and organizations being compelled to provide information under the threat of legal sanction. Whistleblowers draw attention to dangers or abuses which exist within the organization to which they have access. Uncontrollable contingencies are inadvertent happenings that bring to light undisclosed deviance.

Institutionalized discovery mechanisms

Marx suggests that researchers should make much more use of information generated by investigative, legislative and judicial bodies than they do at present. In the United States, the so-called heavy equipment anti-trust cases of the 1950s are a well-documented instance of investigative materials that have attracted the attention of a number of researchers. Suppliers of various kinds of heavy electrical equipment, switch-gear, transformers and generators, engaged in a price-fixing conspiracy that violated anti-trust laws. The grand jury testimony on which the original cases were based was not made public (Geis 1968: 105). However, many of the participants in the original conspiracy (a number of whom had received prison terms) subsequently testified before a US Senate Committee on anti-trust violations. Geis notes that testimony can be used to construct social portraits of white-collar criminals, to uncover techniques of concealment, the processes by which participants are inducted into a conspiracy, and the neutralizations and justifications they use to support their actions. Documents from investigatory tribunals also yield information about interrogatory discourse. Based on extensive and detailed analysis of the hearings into the Watergate and Iran-Contra scandals respectively, Molotch and Boden (1985) and Bogen and Lynch (1989) have explored the discursive strategies used by questioners and witnesses alike during the course of inquiries. In particular, they examine minutely the strategies by which those who examine witnesses try to align their quarries to a particular version of 'what happened'; witnesses in their turn utilize a variety of discursive gambits to resist such alignments.

More generally, evidence before investigatory bodies can be used in complex situations to provide the basic factual parameters of who?, what?, where?, when?, allowing chronologies to be constructed perhaps, or *dramatis personae*. On the basis of testimony before a US Senate subcommittee, Vaughn (1967) was able to reconstruct the natural history of an abortive research project, the furore over which resulted in a law forbidding the secret recording of jury deliberations. (Ironically, in the present context, those being investigated were the social scientists involved.) Loch Johnson's (1989) careful mapping of the myriad linkages between the CIA and the academic community in the 1970s draws in part on testimony to a Senate Select Committee chaired by Senator Frank Church. (This is an unusual case, however, because for a time Johnson was an assistant to the committee.) This last instance provides a reminder that the state creates and maintains what Fuller calls 'forbidden research terrains' (1988). These are 'whole areas of possible investigation, which may be geographically, intellectually or institutionally defined, where social scientists are strongly discouraged from pursuing research' (Fuller 1988: 99). Judicial proceedings can sometimes illuminate such terrains. Foster (1996) explored the nature of government accountability in the United Kingdom based on evidence to the inquiry set up under Sir Richard Scott to examine the export of defence equipment to Iraq. He shows that problems of accountability arise in six distinct areas: the locus of responsibility for policy and policy change, how accountability is exercised when there is a need for confidentiality, and how accountability operated at departmental level, at different levels of ministerial responsibility, between civil servants and civil servants, and between civil servants and ministers.

In some instances, the use of judicial documents might constitute the only feasible way to study a particular topic. Much of what is known about the inner workings of the present-day Sicilian Mafia comes from the testimony of '*pentiti*', former Mafiosi who turned state's evidence (Gambetta 1993). Investigative documents sometimes allow the actual mechanisms of conspiracies to be laid bare. Baker and Faulkner (1993) used accounts witnesses gave before the Senate Committee on anti-trust violations about their meetings with other conspirators to investigate the social networks that underpinned price-fixing agreements in the heavy electrical equipment industry. Sociometric analysis of the ties between conspirators demonstrated that the need for secrecy surrounding the conspiracy worked against the attainment of the industry's ostensible economic goals. Mitchell *et al.* (1998) analysed the evidence presented in a case before the UK High Court in which an accountancy firm was judged to be involved in laundering large sums of money. Not only do documents put before the court reveal the actual processes by which money is laundered, they also point to gaps in the regulatory regimes surrounding accountancy and white-collar crimes.

Material from hearings can provide insight into the social construction of social problems. Binder (1993) examined the rising concern voiced in the

United States in the 1980s over the content of rock music lyrics, particularly in relation to heavy metal and to rap. In 1985, the US Senate held hearings on the issue. Binder notes that testimony portrayed lyrics as having a corrupting effect on listeners and stressed the need to protect the young from such corruption. In addition, lyrics that were sexually explicit and that seemed to glorify violence were seen to be a danger to society. On the basis of a content analysis of song lyrics, Binder suggests that sexual and violent imagery is more prevalent in rap than in heavy metal. In the mass media, however, the corruption and protection themes are more prevalent in stories about heavy metal lyrics; stories about rap more often invoke concerns about the possible danger to society. While heavy metal music is seen by the media as a music of white young people, rap is primarily represented as black music. Binder contends that while young people, white or black, are seen to be socially problematic, black youth is regarded as a threat to the wider society in a way that white young people are not.

Using material from investigative hearings as data can be problematic. The prior work that goes into the hearings is generally not available to the social scientist. In consequence, as Marx points out, 'replication and control of relevant variables are rarely possible' (1984: 99). In addition, it can often be difficult to determine how far witnesses or materials have been selected idiosyncratically or with a particular kind of focus, say on serious cases. Baker and Faulkner (1993) argue that there are strong pressures for witnesses before investigative tribunals to speak frankly. They are under oath, face severe penalties for perjury, and their stories are likely to have been cross-checked against those of others. Treating evidence as surrogate interview data, however, can be problematic. Bulmer (1980b) has noted the tendency for at least some investigative bodies to fall prey to what Schonfield calls the 'pragmatic fallacy': 'just plunge into your subject: collect as many facts as you can; think of them hard as you go along; and at the end, use your common sense . . .' (Schonfield 1980: 59). Such material might not necessarily serve the theoretical interests of social scientists well. Bulmer and others have also noted that public hearings have their limits as an investigative medium. In some cases hearings have become occasions for attempting to elicit responses that accord with a predetermined viewpoint (Vaughn 1967; see also Molotch and Boden 1985). Even in those contexts where participants are questioned under oath, there might still be a strong motivation to lie or obfuscate. In some cases evidence available to an investigative tribunal is not published for security reasons or to avoid, for example, compromising the efforts of law enforcement agencies (Cartwright 1975: 194).

The report of the South African Truth and Reconciliation Commission (1998), a body rather explicit about its methodology, makes clear that the investigation of human rights abuses was hampered by imbalances in the evidence available to it. To put the matter bluntly, the dead can't talk and the traumatized won't, while the evidence of people living in remote areas, who had limited access to the media, the ill, the elderly, and people from constituencies hostile to the work of the commission all were underrepresented in evidence. In addition, an extensive and deliberate process by the previous government of destroying state records as the country made the transition to democratic rule seems to have been clearly aimed at the removal of incriminating information about the activities of state security organs under apartheid. (Ironically, since opponents of the regime kept few records, many of the records have historical value as documents of the struggle *against* apartheid.)

Freedom of information legislation

An additional and potentially powerful weapon that could be of use to researchers is freedom of information legislation. Social scientists in the United States have used the Freedom of Information Act to document a range of topics: (i) the collusion of academics with intelligence-gathering activities, (ii) the surveillance of social scientists by law enforcement agencies, (iii) the attempt by the United States to establish hegemony over cultural production and public opinion in other countries, and (iv) internal political repression. Using, among other sources, records obtained under the Freedom of Information Act, Simpson (1994) documents how the development of communications research as an academic speciality in the aftermath of the Second World War depended heavily on overt and covert funding from defence and intelligence agencies in the USA. On the basis of an FOIA request, Keen (1993) has traced the FBI's interest in Talcott Parsons, perhaps a rather surprising choice for the Bureau's attentions given his current reputation as a conservative social theorist. Pratt (1992) has used the FOIA to conduct research on farm movements and the Left in states such as Montana and North and South Dakota. Rosswurm and Gilpin (1986) note that FBI files are often a source of materials such as personal histories of labour leaders, leaflets, union newspapers and internal records that have otherwise been destroyed. They observe, though, that in many cases newspapers are often heavily excerpted in ways that overemphasize union radicalism.

Researchers who have used the FOIA in the United States generally agree that the process has its limitations. It can be tedious and time-consuming. An agency has 10 working days in which to comply with a request. In practice, however, requesters must often wait while a backlog of requests is processed. As a rule of thumb, it seems the FBI takes on average a year to deliver documents requested under the Freedom of Information Act. Keen (1992) waited eight months to receive FBI records relating to the American Sociological Association. Noakes (1995) points out that because of this problem researchers frequently must have recourse to other sources. Previously released files are available in agency reading rooms, other archives and repositories (see Price 1997: 14), books and microfilm collections. Advice from those who have extensive experience of using the FOIA stresses the importance of being precise about the records required, providing information that will make possible the identification of relevant material and being patient in the face of delay.

Variations in record-keeping practice between agencies can sometimes mean that material missed under one search can turn up under another. Keen warns that material appearing in files can be inaccurate and unreliable. A further difficulty is that a request can produce a great deal of superfluous or unusable material. Much of the material Keen received from the FBI on the American Sociological Association was already in the public domain. In addition, he received only 'segregable' material, those parts of the records not covered by exemptions. What he describes as 'significant portions' of the material were blacked out. It is difficult to judge how representative the material produced through discovery practices might be. Steps might have been taken to ensure that certain kinds of information did not even enter the written record. The researcher, inevitably reliant in these situations on what information is made available, effectively takes a passive role. Pratt notes that through the FOIA one can come to possess discreditable information about other people. This can raise ethical dilemmas concerning confidentiality. Pratt records that he has sometimes been unwilling to approach the relatives of people mentioned in FBI files to confirm their date of birth, and has needed as a consequence sometimes to spend considerable periods of time looking for gravestones in cemeteries. That said, according to Marx, there are relatively few ethical problems in using information provided under freedom of information legislation. A further advantage of such material is that the cost of obtaining data in this way is relatively low. In the United States, researchers based in 'an educational or non-commercial scientific institution whose purpose is scholarly or scientific research' are charged only standard fees for the duplication of documents produced under the Freedom of Information Act (Walter and Adler 1991).

The leaking of documents to journalists has become commonplace. What is rare is the leaking of entire archives. One example is the emergence into the public domain of what became known as 'The Pentagon Papers' (Sheehan 1971), a secret history of US involvement in Vietnam that was made available to the *New York Times* by Daniel Ellsberg, a researcher at the RAND Corporation. Another notable example of whistleblowing is found in the report of the *Brasil: Nunco Mais* (Brazil: Never Again) Project (Archdiocese of São Paulo 1985). This report is based on official proceedings of almost all of the cases tried in secret Brazilian military courts between April 1964 and March 1979. These documents, which were held in the archives of the Supreme Military Court, were surreptitiously photocopied by lawyers for the Archdiocese of São Paulo. Over one-quarter of the defendants appearing in these trials testified that they had been tortured. (An unknown additional number might have been tortured but did not so testify.) From these records a detailed picture emerges of how arrests were made, how prisoners were tortured, how torturers were trained, the participation of medical personnel in the torture process, and the failure of the system of military justice to follow even its own legal procedures.

Marx uses the term 'uncontrollable contingencies' to refer to events such as accidents or mistakes which reveal underlying social patterns. (The term 'uncontrolled contingencies' is a better one, since contingencies do not need to be uncontrollable; only out of control.) Technological accidents, like oil spills, and political scandals, such as Watergate, provide strategic research sites which allow researchers to reveal activities of organizations and elites normally hidden from public view. Marx notes that mishaps shatter the façade of normality and provide an ironic counterpoint to official ideologies by revealing the underlife (Goffman 1968) of institutions and personal lifestyles. Molotch and Lester (1975) examined the local and national news coverage that followed a serious oil spill in the Santa Barbara channel. Although local coverage was evenly balanced between the claims of oil companies and conservationists, non-local coverage was dominated by stories of activities favourable to the oil companies. Molotch and Lester argue that these patterns reflect the differential access powerful groups have to the processes by which newsworthy events are socially produced. According to Marx, uncontrolled contingencies, 'Strictly speaking, . . . offer an opportunity rather than a strategy, for data collection' (Marx 1984: 86). In other words, uncontrolled contingencies are probably more useful for discovering the existence of data than for systematically exploiting it. Since much of the material associated with uncontrolled contingencies appears in the public domain, there are few ethical issues raised by its use. It is also, relatively speaking, a low-cost method. However, relying on accidents and scandals as a source of data suggests that the role of the social scientist is an essentially reactive one. Research agendas thus become shaped by events rather than by a systematic logic, and research studies do not cumulate (Lundmann and MacFarlane 1976).

Analytic strategies

A range of strategies have been developed for the analysis of textual and graphical data. Briefly discussed here are content analysis, grounded theory procedures and semiotic analysis. A wide range of software tools are now available to help in the analysis of textual and, to a lesser extent, graphical data. (Space constraints preclude a full discussion here. See Weitzman and Miles 1995; Fielding and Lee 1998.) Software of this kind is designed to work largely, although not necessarily exclusively, with machine-readable text, and to date packages have been used mostly to analyse transcribed interview data. Many of the sources traditionally used by researchers interested in unobtrusive measures retain their original paper-and-print form. Nevertheless, sources increasingly exist or are being rendered into digital form. Material derived from the Internet is, of course, already machine-readable, and Hansen (1995) points out that the increasing availability of newspapers and magazines in electronic form is set to transform the study of such media.

Content analysis

Content analytic methods stress quantification, systematicity, procedural transparency and theoretical relevance (Holsti 1969; Krippendorf 1980). Content analysis is quantitative in the sense that it is based on procedures that permit categorized data to be translated into nominal, ordinal or interval scales. Once produced, scales can be transformed into multidimensional classifications, or can be used to develop quantitative indices. The analysis is made systematic and transparent through the use of explicitly formulated rules and procedures, with those procedures being carried out ideally in a consistent and reproducible way. Content analysis is usually not a descriptive method (Holsti 1969). It seeks theoretical relevance through hypothesis and theory testing.

The content analysis of text often proceeds from a count of the number of times each word appears in the text. The assumption behind this procedure is that the frequency with which words appear is a reflection of their salience. Quite obviously, this statement needs immediately to be qualified; the words that appear most frequently in a text, like 'a' and 'the', are usually of little interest to social scientists. Lists are an important tool in content analysis. One familiar kind of word list, the index, shows not only which words appear in a text but also the *position* of each. A concordance lists the words in a text, showing for each the immediate *context* in which it appears. Concordances are often generated by computer in a key-words-in-context (KWIC) format. This shows each word, usually centred on a page, surrounded by the words appearing immediately before and after it in the text. The analysis of collocates (that is, co-located words) looks at how words in a text are associated with one another. In specific terms the analyst looks at the range of words that appear within some specified distance of words having analytic interest. An example can be found in Hansen's (1995) account of how British newspapers covered BSE (bovine spongiform encephalopathy or 'mad cow disease'). Hansen found that words such as 'scientist' or 'expert' were typically accompanied by terms like 'top', 'senior' and 'leading'; words used by the newspapers, in his view, to buttress the authority and legitimacy of one set of commentators on the disease.

Weber (1985: 53) notes that word frequencies can be misleading if context is ignored. Because words have different meanings or vary in their meaning across context, a simple count can overestimate the salience of a particular word. Conversely, if one pays no attention to synonyms or words such as pronouns that can be substituted for other words, word frequencies can underestimate salience. Weber also points out that, since a concordance is usually many times longer than the text which produced it, content analysis involves 'data expanding rather than data reducing techniques' (1985: 48). In addition, it might be necessary to go through a number of iterations in order to focus on relevant data. An alternative and rather common way of analysing both textual and graphical content is to code data on the basis of a user-generated category system. Coding is 'the process whereby raw data are systematically transformed and aggregated into units which permit precise description of relevant content characteristics' (Holsti 1969: 94). Category systems need to be constructed according to a number of basic principles; categories should be exhaustive, mutually exclusive, independent and 'derived from a single classification principle' as Holsti puts it (1969: 95). Categories are mutually exclusive and exhaustive where there is only one place in a given classification to put a given item, and no ambiguity exists about what category that should be. The principle of independence stipulates that putting any item of data into a category should have no effect on the classification of any other item. Categorization is derived from the principle of single classification when conceptually different levels of analysis are kept separate. In other words, classification should have a clear conceptual structure that permits no conflation of categories. For many researchers such procedures have a mechanistic, fragmenting and decontextualizing character (see, for example, Dey 1993: 58). Researchers who take this view tend to prefer qualitative approaches of various kinds. A number of these approaches make use of 'coding' procedures, although these differ in important respects from those used in quantitative content analysis (Becker and Geer 1960; Glaser and Strauss 1967; Miles and Huberman 1994; see also Fielding and Lee 1998, Chapter 2). One approach of this kind that has been particularly influential is 'grounded theory'.

Grounded theory

In a number of respects the term 'grounded theory' has become particularly problematic. Some difficulties arise because in later writings its originators, Barney Glaser and the late Anselm Strauss, have themselves disagreed over their interpretation of the method. Some writers attach the label to analytic procedures actually at variance with the method as originally developed, or use the term simply as a synonym for an inductive, data-generated approach to analysis without any recognition that the approach might involve specific analytic procedures (Hood 1996; Locke 1996). This is seen very clearly in Kellehear's (1993) discussion of strategies for the analysis of data produced by unobtrusive methods. Kellehear treats what he calls 'thematic analysis' as being virtually synonymous with grounded theory and narrative analysis, although he then proceeds to describe an analytic approach different from each of them, but similar to that described by Miles and Huberman (1994).

At the heart of what might be called 'classical' grounded theory is the 'constant comparative method' (Glaser 1965; Glaser and Strauss 1967, Chapter V). One begins constant comparison by examining instances in the data of potential analytic interest to the researcher. Each instance is coded into as many theoretical categories as possible. Coding in constant comparison is governed by a basic rule: before doing any further coding the analyst should go back and examine all instances previously coded using the same category. Codes at this stage are conceptual labels. As coding proceeds, one inevitably explores the theoretical properties of a particular category. In other words, the analyst embarked on the constant comparative method will soon begin to think of different types of category, and to explore categories in terms of their conditions and consequences, as well as their relation to other categories and their properties. Glaser and Strauss argue that, from the beginning of the research, the processes of collecting, coding and analysing data should go on at the same time. Data collection in this situation is guided by 'theoretical sampling'. Successive reformulations of theory inform and are informed by the 'ongoing inclusion' (Glaser and Strauss 1967: 50) of relevant materials thought to have comparative relevance for the generation and clarification of conceptual categories. The second stage of constant comparison Glaser and Strauss refer to as 'integrating categories and their properties'. Having generated a set of categories, the analyst now compares further instances against those categories. Glaser and Strauss argue that this process leads to the development of theory. Categories are further clarified, their properties are further specified and the interrelation between categories and their respective properties becomes progressively clearer.

In the writings which appeared after *The Discovery of Grounded Theory*, the initial coding process became known as 'open coding'. According to Glaser (1978) and Strauss (1987), in open coding one should, first of all, constantly question the data. What, for example, do the data say about the emerging topic focus of the study? What theoretical categories can be generated from the data? How do those studied deal with the problems that confront them? Second, data selected for open coding must be treated microscopically; textual data, for example, should be coded line-by-line, sentence-by-sentence, even word-by-word, if need be. Third, coding should be interrupted immediately to record memos detailing the theoretical implications of what is being coded. Finally, the analytic importance of any category should always be demonstrated rather than assumed. This means, for example, that, 'The analyst should not assume the analytic relevance of any "face sheet" or traditional variable such as age, sex, social class, race, until it emerges as relevant. Those, too, must earn their way into the grounded theory' (Strauss 1987: 32).

As coding proceeds, theory emerges, but in the next phase of constant comparison the nature of that theory changes as it becomes 'delimited'. In the first place, the theory itself 'solidifies'. Major modifications become fewer in number. Rather, changes made to the theory involve clarification, simplification and reduction. Reduction is an important step on the way to grounded theory. 'By reduction we mean that the analyst may discover underlying uniformities in the original set of categories or their properties, and can then formulate the theory with a smaller set of higher level concepts' (Glaser and Strauss 1967: 110). Reduction allows categories to be expressed at a greater level of abstraction and generality, and offers the possibility of moving from substantive theory to formal theory. In making such a move, Glaser and Strauss add, one achieves two important goals of theorizing. On the one hand, the theory produced is parsimonious, attaining maximum explanatory power based on a relatively small number of variables. On the other, it has wide scope by virtue of being applicable across a range of situations. In addition, the theory is well grounded in the sense that there is a close relationship between theory and data.

All of this has implications for further data collection. Because one has reduced the range of categories relevant to emerging theory, it is now possible specifically to focus on those categories as analysis proceeds. Furthermore, categories become *theoretically saturated*. One can quickly see whether or not subsequent coding will force a modification of an existing concept. If so, then the concept is coded and compared with existing categories. If not, it can be passed over without coding, because to do otherwise 'only adds bulk to the coded data and nothing to the theory' (Glaser and Strauss 1967: 111). This kind of logic can also be extended to situations where a new category emerges some way into the coding of data or where information from other sources seems to be relevant to the emerging analysis. If new material rapidly leads to theoretical saturation, the need to go back and recode existing coded materials is obviated. A lack of theoretical saturation, on the other hand, might require a reworking of existing categories.

Semiotic analysis

A number of researchers have sought alternatives to what they see as the 'scientistic' character of traditional research methods, based on approaches that share a commitment to the interpretive or hermeneutic understanding of social life. Language from this standpoint does not describe an external reality. Rather, social worlds are socially constructed in and through language. Analysis involves the interpretation of cultural representations treated as texts. Placed in the foreground, therefore, is 'the relationship between the "text" as a social construction and its form or its imputed audience-derived meanings' (Manning and Cullum-Swan 1994: 464). Semiotic analysis, an important strand in this tradition, takes language regarded as a system of signs as a model for analysing other sign systems. A sign is made up of a signifier, or expression, and what is signified, the content, that is, of what is conveyed. Semiotics, the science of signs, seeks 'to explain how the meaning of objects, behaviours, or talk is produced, transformed and reproduced' (Manning 1988: 82). The relationship between expression and content for a given sign is understood in terms of the rules or principles that govern how the connection between the two is made. Metaphor, metonymy and opposition are commonly identified ways through which the connection between sign and signifier produces meaning (Feldman 1995). Eco (1976: 280) describes metaphor as involving 'substitution by similarity'. He gives the example of mendicant friars in the twelfth century who were referred to as 'dogs of God'. Metaphorically speaking, just as a dog is faithful to its master, so the friars were faithful to the Church. Metonymy, on the other hand, involves what Eco calls 'substitution by contiguity'; the drawing of a mortar-board on a road sign to indicate the turning for a university would be an example. A sign in some instances takes its meaning from its contrast with, or opposition to, another sign. In almost all team sports, referees or umpires wear distinctive uniforms that mark them out as having a different (and more formal) role from players.

According to Manning (1987: 35), semiotics provides 'a conceptual apparatus for the analysis of culture'. The meaning of a sign can arise only from its relationship to other signs. The ordering of signs into an integrated system in a given cultural domain can be thought of as a 'code'. (The term 'code' is used here in a way that is different from its usage in qualitative data analysis.) Such codes can be identified, formalized and analysed in a systematic way. The analyst begins by identifying a particular cognitive domain. Attached to the denotative meanings associated with a particular term are further connotative meanings. These might be based on metonymy, metaphor or opposition. For example, person-like qualities such as reputation, need or uniqueness can be attributed to buildings (Feldman 1995). Connotative meanings such as 'home' and 'neighbourhood' are based on metonymy when applied to a residence, but also contain an implicit opposition between 'home' and 'institutional' life. Both Feldman and Manning point out that connotative meaning can be further related to wider organizational or institutional concerns. In this sense, semiotic analysis involves a sequential process of deconstructing the original set of denotative meanings and their reconstruction in a way that aids an understanding of the interrelationships between social organization and socially constructed meanings. Kress and van Leeuwen (1996) have attempted to extend semiotic analysis to the interpretation of images. They suggest that existing approaches focus rather too heavily on connotation and denotation. In a complex analysis, they posit instead the need for a 'grammar of visual design' which describes how visual depictions, whether of people, places or things, combine to form more or less complex wholes. According to Kress and van Leeuwen, such a grammar draws attention to three major aspects of visual design. 'Patterns of representation' can be thought of as ways in which elements such as shape, form and orientation articulate potential meanings within an image. 'Patterns of interaction' refer to the encoding of social relations within an image through the use of elements such as the spatial juxtaposition of those depicted or the position of the viewer that is implied by the image. 'Compositional resources' involve ways of invoking meanings through placing elements in an image to the left or the right, to the top or the bottom, or through framing and cropping.

Conclusion

This chapter has provided an indication of how certain kinds of document can usefully be exploited for research purposes. As Scott (1990) points out, it is sometimes forgotten that documents were the main research tools of classical sociologists such as Marx, Weber and Durkheim, and that the dominance of self-report methods in social research is of relatively recent vintage. At the time there were powerful, and probably good, reasons why direct elicitation methods began to grow in importance. Such methods increasingly seem to many people, however, to fragment and decontextualize the individual lives behind the data they produce. What Ken Plummer (1983) calls 'documents of life' – letters, diaries, journals, memorabilia, family photographs and the like – have begun to re-emerge as a significant source of data in social inquiry. Personal documents, as Plummer points out, present a totalizing view of people's lives, and provide access to subjective meaning and experience, and to the processes, ambiguities and changes that characterize individual biographies. Issues to do with authenticity, credibility, representativeness and meaning (Scott 1990) need to be confronted when personal documents are used as data sources, but, at the very least, when skilfully handled, the illuminative power of personal documents is potentially great.

The mass media are full of visual images, a source somewhat slighted in the social sciences in favour of textual materials. Changes in the composition of such images provide an indication of shifts in the social valuation of particular groups. How images are assembled often gives an insight into how activities, events and roles are socially constructed. Visual materials provide a cheap, effective and readily accessible vehicle for making cross-national comparisons, and in less recognized forms, such as product packaging, attention to the visual can produce insights into the social use of objects.

The judicial and legislative process is an unanticipated source of rich material on the misdeeds of the powerful. Investigative bodies are typically official in their mandate, interrogatory rather than advisory in their function, and relatively focused in their scope. They extend from small-scale inquiries into local bureaucratic malfeasance to the kind of truth commission set up by some countries following their transition to democratic rule. Given the volume and in some cases considerable quality of the material produced by such bodies, it is surprising that social scientists make so little use of investigative records. The factors behind this are complex, but surely reflect, as Marx (1984) points out, both a lack of familiarity with suitable sources and a lack of training in their use. (It can also be argued that, although the evidence will not be rehearsed in detail at this point, networks of social ties in academic disciplines are often structured in ways that inhibit the diffusion of particular methods and data sources.) Despite a degree of resonance between a social scientific interest in unobtrusive methods and the investigative procedures used by detectives and lawyers, the products of 'institutional discovery mechanisms' remain for the moment marginal sources of data for the social scientist.

Finally, analytic issues have not been widely discussed in work on unobtrusive methods. Many of the data sources described in this chapter lend themselves to qualitative analysis. The range of analytic possibilities available to qualitative researchers is rather wide, and only some of them could be discussed here in any detail. However, what some researchers have seen as a greater degree of 'procedural transparency' (Fielding and Lee 1998) in qualitative data analysis should further encourage use of textual and graphical materials as data sources in social research.

Recommended reading

Plummer, K. (1983) *Documents of Life: An Introduction to the Problems and Literature of a Humanistic Method*. London: George Allen and Unwin. (A comprehensive introduction to the use of personal documents in social research.)

Scott, J. (1990) *A Matter of Record: Documentary Sources in Social Research*. Cambridge: Polity Press. (A detailed, comprehensive and well-written treatment of sources and methods in documentary research.)

Williamson, J. (1978) *Decoding Advertisements: Ideology and Meaning in Advertising*. London: Marion Boyars. (An influential book exploring ways of reading the ideologies encoded in advertising images.)

Stanley, L. (1992) *The Auto/Biographical I*. Manchester: Manchester University Press. (Reflexive account of the complex interrelationship between self, biography and documentary research. Provocative in the best sense of the word.)

Marx, G. T. (1984) Notes on the discovery, collection and assessment of hidden and dirty data, in J. W. Schneider and J. Kitsuse (eds) *Studies in the Sociology of Social Problems*. Norwood, NJ: Ablex. (An introduction to, and justification for, the use of 'institutional discovery mechanisms' as a tool for investigative social research.)

Weber, R. P. (1985) *Basic Content Analysis*. Beverly Hills, CA: Sage. (A brief introduction to systematic, computer-based content analysis. Now somewhat dated but a good place to start.)

Fielding, N. G. and Lee, R. M. (1998) *Computer Analysis and Qualitative Research*. London: Sage. (A book, based on empirical research, that tries to chart the opportunities and difficulties associated with computer analysis of qualitative data. Chapter 2 gives an overview of major analytic strands in qualitative research.)

6 Unobtrusive methods and the Internet

Nowadays, few areas of research, teaching or scholarship remain untouched by developments in information technology. Massive increases in computer power at declining cost put on to the desks of researchers ways of dealing with topics and problems thought traditionally to lie beyond the scope of computers (Brent 1993). What might be called 'transformative technologies of social research' (Lee 1995b) provide new means of representing and manipulating information. In particular, computer technologies now provide improved tools for the acquisition, storage and management of data, for worldwide communication and access to widely dispersed sources of information. In the present context, the transformative technology of most interest is the Internet.

The point was made earlier that proponents of unobtrusive methods stress the ubiquity of data, the use of data in multiple ways often not envisaged when the material was originally produced, and the playful exploration of unlikely materials. If these are indeed virtues, then one might say that the Internet is a virtual environment in more ways than one. In the first place, the advent of the Internet instituted a massive shift in the way societies convey information about themselves. Moreover, that shift has been accomplished through technical means that endorse opportunistic, even playful, uses. The character of the Net is such that serendipity is an ever-present possibility. Second, although data can be directly elicited on line, the Internet lends itself to data collection that does not involve the direct intervention of an investigator. Computer-mediated communication (CMC) leaves trails. Thus, how the Internet is used, what material appears on it, how in social terms users are networked together, and the processes of communication they engage in, are all capable of being logged directly and accurately, and free of reactivity bias. Third, the social organization of Internet participation links in complex ways to life off-line. Many such activities and involvements, which are difficult to study directly, leave their traces on-line.

Looked at in broad outline, the Internet has evolved through four stages (Coiera 1997). The first phase of development dates from 1969, when the United States Defense Department commissioned ARPANET. (ARPA stands for Advanced Research Programme Agency.) The research on computer networking that resulted from this enterprise laid much of the foundation for the subsequent development of the Net. This initial experimental phase was followed by a second phase, which can be characterized as one of slow and steady growth, together with an expansion that took on an increasingly international character and entailed heavy use by academics. The third phase of Internet development began with the introduction of the World Wide Web. The Web fostered a period of substantial growth in the use of the Internet by providing a standardized and easy way of accessing the large volumes of remote information that were increasingly being made available in electronic form. The fourth and current phase has seen some slowing in the overall growth of the Internet (Gray 1996). At the same time, however, commercial and institutional exploitation and use of the Internet seem to be growing.

There are a variety of forms of computer-mediated communication. Although it is difficult to arrive at a simple classification, Morris and Ogan (1996) suggest that four main types can be distinguished, depending on the nature of the communication, its purpose and the configuration of the relationship between user and system. First, some forms of communication take place on a one-to-one basis and are 'asynchronous'. In other words, sender and retriever do not need to be present at the same time for communication to take place. The obvious example here is electronic mail. A second type involves many-to-many asynchronous communication in which users sign up or log on to a server to access messages about a particular topic or topics. Examples include Usenet newsgroups, electronic bulletin boards and listservs. Third, there are forms of one-to-one, one-to-few and one-to-many communication that are synchronous and are organized around a topic. These include various multi-user social environments (MUSE), Internet Relay Chat and commercial chat rooms. A final form involves asynchronous communication based on the need of a user to access information and which 'may involve many-to-one, one-to-one or one-to-many source-receiver relationships (e.g. Web sites, gophers and FTP sites)' (Morris and Ogan 1996: 43).

Connectivity and interactivity

Hewson *et al.* (1996) note that in terms of connectivity the Internet has begun to rival more traditional forms of mass communication, such as radio, television and the telephone. Put simply, the Internet, although not yet universal, reaches more and more people in more and more places. In doing so, the familiar constraints of space, time and cost typically juggled by researchers become recast. The Internet differs from existing mass media both in the greater degree of interactivity that it permits and in its ability to handle a variety of communicative forms; text, audio, video, graphics and so on. Indeed, the multimedia capabilities of the Internet lead Newhagen and Rafaeli (1996) to argue that its ability to address people's senses goes far beyond that of any other current medium.

The connectivity and interactivity of the Internet have implications that vary from discipline to discipline. For social psychologists the Internet potentially provides a subject pool larger and more diverse than the undergraduate psychology students who populate so many experiments. Internet methods make feasible (though not necessarily easy) cross-national research without the concommitant monetary and time costs of travel to distant sites needed with traditional methods. In addition, Internet research provides opportunities for researchers in remote, small-scale or resource-poor environments to access wider populations that might not generally be available to them. Smith and Leigh (1997) make the point that researchers located away from large centres of population can have difficulty accessing 'special populations', such as members of rare or deviant groups. In many cases, however, people who fall into these categories have established forums on the Internet, such as newsgroups, potentially accessible to social scientists. 'Therefore, researchers who previously had limited access to some special populations no longer have to be at a disadvantage' (Smith and Leigh 1997: 497).

Hewson *et al.* (1996) point out that many of the kinds of experiments traditionally carried out by social psychologists can be transferred to the Internet. Internet methodologies permit a degree of anonymity, both to researchers and researched, which might mitigate the effects of demand characteristics (Hewson *et al.* 1996; Smith and Leigh 1997). The Internet is also well adapted to research methods, such as those using questionnaires and surveys, in which materials are communicated in a written form. At the same time, Hewson *et al.* point out that not all kinds of experimental research adapt well to networked data collection. Some areas of research require specialist hardware unlikely to be available outside a laboratory context. Some studies involve forms of communication, biofeedback or nonverbal interaction, for example, difficult to accommodate with existing Internet technology. In other cases the absence of control over the experimental environment poses problems. It is difficult, for example, to assess someone's knowledge of a particular topic over the Internet. This is because the researcher has no means of knowing what additional sources of information, reference work, other people and so on, they might have available to them (Hewson *et al.* 1996: 188).

For sociologists, political scientists and other non-experimental researchers, on the other hand, levels of Internet connectivity are still not high enough; those who have access to the Net hardly represent a cross-section of the population. There are some indications that, at least in the United States if not elsewhere, Internet users are becoming more diverse in their social characteristics. According to Kehoe and Pitkow (1996), the age profile of users is flattening somewhat, the gender balance is moving in the direction of equalization, and the Web is becoming truly worldwide. Nevertheless, it is still the case that the typical Internet user is male, North American, educated to graduate level or beyond and – students apart perhaps – relatively affluent. Widespread use of the Internet as a tool for surveying general populations probably awaits the advent of newer and broader networked technologies. These might include so-called 'push' technologies where information is channelled direct to users, web phones and network computers, all of which promise to deliver interactivity to a wide spectrum of the population.

For the moment, given the social profile of users, using the Internet as a survey tool is probably most useful for specific kinds of research. These might include looking at particular topics such as the use of new technologies or the Internet itself, or to investigate specific groups who have ready access to the Internet, such as academics, business people, early adopters of new technologies or perhaps certain groups of young people (Comley 1996). Because the Internet allows rapid data gathering at low cost from potentially huge numbers of widely dispersed respondents (Kehoe and Pitkow 1996), it is a useful tool for piloting. The Internet also holds some promise for research on sensitive topics. Ross Coomber (1997), for example, has used the Internet to gather information from drug users and dealers on the adulteration of illegal drugs, an extremely sensitive issue.

The Internet as an information resource

Webb *et al.* remark that 'Archives are where you find them' (1981: 139). One might add that they are found increasingly on the Internet. Placed on the Internet, information produced and processed by someone else can easily be retrieved even when that information is located at a site thousands of miles away. In addition, the Internet has an 'anything goes' character that fits well with a 'data are where you find them' orientation to social research. For example, a random search of the Web, using a search page that returns a list of URLs selected at random, produced sites dealing with: electronic dog collars, ancient Eygpt, cigars, state government in California, William Hearst's house at San Simeon, a chronicle of Russian history, equine law, software development, and the philosophy department at an Italian university.

The diffuse and democratic character of the Internet, the very attributes that make it such a valuable source for information, also make the finding of available information difficult. Fortunately, the Internet provides a variety of means for homing in on likely information and data sources. **Search engines**, as the name implies, allow the retrieval of Internet material that matches keywords specified by the user. (Although engines can access a variety of resources on the Internet, the discussion that follows focuses on the World Wide Web.) There are different types of search engine, with disagreement over the appropriate terminology for describing them. A distinction is sometimes made between 'active' and 'passive' search engines (Barrett 1997). In the former, a computer program called a 'spider' or 'crawler' travels through the Web locating and cataloguing Web pages. By contrast, the listings maintained by a passive search engine depend on a registration procedure; users submit a detailed description of their own site. (In practice, a number of search engines now combine both active and passive cataloguing strategies.) Meta-search engines (or multi-search engines) simultaneously query other individual search engines. This obviously broadens the range of material covered. Equally obviously, meta-searches take longer and the results of searches are not always displayed in a convenient form. There are advantages and disadvantages to both types of engine. Search engines based on crawlers tend to generate more up-to-date 'hits', since they access what is actually on the Internet rather than what happens to have been submitted. They also tend to generate a large number of hits, although many of these can be redundant or irrelevant. Catalogued by humans, passive search engines tend to generate more relevant hits, although the number of hits produced overall may be smaller than with an active engine. Also, since they rely on registration, passive engine catalogues tend to be updated less regularly.

An important skill in using the Internet effectively is knowing how to use search engines and the associated tools that allow one to locate relevant material within the vast sea of information that the Net contains. For example, a search for 'survey' without any further specification yields Web pages on the US Geological Survey and the British Antarctica Survey, as well as surveys of a kind potentially more useful to a social scientist. How precisely one enters anything more than a simple search varies from search engine to search engine. Help in formulating more complex queries is usually available from the search page. (See Peters (1998) for advice on accessing resources not discussed here, such as software and bibliographical information.)

Just as search engines vary in their operation, they also vary in their

Popular search engines

Search Engine	URL
AltaVista	http: //www.altavista.digital.com
Excite	http: //www.excite.com
HotBot	http: //www.hotbot.com
InfoSeek	http: //www.infoseek.com
Lycos	http: //www.lycos.com
Webcrawler	http: //www.webcrawler.com
Yahoo	http: //www.yahoo.com

organization. Although some search engines provide only the front end to a keyword search, some allow the user to move through a hierarchically organized system of categories. This directory-style organization is probably more useful than a search when the user knows broadly what information is being sought. In a similar way, one can often focus on a particular area by going to a specialist website. The Internet Public Library <http://www.ipl.org> makes available a very wide variety of resources of the kind likely to be found in a well-stocked reference library, including a range of biographical material and many different kinds of almanac and encyclopaedia. The Project Gutenberg site <http://www/promo.net/pg> contains a very large volume of out-of-copyright literary texts. Although both of these sources are exemplary in terms of their accessibility, it does need to be remembered that information available on the Internet might not always be found in a particularly searchable or retrievable form.

An important Internet resource are 'subject gateways' which contain lists of websites for a particular discipline. Such lists are usually organized with a description of each listed site as well as a link to it. As Stuart Peters comments (1998: 2): 'The advantage that these gateways have over search engines is that they list only reliable, high content sites and the smaller number of catalogued sites make searching less daunting.' Sociologists will find sites such as the Social Science Information Gateway (SOSIG), Sociosite and Socioweb particularly useful. Although he chides anthropologists for making less use than they might of the Internet for dissemination, Schwimmer (1996) points to a wide range of anthropological resources on-line. These include film and photographic archives, museum collections and area studies material, including handbooks produced by the CIA and the US Army. A different kind of resource, The Scout Report, compiles lists of up-to-date resources for social scientists. These lists are distributed to subscribers by email.

Useful resources	
Internet Public Library	http://www.ipl.org/
Project Gutenberg	http://www.promo.net/pg/
Research Resources for the Social Sciences	http: //www.socsciresearch.com/
Social Sciences Data Collection	http://ssdc.ucsd.edu/
Sociosite	http://www.pscw.uva.nl/sociosite/
Socioweb	http://www.socioweb.com/~markbl/socioweb/
SOSIG	http://www.sosig.ac.uk/
WWW Virtual Library for Anthropology	http://www.anthropology.org/

The sheer volume of information on the Internet tends to mask, except at the broadest level of generality, the social processes that shape what is made available on it and what is not. It is certainly the case that a very wide range of statistical information is available, as are survey datasets for secondary analysis. This is perhaps not entirely surprising. Despite other influences, 'the Net can be considered an academic accomplishment. . . . Much of the morphology and culture of the Net, the practice of information exchange, and the very emphasis on information and the symbolic are all traditional academic messages' (Newhagen and Rafaeli 1996). One can add to this Sieber's (1991) observation that data sharing has a long history in some disciplines, that it enjoys support by funding bodies and government agencies, and that data archives and statistical providers have long been early adopters of dissemination technologies. Accessing data on-line is convenient and efficient for users (Clark and Maynard 1998). It obviates the need for paper catalogues that were expensive to produce and that dated quickly. By contrast, on-line catalogues are searchable, can link the user to other resources and allow data to be retrieved quickly and with little effort. Against this one can note the growing commercialization of the Internet. The number of commercial Internet hosts (those denoted by 'com') reached almost 4 million in 1996. By late 1994 the number of commercial sites had already begun to exceed academic sites and had shown a sharper rate of increase. (Data on these trends can be found at http://www.genmagic.com/ Internet/Trends/)

Tang (1998), citing industry figures, suggests that the global market for on-line information sales will reach US$24bn by 1999, showing an increase over a 5-year period of some 75 per cent. One aspect of the trend towards greater use of the Internet by commercial companies is a growing commodification of information. To take a rather relevant example, information on Web demographics is useful to social scientists developing Internet survey methodologies. As Christine Smith (1997) points out, however, much of the demographic research done to date has been carried out by market research firms. The data from these studies have a proprietary character and remain largely confidential. Commodification of information potentially favours those with resources. In academic terms this means researchers at prestigious research-led universities, against their resource-poor colleagues at undergraduate teaching institutions (Bainbridge 1995). For the time being at least, one major fear – the monopolization of content provision by a few very large companies – has not materialized. Companies that provide on-line information services operate for the most part in niche markets. For such providers, there is a tension between 'getting the product to market' and protecting intellectual property. As Tang (1998) shows, that tension is not always resolved in restrictive ways. Overprotection, indeed, is often seen by electronic publishers as inimical to commercialization and innovation. As far as quantitative data are concerned, a trend towards the commodification of information pre-dates the Internet. What Starr and Corson (1987) call the 'statistical services industry' began in the 1970s, providing data and data services to commercial companies often based on official data obtained at low cost. As Starr and Corson point out, most companies involved in the provision of statistical services attempt to exploit either the size of their accumulated databases or the speed with which they can track market and other trends. (Ironically in the present context, some kinds of rapid trend data are obtained unobtrusively, for example from barcode readers in supermarkets.) Statistical service companies trade most often in geodemographics (the linking of consumer data to small geographical areas), consumer trends, credit information data and market analysis. Most likely to be affected, therefore, by the uneven distribution of available content produced by information commodification are researchers for whom time, space and economic behaviour are important variables.

Two important sources of data that Webb *et al.* (1966, 1981) discuss, institutional records and sales records, have tended traditionally not to be found in the public domain. Analysis of such records depended on being granted access to them by those who controlled them. (For those granted access, the fact that such data increasingly take a digital form might, of course, be advantageous.) The advent of the Internet has not removed barriers to access, although one can point to instances where greater volumes of information about institutions and organizations have come into the public domain. The Oyez Project has produced a website devoted to the operation of the US Supreme Court <http://oyez.nwu.edu>. It allows access to a wide range of information about the Court and its relationship to wider social and political issues, the Justices and their decisions and the legal background to cases (Goldman 1998). It is intended to extend the scope and usefulness of the material made available by the Oyez Project through a wide incorporation of multimedia materials. Bainbridge (1995) has explored the usefulness of the World Wide Web for researchers studying new religious movements. He notes that a number of the larger movements disseminate literature, sacred texts and various kinds of membership information by electronic means. Some smaller and more obscure movements maintain a presence on the World Wide Web, perhaps prolonging what might otherwise be a rather precarious existence. As Bainbridge (1995) points out, the Internet is potentially a useful source of information about disputes and controversies. In the case of some new religious movements, for example, supporters and detractors of the movements have sometimes vied with one another to make available information they believe detrimental to their opponents, including what are purported to be internal movement documents. Zelwietro (1998) has documented a fairly steady rise in the number of environmental groups that make use of the Internet. He notes that such groups make many different kinds of information available on line. They primarily use the Internet, however, to disseminate news about their activities and information about the organization itself. One important consideration from a research point of view is whether groups using the Internet differ significantly from those that do not. For environmental groups at least, Zelwietro found relatively little difference between on-line and off-line groups. Broadly speaking, though, on-line groups had more contact with other individuals and groups, were more international in character, and dealt with more requests for information.

Computer-mediated communication

Williams *et al.* (1988) point out that computers automatically generate data on a variety of topics. These include usage of the system itself, the networks that exist between users, the content of messages that pass through the system and, over time, the processes involved in computer-mediated communication. Moreover, with computer-generated data, the total volume of information relevant to a particular topic can typically be obtained. Unlike in a survey, for example, the analyst might not therefore need to deal with problems caused by missing data, small or unrepresentative samples and the like.

Internet usage

Newhagen and Rafaeli (1996: 3) comment on what they describe as the 'inviting empiricism inherent in Net behavior':

. . . communication on the Net leaves tracks to an extent unmatched by that in any other context – the content is easily observable, recorded, and copied. Participant demography and behaviors of consumption, choice, attention, reaction, learning, and so forth, are widely captured and logged. Anyone who has an opportunity to watch logs of WWW servers, and who is even a little bit of a social scientist, cannot help but marvel at the research opportunities these logs open.

(p. 3)

Newhagen and Rafaeli's reference to being 'a little bit of a social scientist' might be apposite. Despite the considerable degree of media attention paid to the World Wide Web, for example, there has been relatively little empirical study of its use (Bates and Lu 1997). In part, this probably reflects technical barriers to data collection. Research on Web use has, to some extent, been the province of computer scientists involved in research and development work. This situation arises because they, rather than social scientists, had the skills required to build new tools capable of capturing the data needed. Woodruff *et al.* (1996) examined 2.6 million documents collected from the World Wide Web by the Inktomi web crawler, a piece of software that 'crawls' through the Web retrieving documents. Their interest was in HTML (HyperText Markup Language), the language used to write Web pages. Woodruff *et al.* observe that 'many interesting sociological observations may be derived from the content of Web pages'. In their case, patterns of high and low prevalence for new features and functions on Web pages potentially give insight into how innovations diffuse. They also shed light on the marketing tactics of companies producing Internet software. Companies sometimes claim widespread acceptance of proprietary features in order to create an impression of strength in the marketplace. The success or otherwise of these attempts can be judged empirically.

At a more global level there has been a good deal of research on the statistical geography of the Internet (Dodge 1998). Charted in this work is the explosive growth of the Net as well as the uneven distribution of Internet usage between rich and poor countries, and for particular groups within individual countries. As Press comments: 'Everyone knows the Internet is growing like a weed, but measuring that growth with a degree of precision is difficult' (1997: 11). This has partly to do with changes to the underlying infastructure of the Internet as well as problems associated with what is actually to be counted. However one measures usage, it is clear that there are wide disparities in Internet availability between countries. Press examined the relationship between the United Nations Human Development Index, which encompasses data on life expectancy, adult literacy, postprimary school enrolments and GDP per capita, and the number of Internet hosts per 1000 population. The resulting graph shows a clear linear upward trend. In other words, the more socially developed a country is, the greater its level of Internet usage tends to be. As Goodman *et al.* (1994) point out, Internet inequalities are not simply a matter of quantity; quality and cost are also important issues. Users in some parts of the world have access to only rather basic facilities. They may also have to bear directly rather substantial connection costs, in contrast to the situation in First World countries where Internet access is, in many instances, provided effectively free for academic purposes. In particular countries levels of Internet access depend on a variety of factors. Technical and economic factors are clearly important, but government policies, legislative frameworks and cultural factors also clearly play a part. In some countries Internet penetration has been inhibited by curbs on freedom of expression and government restrictions (Connors 1997).

Marc Smith (1997) notes that where communication is not mediated by computer, it is relatively easy to identify where people are located, where they travel, how they group together and what they do. In computer-mediated contexts, by contrast, it is difficult to establish how many and what kinds of people are on line, and how they are spatially and socially distributed. Smith has developed a software package called Netscan which collects information about the structure and dynamics of Usenet. Netscan collects all the messages for all the newsgroups carried on a Usenet news server. It extracts and stores in a database information extracted from message headers. The data collected can be used to explore posting and cross-posting behaviour within and between newsgroups and to look at temporal patterns in newsgroup use. In the future Netscan might permit the visualization of cross-posting behaviour and could be extended to other forms of electronic communication such as email.

There has been a degree of interest in the relationship between the behaviour of individual users and the operation of the electronic infrastructure that supports the Internet. This work, which partly reflects pressures towards the growing commercialization of the Internet, has again mostly been carried out by computer scientists. Huberman *et al.* (1998) claim to detect 'strong regularities' in the behaviour of users surfing the World Wide Web. The behaviour of users, looked at in aggregate terms, tends to fit rather closely well-known statistical distributions. For example, the number of 'hits' received at a website follows a Zipf-like distribution. That is, the second most popular page receives approximately half the hits of the first-ranked page, the third most popular page one-third of the hits, the fourth one-quarter, and so on. These regularities come about, according to Huberman *et al.*, because users looking for information typically make judgements about the usefulness of further surfing based on the utility of the information they have already before them.

The report of Kenneth Starr, the special prosecutor looking into President Clinton's relationship with Monica Lewinsky, was published on the Internet. Reportedly, access times to those portions of the report containing details of their sexual relationship were considerably slower than to those sections dealing with legal issues, an indication of where the public's interest apparently lay. Latency measures are an important class of nonreactive measures (Webb *et al.* 1981: 295). Latency is the time taken from one event to a subsequent event. A number of writers have argued that latencies on the Internet provide information about the relationship between individuals and the virtual community. Anyone using the Web will have experienced the frustration of clicking on a link in a web page and having nothing happen, or of waiting interminably for a web page to download. Sometimes these delays are the result of 'Internet storms', brief spikes of congestion that appear intermittently and for no apparent reason. Huberman and Lukose (1997) have argued that such 'weather patterns' are the collective consequence of individual-level decision-making about Internet usage in the absence of information about the activity levels of other users. Lacking knowledge about overall levels of usage, individuals consume as much bandwith as they can, creating problems for others doing the same thing at the same time. In contrast to this view, which sees users as (rather greedy) consumers, Chen and Gaines (1998) ask why individuals provide information to others on the Internet without any apparent immediate advantage to themselves. Here, the latency involved is the frequency with which web pages are updated. The frequency and duration of such changes can be detected using specialist software. Using a social exchange perspective, Chen and Gaines suggest that a variety of mechanisms encourage the continued flow of information on to the World Wide Web. These include reinforcers such as positive self-image and a desire for name recognition, as well as institutionalized forms of social learning.

Although as yet not widely studied, one rather visible and important component of communication on the World Wide Web has begun to attract attention – the home page. The importance of home pages is that they represent a form of self-presentation (Miller 1995; Wynn and Katz 1997). Unlike many other forms of self-presentation however, there can be little certainty about the size, character or likely reactions of the possible audience. On the basis of an unsystematic sample, Miller (1995) suggests that home pages take a variety of forms. These include pages that are informational about individuals, organizations or groups, pages that display personal style, and pages seeking employment or offering a service. Although they found many of the same features, Bates and Lu (1997) conclude from a sample of 117 home pages drawn from a web page directory that, as yet, no standardized documentary format exists for the home page. Contrary to their expectation, 'home' did not seem to be taken very seriously as a metaphor on home pages. The notion of 'home' as in 'home, sweet home' or 'my humble abode' was not found to any great degree in their sample. On the other hand, almost half of the pages they examined had some resemblance to a curriculum vitae in the sense that they displayed information about the professional capabilities and experience of their creators. Bates and Lu suggest that in American society information about one's professional background is often routinely exchanged on first meeting. They also note that there might be parallels between the home page and the nineteenth-century *carte-de-visite*, a rather large calling card that often featured a photograph, and Miller (1995) points to continuities of form between home pages of this kind and the penpal letter. The purpose of slightly more than one-quarter of the pages Bates and Lu examined was simply to display the creator's ability to create a home page, as in the phrase, 'I have no idea why I'm creating this Web page except for the sake of doing it' (Bates and Lu 1997: 334). Features such as counters recording the number of times the page had been visited and the date of its last update also suggest a self-presentation of competence. About one-third of the pages announced themselves as 'under construction', perhaps a device for saving face should one's site be perceived as technically or aesthetically wanting.

Wynn and Katz (1997) argue that home pages often suggest that their creators possess and value a rather stable social identity. In doing so, they question claims made by some writers (for example, Turkle 1995) who see the self in computer-mediated communication as being disembodied and fragmented. Although the details of this debate cannot be rehearsed here, one point of interest is the preference in later work for nonreactive measures and the use of multiple methods. Apparent in the research by Wynn and Katz, this preference can also be seen in Schiano's (1997) research on MUDs (multi-user domains). Schiano notes that a number of themes that have emerged out of existing work on MUDs and MOOs (MUD, Object Oriented). These include claims that MUDs are addictive, that they encourage communal forms of sociability, and that users frequently swap identities and genders. In addition to an on-line survey and personal interviews with participants in LamdaMOO, a longstanding and much-studied MUD, Schiano also logged anonymous data on use of the system. Data from user logs suggested that some of the more dramatic claims made about interaction in MUDs might well be exaggerated. On average, users spent just over an hour a day in LamdaMOO, a figure hardly indicative of widespread addiction. Users tended to engage in one-to-one interaction with others rather than in the larger social aggregates some have seen as typical of on-line communities. Schiano also found lowish levels of 'morphing' or changing character within the MOO. Even those who did morph remained with a single 'main character' much of the time, and fewer than half of those who morphed changed gender.

Network analysis

One can begin by making a rather obvious point, but one that often is overlooked – the Internet *is* a network. Yet, as Jackson (1997) points out, the models and tools of social network analysis have rarely been applied to computer-mediated communication. Social network analysis concerns itself with mapping patterns of interrelationship between sets of social entities (persons, roles, locations, organizations and so on). The messages that flow back and forth on a computer network, whether local or global, can be captured. Both the messages themselves and the computer-generated infomation concerning the sender, the recipient, the time sent and so on, all provide data of interest to the social scientist. In early work, how groups interacted, operated and developed was typically linked to particular features of computer-mediated communication, such as the absence of verbal and non-verbal cues (pitch, tone, body language) or the unavailability of information about physical arrangements or the social characteristics of participants. Based primarily on laboratory research, these studies tended to ignore the social characteristics of participants, and their relative power and social embeddedness (Wellman *et al.* 1996).

Particularly in organizational contexts, who sends what to whom can be revealing about patterns of informal organization, influence and so on. Garton *et al.* (1997) looked at the introduction of a desktop video-conferencing system into an organization. For lower-level staff, links previously based on physical location began to be mediated by the new technology. At the uppermost level of the organization, relations between the most senior official in the organization and his immediate deputy shifted. The latter, who had previously enjoyed high levels of access and who played something of a gatekeeping role, increasingly became isolated as the computer-based system blurred boundaries between remote sites. McKenney *et al.* (1992) compared patterns of email and face-to-face communication in a work group involved in developing a complex project. They noticed that over the course of a work day, who communicated with whom and by what means shifted in rather predictable ways relating to patterns of organizational and task structure. They also note, however, that there seemed to be clear preferences for using one or other form of communication in problem-solving situations. Electronic mail was preferred in situations of uncertainty, where, for example, there was not enough information to make a decision. Face-to-face communication was preferred in situations of 'equivocality', where it was the nature of the problem itself that was at issue. In other words, there seems to be a trade-off between the efficiency of email and the ability to develop complex shared understanding of particular situations using face-to-face communication.

Rice and Love (1987) explored the relationship between content and connectivity on a computer bulletin board they studied. Specifically, they were interested in whether socioemotional content varied by network role. Although they were able to discern a variety of network roles, from individual isolates, through dyads and 'trees' to groups, they report little variation between roles and the extent of socioemotional communication. Rice and Love note, however, that different methods of network analysis depend on different implicit conceptualizations of network structure, which might in turn be more or less sensitive to measures of socioemotional content. It is important to note, however, that computer-generated data do not necessarily measure well social recognition in networks. In Eveland and Bickson's (1988) study, some people reported having had no communication with another individual, even though communication was recorded in message logs. Much of the disparity is accounted for by messages addressed to a group rather than an individual. It seems that it is the exchange of messages rather than their receipt that is regarded as relationally significant. Garton *et al.* comment that network researchers typically combine methods. Surveys and ethnographic methods can both be used as 'a way for [*sic*] integrating the analysis of social networks of persons and offices with cognitive networks of meaning' (1997).

One advantage of network methods is that they often reveal patterns not necessarily discernible by the participants involved. Schwartz and Wood (1993) collected email logs from a number of sites around the world. Using rather powerful computer algorithms they represented the patterns of who-to-whom communication in a graphical form. Eventually, they were able to isolate on the basis of their communication patterns people who shared similar interests in particular topics, not all of whom were known to each other. Schwartz and Wood argue that their work has 'powerful potential for supporting resource discovery and various types of collaboration' (1993: 88). Nevertheless, they note that the ability to derive the content of people's interests from the pattern of their communication raises privacy issues that are not necessarily easy to resolve. Larson (1996) examined the underlying intellectual structure of the World Wide Web. Search engines on the Web can return information not just about the content of particular web pages, but also about their links to other pages. Links between documents, according to Larson, can be regarded as analogous to patterns of citation and co-citation in academic journal articles. Examining web pages dealing with a specific range of topics (Earth Sciences, Remote Sensing and Geographical Information Systems), Larson uncovered patterns of linkages between pages that seem to reflect the organization of existing academic specialisms. The implication is that, if the Web is – as is sometimes assumed – a vast digital library, its intellectual structure is capable of being mapped through the linkages embedded within it. A final example of network analysis has a more qualitative and interpretive feel to it. As noted earlier, Wynn and Katz (1997) examined a variety of home pages on the World Wide Web in a study of how people present identity on line. For a chosen individual, Wynn and Katz followed links from that person's home page to the pages of other individuals apparently relationally important to them. (The procedure is analogous to 'chain referral' or 'snowball' sampling in qualitative research. On the problematic status of the term 'snowball' in this context, see Lee

(1993).) According to Wynn and Katz, the content of these linked pages provides a context for the identity presented on the starting page.

The content of computer-mediated communications

For many qualitative researchers, there has been a growing recognition that the Internet presents considerable opportunities for first-hand naturalistic investigation into the character of computer-mediated communication itself. Computers have 'built-in external memory' (Sproull 1991: 182). Once downloaded, computer-mediated communications can be stored electronically and retrieved later. In addition, what is retrieved is computer processable. It can be searched, counted, coded and so on. Both these aspects have important methodological consequences. First of all, data capture is extremely easy. For example, all the messages sent to a particular newsgroup about a particular topic for a particular period can be retrieved in their entirety in a matter of minutes. Second, the data already take a machine-readable form. They do not require transcription, a major bottleneck in many kinds of text-based research, and they are amenable to a variety of computer-based strategies for analysing text (see Fielding and Lee 1998).

Studies of computer-mediated communication have taken in a wide range of so-called 'virtual environments'. A good deal of work has been done on MUDs and MOOs. Attention is now also being directed to Multi-User Virtual Reality, computer-generated display systems that give users a sense of being present in an environment other than the one they are actually in, and that allows them to interact with that environment (Schroeder 1996: 25). Research in these environments usually takes the form of virtual ethnography, with the researcher openly present in the world, often conducting on-line interviews with users. In what follows, by contrast, the focus will be on Usenet newsgroups, which provide vast stocks of unobtrusive data.

Newsgroups are on-line discussion groups. The most popular forum for the distribution of such discussions is Usenet. There are thousands of newsgroups on Usenet, each devoted to a particular topic and each with its own name. Newsgroup names are organized hierarchically. For example, a newsgroup might be named rec.music.classical. The top-level hierarchy indicates in a general way what the group is about; 'rec' indicates that this is a group concerned with a recreational topic. The second and third terms (and occasionally beyond) indicate levels of greater specificity. In this case the group is about music rather than film and about classical rather than folk music. There are seven standard newsgroup categories, such as 'comp', the hierarchy to do with computing, 'soc' for social affairs, 'sci' for scientific matters, and so on. Unofficial hierarchies also exist, the most extensive of which is the alt.* hierarchy. (For a detailed discussion of Usenet, see Pfaffenberger 1995.)

To access Usenet, one typically subscribes to a particular newsgroup or set of newsgroups. Users post messages to the group. These messages can be downloaded from a server that makes available Usenet postings by using a 'newsreader', a software program that acts as a 'client' to the server. Newsreaders typically organize postings sequentially into 'threads' sharing a common subject. This makes it possible to follow the discussion of a particular topic. Postings contain a 'header' and a 'body' (and often a 'signature', a personalized footer). The header contains a number of fields showing information about the posting, including who sent it and what it is about. The body contains the message to which the user can append a further text which can then be reposted.

The postings on abortion analysed by Schneider (1996) amounted to 46,592 messages over 12 months. These articles had 3276 different authors distributed across 7831 threads. Baym (1995) analysed 32,000 posts which she collected in a systematic way over a 10-month period. She gives an example of a post that is 'fairly typical in content, tone and length' (Baym 1995: 34). It is 25 lines long. If we assume six words to a line, then Baym's data corpus contains $25 \times 6 \times 32,000 = 4.8$ million words. Because the volume of data collected from a newsgroup can be very large, how postings are to be analysed is an important consideration. It seems that much of the work that uses newsgroup data has taken a rather structured analytic approach that allows data to be dealt with in a manageable way. Without this, one might be faced by massive problems of data management that potentially interfere with the process of analysis.

In analysing newsgroup data, researchers have either made use of traditional content analytic methods, or have focused on particular communicative features of the postings they studied. An example of the former is a study by Steve Jones (1997) which looked at how stories appearing in the mass media were redistributed on a Usenet newsgroup devoted to Yugoslavia. Each message which mentioned a news source was systematically coded for name, type, location, method of use and so on. Using the coded data, Jones explored preferences for different types of news source, and how the perceived credibility of sources was used to buttress conflicting positions, while at the same time avoiding a descent into rancorous dispute. Schneider (1996) analysed how the Internet operates as a sphere for democratic discussion. He reasoned that a highly democratic forum would be one where participants contributed in broadly equal measure. Schneider notes that the individual levels of participation on the newsgroup he studied were highly unequal. Fifteen participants contributed 43 per cent of the posts over the period studied. By contrast, Baym (1995) notes that the users who contributed to the newsgroup on TV soaps she studied used a variety of linguistic conventions to create a sense of community and 'fandom', and to further enhance their enjoyment of the soaps they watched. She also points out that commenting on the sometimes convoluted plotlines of particular soaps allowed participants to discuss parallel difficulties in their own lives within a safe and supportive context. A different kind of analytic strategy is to focus on some dramatic event. Phillips (1996), for example, examined in detail an escalating on-line quarrel that resulted from a new member of a newsgroup taking to task one who had been a participant for a long time. Phillips argues that what these events reveal is the complex relationship between technical resources, group membership and cultural meanings in computer-mediated communication.

Process

Williams *et al.* comment that using computer-logged data allows 'researchers to study how users develop patterns of interaction over time, how themes in computer conferences develop and eventually disappear, and how group members interact with different other individuals as a network matures over time' (1988: 97). Putting this another way, the Internet opens up opportunities previously unavailable to study behaviour prospectively. The transmission of rumours, arguments, the development of relationships, the unmasking of previously unsuspected selves, all of which previously could be captured only in retrospect, if at all, can now be followed in their electronic manifestations from their inception to their conclusion (see, for example, Bordia 1996). Rumour transmission is difficult to study since the processes involved are rather fleeting. The laboratory procedures that have had to be used to study transmission processes do not, however, mimic very well the real-life conditions under which rumours spread. Nor do they permit investigation of the motivational factors in rumour transmission (Bordia 1996). Bordia points out, however, that the Internet allows the processes involved in rumour transmission to be studied naturalistically and unobtrusively. Rumours are apparently fairly common in newsgroups and electronic discussion forums and can be retrieved fairly easily from their archives. In this way, both the content of rumours and the communicative events surrounding their transmission become accessible to empirical study in a way not previously feasible.

Internet Relay Chat (IRC) is an Internet system in which users 'talk' to one another in real time by typing at their computer keyboards. Danet *et al.* (1998) analyse the structure and development of an on-line IRC 'party' based on an electronic log of the participants' typed contributions to the session. The party involves seven participants in widely dispersed locations in more than one country. Analytically, the on-line interaction between the participants is conducted within a series of dominant, but implicit, definitions of the situation, or frames, embedded within each other. In one interaction sequence, closely analysed by Danet *et al.*, the participants engage in a sustained and playful exchange in which they simulate on line the smoking of marijuana. In this 'performance frame', the participants produce representations of smoking the drug using nothing more than their quick wits and the characters available on their computer keyboards. As they do so, they scatter throughout their discourse puns, in-jokes and compliments on each other's typographical virtuosity. Danet *et al.* point out that what they describe is a rather benign example of CMC. They accept that aggressive and possible addictive involvement can also be features of IRC. They note too, however, that the illustrative material they present has wider theoretical and cultural significance. It helps to extend analytic understandings of play and performance and other 'liminoid' spheres of social life (Turner 1986). Citing the growth of virtual pubs and internet cafés, they also suggest that IRC might ironically prefigure a return to forms of conviviality more typical of pre-industrial times.

Coordinated by Sheizaf Rafaeli at the Hebrew University and Fay Sudweeks at the University of Sydney, what became known as ProjectH involved more than 100 researchers from 21 different disciplines distributed over 15 countries. In order to complement existing laboratory-based studies of CMC and qualitative single-group studies, ProjectH adopted a quantitative methodology. A total of 4322 messages from three networks, Usenet, Bitnet and Compuserve, were sampled and their contents analysed. The content analysis was based on a collaboratively developed codebook containing 46 closed items designed to permit a wide range of possible analyses of interest to project members (although there are some indications that the coding scheme was not sufficiently fine-grained for some kinds of analysis (Witmer and Katzman 1998)). One notable feature of ProjectH is that its organization, coordination and operation were largely effected electronically through email and on-line discussion groups.

Marby (1998) used the ProjectH corpus to analyse the structure of argumentation within messages. He found a complex, but discernible, pattern of relationships between the emotional tone of a message and a variety of other communicative features. Tone, rated on a scale running from neutrality to outright hostility, was related to the use of various 'message framing devices', such as reference to, or quotation from, previous messages. It was also related to aspects of message content including the use of an explicit statement of agreement or disagreement with previous statements, and the deployment of conciliatory or apologetic statements. Marby makes the point that these patterns suggest that important continuities exist between face-to-face and computer-mediated communication.

Rafaeli and Sudweeks (1998) used the ProjectH database to explore interactivity in computer-mediated communication – the extent to which messages take into account not just previous messages, but the relationship between those messages. In contrast to existing experimental and survey-based studies, Rafaeli and Sudweeks found that the messages they studied tended overall to be factual in character, conversational in texture and to be agreeable and supportive in tone. Interactive messages, those that referred to the relationship between previous messages and those that had preceded them, showed higher levels of agreement, humour and self-disclosure, and made more use of the word 'we'. Rafaeli and Sudweeks suggest that these features might have implications for the stability and longevity of on-line groups.

Romm and Pliskin (1998) describe a situation where the enthusiasm of university administrators for email was moderated when opponents of the university's president began to use the technology to mobilize opposition to his policies. Romm and Pliskin argue that email can act as a mobilizing technology because of its speed and the ease to which it can be transmitted simultaneously to a large number of people. Those involved in the protest could add their own politically inspired gloss to the email they received and forwarded. The ability to retransmit messages so that they are received by people other than those for whom they were originally intended was also important. Because messages were electronically stored, they could be retrieved and redistributed with their potential significance highlighted. As the conflict proceeded, earlier messages could subsequently come to be seen in a new light.

Goffman has skilfully dissected the interactional and ritual dynamics of social forms such as embarrassment (1956b). The 'disembodied' character of the Internet does not permit exploration of the gestural components of embarrassment such as blushing, fidgeting and so on. On-line communications do, however, provide data on the remedial strategies used to reinstate the good character of those who trangress against normative expectations. Wynn and Katz (1997) record an incident on an electronic discussion list where a list member, J., posted a message extolling the virtues of a particular software package. Another list member, S., made suspicious by the tone of the message, determined that J. worked for the company that produced the software. S. privately remonstrated with J. by email, but also posted a message to the list exposing the deception. J. subsequently posted to the list a lengthy and fulsome apology (Wynn and Katz 1997: 314). In his apology J. attempts to show that his original posting was motivated by inexperience, misplaced enthusiasm and bad advice. He also offers various indications of his own good faith and tries to ensure that no disrepute is attached to the company he works for, and by extension its products, as a result of his actions.

Ethical issues in research on computer-mediated communication

In the United States the Belmont Report (National Commission for the Protection of Human Subjects 1978) set forward a series of principles stressing the voluntary participation and protection from harm of human subjects in research projects, especially those participants who for a variety of reasons might be judged to be vulnerable. Such principles have been widely accepted by social scientists. However, regulatory systems for ensuring the ethical conduct of researchers vary from country to country (Lee 1993). The system of ethical regulation in the United States depends on the prior review of research projects by a local Institutional Review Board (IRB). IRBs assess the balance of risks and benefits arising from participation in a proposed research project (Reynolds 1982), as well as examining procedures for securing the informed consent of those being studied. The system in the United States, and other countries such as Sweden which insist on prior ethical regulation, is rather strict from the point of view of researchers. In other countries, the United Kingdom is an example, norms of ethical behaviour in social research remain embodied for the most part in professional codes of ethics and are without regulatory force. Jones (1994), Schramm (1995) and J. Thomas (1996) have examined research in computer-mediated communication in the light of the principles enunciated in the Belmont Report. They agree that research in cyberspace falls within the scope of existing guidelines on ethical research practice in respect of informed consent, privacy and confidentiality and the need to protect research participants from harm. They are less clear, however, that existing guidelines are entirely adequate.

Allen (1996) points out that the technical, rhetorical and administrative structure of sites on the Internet often signal understandings of the rights and obligations of participants, including researchers. For example, both 'public' and 'private' spaces and public and private communication channels existed within the MOO she studied. Nevertheless, one difficulty in applying broad ethical principles to the study of computer-mediated communication is that it is not clear where the boundary between public and private lies in cyberspace. Some kinds of communication are clearly bounded; email sent between two individuals is generally considered to be private and could not be reproduced without their permission. Where one has an open distribution system, as is the case for much of the information on the World Wide Web, few problems might arise in the reproduction of posted materials. It is much less clear where the boundaries are in between. Some people take the view that postings to listservs, bulletin boards and Usenet newsgroups are in the public domain and can be reproduced without permission and without the need to anonymize their content. Synchronous communication systems, including multi-user VR, may form an intermediate case. Reid (1996) usefully distinguishes between the ethics of access to information and the ethics of its use. She notes that some kinds of information while easily accessible are not necessarily intended for use.

Paccagnella has commented that 'many of the most interesting virtual communities are . . . very proud of their exclusive culture' (1997). Reid (1996) found, on the other hand, that the MUD users she studied were rather willing to be studied and placed little restriction on her work. The irony here, as Reid points out, is that in doing so research participants often did not recognize the possible negative consequences of being studied. She argues that the well-known disinhibiting effects of computer-mediated communication produces what she calls an 'allure of self-revelation' that can encourage participants to consent rather too readily to being studied. However, as Reid goes on to point out, not to accept at face value decisions to participate in the research can be to adopt a patronizing attitude towards those researched.

It is worth pointing out that there are practical problems involved in obtaining informed consent in cyberspace (Reid 1996). The population that comprises a virtual group is often a rather shifting one. Herring comments: 'Informed consent from whom? To get all participants to consent to any project, no matter how unintrusive, is a difficult task. If the project is at all controversial, the chances that everyone will agree are virtually nil. Should the researcher then abandon the project?' (Herring 1996: 161). Herring goes on to point out that an alternative to this is to gain the consent from the list owner on behalf of the group. It is not entirely clear, though, that those who 'own' or 'manage' groups can give consent on behalf of others.

The seeking of informed consent is itself reactive. Participants often change their behaviour once they become aware they are being studied. Methodologically, this problem is often dealt with by lengthening the period of observation and by building bonds of trust with those studied. The establishment of trust in the research relationship typically depends on guarantees that those studied will be protected from harm. It is also assumed that where research participants cannot be identified they cannot be harmed by information about them appearing in the public realm. Anonymity protects not just the interests of those studied, but also their privacy. It can be argued that pseudonyms or, in the case of Internet studies, site disguises, have a largely symbolic function. Their importance lies in the illusion they give to those studied that possibly unflattering portrayals of themselves are hidden from outsiders (Barnes 1979). However, while some writers have been meticulous about disguising those they have studied, others have dissented from the practice of anonymization, arguing that such disguises make difficult the assessment or replication of existing studies (Lee 1993). A further complication, King points out, is that 'In the past, one of the factors that helped to protect the human subjects of naturalistic observations was the statistical improbability of their exposure to the often esoteric and expensive academic journals in which the results were reported' (King 1996: 200). The insulation of research participants from research findings discussing them is more difficult in research on computer-mediated communication. Given some basic information, powerful search facilities on the Internet allow sites and the information they contain to be tracked down relatively easily. Beyond this, as Allen (1996) points out, those studied can be knowledgeable about research on computer-mediated communication. Participants in the MOO she studied were quite familiar with existing studies and research on computer-mediated communication in general. By contrast, Reid records that her study of a MUD attracted attention from other social scientists. The group, which by then was undergoing a somewhat traumatic period, began to close access to researchers.

Reynolds (1982) notes that how a particular field is researched depends on the state of knowledge within it. For example, structured methods such as survey research can be used where knowledge about an aspect of social life is already widely available or can be obtained in an open manner. Where little accurate or relevant information is available, as is often the case in relation to novel social phenomena, less structured, but possibly more ethically problematic, methods such as participant observation might be more appropriate. One attraction of research on computer-mediated communication is that it permits researchers to obtain high volumes of data already in a machine-readable form at low cost, and with relatively little effort compared with traditional methods of data collection. The difficulty is that data collection sometimes follows the path of least resistance. Ironically, much social research on computer-mediated communication assumes that technology has 'relatively fixed, invariant attributes that influence all users in similar ways' and ignores social contexts of use (Thompsen 1996: 302). The associated ethical danger lies in objectifying research participants as disembodied selves devoid of rights (Reid 1996).

Conclusion

One does not need to be much of a futurologist to recognize that new technologies will increasingly transform research processes in the social sciences, perhaps even in ways presently hard to envisage. Because of its interactivity and connectivity the Internet offers a range of possibilities for new ways of working across a number of disciplines. In particular, the ability to bridge vast distances at speed and at relatively low cost will clearly affect some of the traditional barriers and contingencies that place limits on the research process. For some kinds of work the constraints of time, cost and distance will simply become less salient.

It is no part of the case for unobtrusive methods that 'data speak for themselves', but there is a preference for data to speak without prompting. The self-monitoring and information-generating capabilities of modern computer networks allow precisely this. Data on computer usage, patterns of networking, communication processes and the content of electronic messages are all available to the researcher with little effort. The Internet opens major possibilities for the retrieval of secondary data and on-line archival material. Indeed, the skills and tools necessary for accessing these resources are rapidly becoming a standard part of the social scientist's toolbox. One possible implication of this is that the use of running records and some kinds of documents will become increasingly popular. The shift to electronic access and delivery does not, of course, reduce in any way the need for methodological awareness in the use of such sources.

Some research on computer-mediated communication chimes readily with postmodern concerns in social science to do with the meaning of culture, identities and the fragmentation of selves in modern society. This work has raised again in a new guise many well-established ethical issues in social research. Specifically, as social scientists explore research uses of computer-mediated communications, they will need to think carefully about where the boundary between public and private lies, about issues of informed consent, how confidentiality is to be maintained, and the potential for harm to research participants.

Recommended reading

Barrett, D. J. (1997) *NetResearch: Finding Information Online.* Sebastopol, CA: Songline Studios and O'Reilly and Associates. (A clear introductory text which explains a variety of strategies for searching the Internet.)

Pfaffenberger, B. (1995) *The USENET Book: Finding, Using and Surviving News-groups on the Internet.* Reading, MA: Addison-Wesley. (Everything you ever wanted to know about newsgroups but were afraid to ask.)

Sudweeks, F., McLaughlin, M. and Rafaeli, S. (1998) *Network and NetPlay: Virtual Groups on the Internet.* Cambridge, MA: MIT Press. (A collection of articles exploring the varied work of ProjectH, a large-scale collaborative study of computer-mediated communication.)

$$\left(\; 7 \; \right)$$ Conclusion

Reviewing *Unobtrusive Measures* soon after its publication, James A. Davis likened it to a sermon 'illustrated with anecdotes, aphorisms and parables' (1966: 290). He went on to speak of its 'interesting' examples and its 'agreeable' writing. Davis (1966) goes on in parodic style to coin the notion of a 'Gee Whiz Ratio' to summarize this aspect of the book's appeal. Calculated by 'tape recording the verbal reactions of reviewers and dividing the number of "Gee Whizzes" by the number of "Are you kidding?s" ', Davis concluded that the ratio 'seems to be positive – in a small sample' (1966: 291). Quite possibly, the appeal of *Unobtrusive Measures* was carefully crafted. In both the 1966 and 1981 editions Webb *et al.* provide (slightly different) lists of examples, each intended to illustrate a particular kind of unobtrusive measure: wear on floor tiles around a museum exhibit showing hatching chicks (erosion), counting bottles in dustbins to estimate alcohol consumption (accretion), the extent to which children sit together when listening to ghost stories as an index of fear (simple observation), Chinese jade dealers' use of pupil dilation as an indicator of a buyer's interest (simple observation), library withdrawals and the arrival of television (running records), recruitment to managerial positions in baseball (running records), Galton's use of a sextant to make anthropometric measurements of African females at a distance (**contrived observation**), the size of Santa Claus figures in children's drawings (written documents), spatial clustering as an indicator of racial attitudes (simple observation), and toilet flushes as an indicator of political popularity (simple observation). One suspects that these examples are meant in various ways to present an engaging aspect to readers. Those relating to racial and political attitudes and to television as a new medium may have had some degree of (lagged?) topicality at the time of writing. There is a certain 'masculine interest' in the items on alcohol and sports. Examples such as the Chinese jade dealers speak to exoticism while the items involving children, to which we might add the hatching chicks, could be thought of as 'cute', perhaps because associated with them are emotions that adults hold but rarely reveal.

It might not be surprising, then, that by 1972 *Unobtrusive Measures* had gone into its eighth printing, and by 1979 it had sold 125,000 copies (Sechrest and Phillips 1979). Yet, in the preface to the second edition Webb *et al.* complained that 'despite the widespread acceptance of the *concept* of nonreactive measurement, the *practice* was still sporadic and undependable' (1981: viii, emphasis added). There seems little reason to revise this assessment. An inspection of the *Social Science Citation Index* suggests that, where the work of Webb *et al.* is cited today, it is predominantly in the context of methodological discussion of multiple methods rather than specifically in relation to unobtrusive methods. This relative invisibility might signal what Merton (1987) called 'obliteration by incorporation', the process by which an idea becomes so accepted that its originator(s) are no longer cited. Perhaps, on the other hand, one can simply conclude that the success of *Unobtrusive Measures* has been greater than its impact. Why should this be? Webb and Weick (1983) point to a variety of reasons for the non-use of unobtrusive methods. They note, for example, that the commitment to multiple methods implicit in the use of unelicited data can often be a disincentive to the use of unobtrusive measures. Multiple methods are costly in time and resources, and their use can be complex. Some researchers additionally feel that, even within a multi-method design, unobtrusive measures add relatively little additional information, or increase the possibility of generating inconsistent findings. Not everyone accepts the overtly opportunistic attitude towards data typical of unobtrusive measure enthusiasts. Many researchers instead feel that the best data are those produced, designed or created for a specific purpose. 'Unobtrusive measures buy a lot of dirty details. To some that is their strength, to others it is their greatest liability' (Webb and Weick 1983: 212). Webb and Weick also note that there is an association between eclecticism and the use of unobtrusive measures. Presumably, however, eclecticism is not always well regarded by one's peers. In a similar way, the playfulness associated with unobtrusive measures can meet with disapproval from colleagues. Even where this is not the case, as a matter of personal preference, a playful attitude might be difficult for some to adopt, while Webb and Weick suggest that being playful in a hesitant, self-conscious or apologetic manner is rarely successful.

Many of these problems reflect the difficulties inherent in the kind of orientational approach taken by Webb and Weick. At the same time, a taxonomic solution to the problem of generating unobtrusive measures in specific research situations remains elusive. Perhaps all one can hope for is a greater transparency about the heuristic strategies researchers use when seeking appropriate sources of unelicited data. On the positive side, one can stress, as Kellehear (1993) does, the simplicity and accessibility of unobtrusive methods. They rarely require great technical or technological sophistication. Kellehear also applauds their role in contextualizing and complexitizing social science understanding. Positively in his view, elicited and unelicited data in conjunction speak to the relationship between attitudes and behaviour as well as the interrelationship between past and present. Unobtrusive methods provide a pathway, however narrow and winding, to the verbally inaccessible. In this context it will be interesting to see precisely how some of the newer information technologies will affect social research in the longer term. Increasingly, in the future the collection of data will be mediated not only by the literal presence or absence of the researcher, but also, in probably complex ways, by whether or not he or she is also virtually present. Novel methods of research and sources of data will both pose new methodological issues and encourage the revisiting of old ones.

The quirky character of Webb *et al.*'s work is demonstrated by the unconventional ending of the book itself. The penultimate chapter, headed 'A Statistician on Method', consists solely of one paragraph, a quotation from Binder (1964) extolling the importance of judgement in the use even of imperfect data. The last chapter is made up in its entirety of Cardinal Newman's epitaph, 'From symbols and shadows to the truth'. The final word here will be left to Webb *et al.* themselves (1981: 324): 'There are no rewards for ingenuity as such, and the payoff comes only when ingenuity leads to new means of making more valid comparisons.'

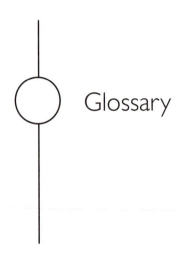# Glossary

Accretion measure: A type of unobtrusive measure arising from the deposit of material in some setting. An example is the litter left behind in a particular area.

Ad libitum **sampling:** Observational sampling method in which there are no systematic constraints on what is observed and when. The observer notes what is visible and apparently relevant as it occurs.

Artefact: A feature of a particular research design that has an effect (usually unwelcome) on the results produced.

Behaviour sampling: An observational sampling method in which a group of research subjects is observed and occurrences of particular types of behaviour are recorded.

Content analysis: The systematic quantitative study of the manifest content of texts.

Continuous recording: Observational procedure that aims to produce a precise and faithful record of how often and for how long particular behaviours occur, with accurate recording of start and stop times.

Contrived observation: Observation in which some feature of the setting is altered in order to make aspects of what is observed more visible.

Demand characteristics: In experimental settings, the clues research subjects use to identify an ostensible purpose for the experiment.

Episodic records: Archival records having a discontinuous form which does not permit the identification of trends.

Erosion measure: A type of unobtrusive measure produced by selective wear on some material. An example is wear on floor tiles as a measure of the volume of traffic passing over them.

Field experiment: An experiment conducted outside the laboratory context.

Focal sampling: An observational sampling method in which a particular sample unit is observed for a specific time period and all instances of its behaviour are recorded.

Grounded theory: An analytic tradition in qualitative research that uses a systematic set of procedures to derive a theory of high generality inductively grounded in data.

Hawthorne Effect: A change in the outcome of an experiment that arises from research subjects' awareness that they have been selected for study.

Meta-analysis: A set of quantitative techniques for synthesizing the results of a large number of studies relevant to a specific issue or topic.

Newsgroup: An on-line discussion group organized around a particular topic.

One-zero sampling: Observational procedure in which an observer records at each sampling point whether some behaviour of interest did or did not occur during the preceding sample interval. Because of the biases it introduces, one-zero sampling needs to be used with care.

Personal documents: Documents produced by individuals for a personal rather than an official purpose. Examples include letters, diaries, memoirs, family photographs and so on.

Reactivity: The potential for the behaviour of research participants to change because of the presence of an investigator.

Running records: Type of unobtrusive measure taking the form of ongoing, continuous documentary records that allow trends to be established.

Scan sampling: An observational sampling method in which a group of research subjects is visually scanned at regular intervals and the behaviour of each individual at the moment of scanning is recorded.

Search engine: Software, usually Web-based, that allows the retrieval of Internet material matching keywords specified by a user.

Semiotics: The study of signs, systems of signs and the processes of signification.

Simple observation: Observational method in which the observer has a largely passive and non-intrusive role in the setting.

Time sampling: Observational method in which data are collected at periodic intervals.

Traces: A type of unobtrusive measure using physical evidence to provide information about social behaviour.

Triangulation: The use of multiple data collection methods with the aim of compensating for the weakness of particular methods by drawing on the strength of others.

Unobtrusive measure: Data collected without the direct elicitation of information from a respondent or informant. Data collected in this way avoid problems of data quality that arise because people who are aware of being studied often change their behaviour.

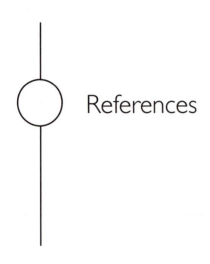

References

Abel, E. L. and Buckley, B. E. (1977) *The Handwriting on the Wall: Toward a Sociology and Psychology of Graffiti*. Westport, CT: Greenwood Press.

Akeroyd, A. V. (1991) Personal information and qualitative research data: some practical and ethical problems arising from data protection legislation, in N. G. Fielding and R. M. Lee (eds) *Using Computers in Qualitative Research*. London: Sage.

Alasuutari, P. (1995) *Researching Culture: Qualitative Method and Cultural Studies*. London: Sage.

Allen, C. (1996) What's wrong with the Golden Rule? Conundrums of conducting ethical research in cyberspace, *Information Society*, 12: 175–87.

American Statistical Association (1974) Report of the American Statistical Association Conference on Surveys of Human Populations, *The American Statistician*, 28: 30–3.

Archdiocese of São Paulo (1985) *Torture in Brazil: A Shocking Report on the Pervasive Use of Torture by Brazilian Military Governments: 1964–79*. Austin, TX: University of Texas Press.

Archer, D. (1997) Unspoken diversity: cultural differences in gestures, *Qualitative Sociology*, 20: 79–105.

Archer, D. and Erlich, L. (1985) Weighing the evidence: a new method for research on restricted information, *Qualitative Sociology*, 8: 345–58.

Archer, D. and Erlich-Erfer, L. (1991) Fear and loading: archival traces of the response to extraordinary violence, *Social Psychology Quarterly*, 54: 342–52.

Arthur, L. B. (1997) Role salience, role embracement and the symbolic self-completion of sorority pledges, *Sociological Inquiry*, 67: 364–79.

Atkinson, P. (1992) *Understanding Ethnographic Texts*. Thousand Oaks, CA: Sage.

Atkinson, P. (1999) Review essay: voiced and unvoiced, *Sociology*, 33: 191–7.

Bainbridge, W. S. (1995) Sociology on the World Wide Web, *Social Science Computer Review*, 13: 508–23.

Baizerman, S. (1993) The Jewish *Kippa Sruga* and the social construction of gender, in R. Barnes and J. B. Eicher (eds) *Dress and Gender: Making and Meaning in Cultural Contexts*. Oxford: Berg.

Baker, W. E. and Faulkner, R. R. (1991) Role as resource: the Hollywood film industry, *American Journal of Sociology*, 97: 274–304.

Baker, W. E. and Faulkner, R. R. (1993) The social organization of conspiracy in the heavy electrical equipment industry, *American Sociological Review*, 58: 837–60.

Barber, T. X. (1976) *Pitfalls in Human Research: Ten Pivotal Points*. New York: Pergamon.

Barnes, J. A. (1979) *Who Should Know What?: Social Science, Privacy and Ethics*. Harmondsworth: Penguin.

Barrett, D. J. (1997) *NetResearch: Finding Information Online*. Sebastopol, CA: Songline Studios and O'Reilly and Associates.

Bates, M. J. and Lu, S. (1997) An exploratory profile of personal home pages: content, design, metaphors, *Online and CDROM Review*, 21: 331–40.

Bateson, N. (1984) *Data Construction in Social Surveys*. London: Allen & Unwin.

Baym, N. K. (1995) From practice to culture on Usenet, in S. L. Star (ed.) *The Cultures of Computing*. Oxford: Blackwell.

Becker, H. S. and Geer, B. (1960) Participant observation: the analysis of qualitative field data, in R. N. Adams and J. J. Preiss (eds) *Human Organization Research*. Homewood, IL: Dorsey Press.

Behrens, C. A., Baksh, M. G. and Mothes, M. (1994) A regional analysis of Barí land use intensification and its impact on landscape heterogeneity, *Human Ecology*, 22: 279–316.

Beniger, J. R. (1983) Does television enhance the shared symbolic environment? Changes in the labeling of editorial cartoon, 1948–1980, *American Sociological Review*, 48: 103–11.

Berman, H. J. (1995) Claire Philip's Journal: from life to text, from text to life, *Journal of Aging Studies*, 9: 335–42.

Bernard, H. R. (1994) *Research Methods in Anthropology: Second Edition: Qualitative and Quantitative Approaches*. Thousand Oaks, CA: Sage.

Berry, D. S., Koon, K. J., Misovich, S. J. and Baron, R. M. (1991) Quantised displays of human movement: a methodological alternative to the point-light display, *Journal of Nonverbal Behaviour*, 15: 81–9.

Best, J. and Luckenbill, D. (1980) The social organization of deviants, *Social Problems*, 28: 14–31.

Biddle, S. and Armstrong, N. (1992) Children's physical activity: an exploratory study of psychological correlates, *Social Science and Medicine*, 34: 325–32.

Binder, A. (1964) Statistical theory, *Annual Review of Psychology*, 15: 277–310.

Binder, A. (1993) Constructing racial rhetoric: media depictions of harm in heavy metal and rap music, *American Sociological Review*, 58: 753–67.

Bird, A. M. (1976) Nonreactive research: applications for sociological analysis of sport, *International Review of Sport Sociology*, 11: 83–9.

Bishop, G. F., Oldendick, R. W., Tuchfarber, A. J. and Bennett, S. E. (1980) Pseudo-opinions on public affairs, *Public Opinion Quarterly*, 44: 198–209.

Blake, C. F. (1981) Graffiti and racial insults: the archaeology of ethnic relations in Hawaii, in R. A. Gould and M. B. Schiffer (eds) *Modern Material Culture: The Archaeology of Us*. New York: Academic Press.

Blumberg, P. M. and Paul, P. W. (1975) Continuities and discontinuities in upper-class marriage, *Journal of Marriage and the Family*, 37: 63–77.

Bochner, S. (1979) Designing unobtrusive field experiments in social psychology, in L. Sechrest (ed.) *Unobtrusive Measurement Today*. San Francisco, CA: Jossey-Bass.

Bogen, D. and Lynch, M. (1989) Taking account of the hostile native: plausible deni-ability and the production of conventional history in the Iran-Contra Hearings, *Social Problems*, 36: 197–224.

Bordia, P. (1996) Studying verbal interaction on the Internet: the case of rumour transmission research, *Behaviour Research Methods, Instruments and Computers*, 28: 149–51.

Boruch, R. F. and Cecil, J. S. (1979) *Assuring the Confidentiality of Research Data*. Philadelphia, PA: University of Philadelphia Press.

Bouchard, T. J., Jr. (1976) Unobtusive measures: an inventory of uses, *Sociological Methods and Research*, 4: 267–300.

Bowen, L. and Schmid, J. (1997) Minority presence and portrayal in mainstream magazine advertising: an update, *Journalism and Mass Communication Quarterly*, 74: 134–46.

Box, S. (1981) *Deviance, Reality and Society*. London: Holt, Rinehart and Winston.

Bradburn, N. M., Seymour Sudman, E. B. *et al.* (1979) *Improving Method and Questionnaire Design*. San Francisco: Jossey-Bass.

Braithewaite, J., Fisse, B. and Geis, G. (1987) Covert facilitation and crime: restoring the balance to the entrapment debate, *Journal of Social Issues*, 43: 5–42.

Brannen, J. (1988) The study of sensitive subjects, *Sociological Review*, 36: 552–63.

Brent, E. (1993) Computational sociology: reinventing sociology for the next millennium, *Social Science Computer Review*, 11: 497–9.

Brodisio, E. S., Moran, E. F., Mausel, P. and Wu, Y. (1994) Land use change in the Amazon estuary: patterns of Caboclo settlement and landscape management, *Human Ecology*, 22: 249–78.

Bryant, C. D. and Snizek, W. E. (1975) The last will and testament: a neglected document in sociological research, *Sociology and Social Research*, 59: 219–30.

Bulmer, M. (1980a) Why don't sociologists make more use of official statistics? *Sociology*, 14: 505–24.

Bulmer, M. (1980b) Introduction, in M. Bulmer (ed.) *Social Research and Royal Commissions*. London: George Allen and Unwin.

Bulmer, M. (1984) *The Chicago School of Sociology: Institutionalization, Diversity, and the Rise of Sociological Research*. Chicago, IL: Chicago University Press.

Bumpass, L. L. and Sweet, J. A. (1972) Differentials in marital instability, *American Sociological Review*, 37: 754–66.

Burchinall, L. S. and Chancellor, L. B. (1963) Survival rates among religiously homogamous and interreligious marriages, *Social Forces*, 41: 353–62.

Burma, J. H. (1959) Self-tattooing among delinquents: a research note, *Sociology and Social Research*, 41: 341–5.

Burns, T. (1992) *Erving Goffman*. London: Routledge.

Bushnell, J. (1995) Organizing a counter-culture with graffiti, in T. Triggs (ed.) *Communicating Design*. London: Batsford.

Bytheway, B. (1993) Ageing and biography: the letters of Bernard and Mary Berenson, *Sociology*, 27: 153–65.

Cain, P. S. and Treiman, D. J. (1981) The *DOT* as a source of occupational data, *American Sociological Review*, 46: 253–78.

Cameron, P., Playfair, W. L. and Wellum, S. (1994) The longevity of homosexuals: before and after the AIDS epidemic, *Omega: The Journal of Death and Dying*, 29: 249–72.

Campbell, D. T. (1969) Reforms as experiments, *American Psychologist*, 24: 209–29.

Campbell, D. T. (1981) Comment: another perspective on a scholarly career, in M. B. Brewer and B. E. Collins (eds) *Scientific Inquiry and the Social Sciences: A Volume in Honor of Donald T. Campbell*. San Francisco, CA: Jossey-Bass.

Campbell, D. T., Boruch, R. F., Schwartz, R. D. and Steinberg, J. (1977) Confidentiality-preserving modes of access to files and to interfile exchange for useful statistical analysis, *Evaluation Quarterly*, 1: 269–300.

Cannell, C. F. and Kahn, R. L. (1968) Interviewing, in L. Gardner and E. Aronson (eds) *The Handbook of Social Psychology*. Reading, MA: Addison-Wesley.

Caplan, A. L. (1982) On privacy and confidentiality in social science research, in T. L. Beauchamp, R. R. Faden, R. J. Wallace *et al.* (eds) *Ethical Issues in Social Science Research*. Baltimore, MD: Johns Hopkins University Press.

Capron, A. M. (1982) Is consent always necessary in social science research? in T. L. Beauchamp, R. R. Faden, R. J. Wallace and L. Waters (eds) *Ethical Issues in Social Science Research*. Baltimore, MD: Johns Hopkins University Press.

Carley, M. (1981) *Social Measurement and Social Indicators: Issues of Policy and Theory*. London: Allen & Unwin.

Cartwright, T. J. (1975) *Royal Commissions and Departmental Committees in Britain*. London: Hodder and Stoughton.

Caudill, S., Caudill, E. and Singletary, M. W. (1987) 'Journalists wanted': Trade journal ads as indicators of professional values, *Journalism Quarterly*, 64: 576–80.

Cavan, R. S. (1928) *Suicide*. Chicago, IL: University of Chicago Press.

Cavan, S. (1966) *Liquor License: An Ethnography of Bar Behavior*. Chicago, IL: Aldine.

Chai, T. R. (1977) A content analysis of the obituary notices on Mao Tse-Tung, *Public Opinion Quarterly*, 41: 475–87.

Chalfen, R. (1992) Picturing culture through indigenous imagery: a telling story, in P. I. Crawford and D. Turton (eds) *Film as Ethnography*. Manchester: Manchester University Press.

Chalfen, R. (1998) Interpreting family photography as pictorial communication, in J. Prosser (ed.) *Image-based Research: A Sourcebook for Qualitative Researchers*. London: Falmer.

Chen, L.L.-J. and Gaines, B. R. (1998) Modeling and supporting virtual cooperative interaction through the World Wide Web, in F. Sudweeks, M. McLaughlin and S. Rafaeli (eds) *Network and NetPlay: Virtual Groups on the Internet*. Cambridge, MA: MIT Press.

Christensen, H. T. and Barber, K. E. (1967) Interfaith versus intrafaith marriages in Indiana, *Journal of Marriage and the Family*, 29: 461–9.

Cialdini, R. B. and Baumann, D. J. (1981) Littering: a new unobtrusive measure of attitude, *Social Psychology Quarterly*, 44: 254–9.

Clark, H. H. and Schober, M. F. (1982) Asking questions and influencing answers, in J. M. Tanur (ed.) *Questions about Questions: Inquiries into the Cognitive Bases of Surveys*. New York: Russell Sage Foundation.

Clark, L. and Werner, O. (1997) Short Take 23: protection of human subjects and ethnographic photography, *Cultural Anthropology Methods Journal*, 9: 18–20.

Clark, R. and Maynard, M. (1998) Research methodology: using online technology for secondary analysis of survey research data – 'Act globally, think locally', *Social Science Computer Review*, 16: 58–71.

Cloyd, J. W. (1976) The market-place bar: the interrelation between sex, situation, and strategies in the pairing ritual of *Homo Ludens*, in C. Warren (ed.) *Sexuality: Encounters, Identities and Relationships*. Beverly Hills, CA: Sage.

Coiera, E. (1997) *Medical Informatics, the Internet and Telemedicine*. London: Chapman & Hall.

Colfax, D. and Frankel, S. (1972) The perpetuation of racial stereotypes: Blacks in mass circulation magazine advertisements, *Public Opinion Quarterly*, 36: 8–18.

Collier, J. Jr. and Collier, M. (1986) *Visual Anthropology: Photography as a Research Method*. Albuquerque, NM: University of New Mexico Press.

Collins, R. (1980) Erving Goffman and the development of modern social theory, in J. Ditton (ed.) *The View from Goffman*. London: Macmillan.

Comley, P. (1996) The use of the Internet as a data collection method. http: //www.sga.co.uk/esomar.html

Connors, L. (1997) Freedom to connect, *Wired*, 5: 106–7.

Conrad, P. (1997) 'It's boring': notes on the meaning of boredom in everyday life, *Qualitative Sociology*, 20: 465–75.

Cook, T. D. and Campbell, D. T. (1979) *Quasi-experimentation: Design and Analysis Issues for Field Settings*. Boston, MA: Houghton-Mifflin.

Coomber, R. (1997) Using the Internet for survey research, *Sociological Research Online*, 2. http: //www.socresonline.org.uk/socresonline/2/1/2.html

Cort, L. A. (1993) 'Whose sleeves . . . ?' Gender, class and meaning in Japanese dress of the seventeenth century, in R. Barnes and J. B. Eicher (eds) *Dress and Gender: Making and Meaning in Cultural Contexts*. Oxford: Berg.

Croll, P. (1986) *Systematic Classroom Observation*. Lewes: Falmer.

Cronin, B. and Hert, C. A. (1995) Scholarly foraging and network discovery tools, *Journal of Documentation*, 51: 388–403.

Dabbs, J. M., Jr. (1982) Making things visible, in J. Van Maanen, J. M. Dabbs Jr and R. B. Faulkner (eds) *Varieties of Qualitative Research*. Beverly Hills, CA: Sage.

Danet, B., Ruedenberg, L. and Rosenbaum-Tamari, Y. (1998) 'Hmmm . . . Where's that smoke coming from?' Writing, play and performance on Internet Relay Chat, in F. Sudweeks, M. McLaughlin and S. Rafaeli (eds) *Network and Net-Play: Virtual Groups on the Internet*. Cambridge, MA: MIT Press.

Dann, G. (1996) The people of tourist brochures, in T. Selwyn (ed.) *The Tourist Image: Myths and Myth Making in Tourism*. London: Wiley.

Darley, J. M. and Latané, B. (1968) Bystander intervention in emergencies: diffusion of responsibility, *Journal of Personality and Social Psychology*, 8: 377–83.

Davidoff, L. (1979) Class and gender in Victorian England: the diaries of Arthur J. Munby and Hannah Cullwick, *Feminist Studies*, 5: 87–141.

Davis, D. L. (1975) The shadow scale: an unobtrusive measure of door-to-door interviewing, *Sociological Review*, 23: 143–50.

Davis, J. A. (1966) Review of Webb et al., *Unobtrusive Measures, Social Forces*, 45: 290–1.

Denzin, N. K. (1970) *The Research Act in Sociology: The Theoretical Introduction of Sociological Methods*. London: Butterworth.

Denzin, N. K. (1989) *Interpretive Biography*. Thousand Oaks, CA: Sage.

Dethlefsen, E. S. (1981) The cemetery and culture change: archaeological focus and ethnographic perspective, in R. A Gould and M. B. Schiffer (eds) *Modern Material Culture: The Archaeology of Us*. New York: Academic Press.

Dey, I. (1993) *Qualitative Data Analysis: A User-Friendly Guide for Social Scientists*. London: Routledge.

Diener, E. and Crandall, R. (1978) *Ethics in Social and Behavioral Research*. Chicago, IL: University of Chicago Press.

Dilevko, J. and Harris, R. M. (1997) Information technology and social relations: portrayals of gender roles in high tech product advertisements, *Journal of the American Society for Information Science*, 48: 718–27.

Dilnot, A. and Morris, C. N. (1981) What do we know about the black economy?, *Fiscal Studies*, 2: 58–73.

Dingwall, R., Tanaka, H. and Minamikata, S. (1991) Images of parenthood in the United Kingdom and Japan, *Sociology*, 25: 423–46.

Dodge, M. (1998) The geographies of cyberspace, paper presented at the Annual Meeting of the Association of American Geographers, Boston, MA, March.

Douglas, J. D. (1967) *The Social Meanings of Suicide*. Princeton, NJ: Princeton University Press.

Downes, D. and Rock, P. (1988) *Understanding Deviance*. Oxford: Clarendon.

Durkheim, E. (1933) *The Division of Labor in Society*. New York: Macmillan.

Dworkin, G. (1982) Must subjects be objects?, in T. L. Beauchamp, R. R. Faden, R. J. Wallace and L. Walters (eds) *Ethical Issues in Social Science Research*. Baltimore, MD: Johns Hopkins University Press.

Eco, U. (1976) *A Theory of Semiotics*. Bloomington, IN: Indiana University Press.

Edge, S. (1999) 'Why did they kill Barney?': media, Northern Ireland and the riddle of Loyalist terror, *European Journal of Communication*, 14: 91–116.

Edwards, E. (1996) Postcards: greetings from another world, in T. Selwyn (ed.) *The Tourist Image: Myths and Myth Making in Tourism*. London: Wiley.

Evans, W. (1996) Divining the social order: class, gender and magazine astrology columns, *Journalism and Mass Communication Quarterly*, 73: 389–400.

Eveland, J. D. and Bickson, T. (1988) Work group structures and computer support, *ACM Transactions on Office Information Systems*, 6: 354–79.

Eyre, L. A. (1984) Political violence and urban geography in Kingston, Jamaica, *Geographical Review*, 74: 24–37.

Feige, E. L. and Watt, H. W. (1970) Protection of privacy through microaggregation, in R. L. Biscoe (ed.) *Data Bases, Computers and the Social Sciences*. New York: Wiley.

Feldman, M. S. (1995) *Strategies for Interpreting Qualitative Data*. Thousand Oaks, CA: Sage.

Fielding, N. G. and Lee, R. M. (1998) *Computer Analysis and Qualitative Research*. London: Sage.

Fine, G. A. (1994) The social construction of style: Thorstein Veblen's *Theory of the Leisure Class* as contested text, *Sociological Quarterly*, 35: 457–72.

Fine, G. A. and Martin, D. D. (1990) A partisan view: sarcasm, satire and irony as voices in Erving Goffman's *Asylums*, *Journal of Contemporary Ethnography*, 19: 89–115.

Firth, R., Hubert, J. and Forge, A. (1970) *Families and their Relatives*. London: Routledge & Kegan Paul.

Flaherty, M. G. (1987) Multiple realities and the experience of duration, *Sociological Quarterly*, 28: 313–26.

Fligstein, N. (1987) The intraorganizational power struggle: the rise of finance personnel to top leadership in large corporations, 1919–1979, *American Sociological Review*, 52: 44–58.

Foster, C. (1996) Reflections of the true significance of the Scott Report for government accountability, *Public Administration*, 74: 567–92.

Freud, S. ([1901] 1975) *The Psychopathology of Everyday Life*. Harmondsworth: Penguin.

Frey, B. S. and Pommerehne, W. W. (1982) Measuring the hidden economy: though this be madness there be method in it, in V. Tanzi (ed.) *The Underground Economy in the United States and Abroad*. Lexington, MA: D. C. Heath.

Fuller, L. (1988) Fieldwork in forbidden terrain: the US state and the case of Cuba, *American Sociologist*, 19: 99–120.

Gambetta, D. (1993) *The Sicilian Mafia: The Business of Private Protection*. Cambridge, MA: Harvard University Press.

Garner, A., Sterk, H. M. and Adams, S. (1998) Narrative analysis of sexual etiquette in teenage magazines, *Journal of Communication*, 48: 59–78.

Garton, L., Haythornthwaite, C. and Wellman, B. (1997) Studying online social networks, *Journal of Computer-Mediated Communication*, 3. http: //cwis.usc.edu/dept/annenberg/vol3/issue1/garton.html

Geary, P. (1986) Sacred commodities: the circulation of medieval relics, in A. Appadurai (ed.) *The Social Life of Things: Commodities in Cultural Perspective*. Cambridge: Cambridge University Press.

Geis, G. (1968) The heavy electrical equipment antitrust cases of 1961, in G. Geis (ed.) *White-Collar Criminal: The Offender in Business and the Professions*. New York: Atherton Press.

George, A. (1983) 'You know. . . , You know': the theoretical and methodological implications of what is not said in interviews, paper presented at the Annual Conference of the British Sociological Association, Cardiff, April.

Ginsburg, R. (1996) 'Don't tell, dear': The material culture of tampons and napkins, *Journal of Material Culture*, 1: 365–75.

Giordano, P. C. (1995) The wider circle of friends in adolescence, *American Journal of Sociology*, 101: 661–97.

Gittelsohn, J., Shankar, A. V. and West, K. P. Jr. (1997) Estimating reactivity in direct observation studies of health behaviors, *Human Organization*, 56: 182–9.

Glaser, B. G. (1965) The constant comparative method of qualitative analysis, *Social Problems*, 12: 436–45.

Glaser, B. G. (1978) *Theoretical Sensitivity*. Mill Valley, CA: Sociology Press.

Glaser, B. G. and Strauss, A. L. (1967) *The Discovery of Grounded Theory*. Chicago, IL: Aldine.

Glassner, B. and Corzine, J. (1982) Library research as fieldwork: a strategy for qualitative content analysis, *Sociology and Social Research*, 66: 305–19.

Goffman, E. (1956a) *The Presentation of Self in Everyday Life*. Edinburgh: University of Edinburgh Social Sciences Research Centre.

Goffman, E. (1956b) Embarrassment and Social Organization, *American Journal of Sociology*, 62: 264–74.

Goffman, E. (1968) *Asylums: Essays on the Social Situation of Mental Patients and Other Inmates*. Harmondsworth: Penguin.

Goffman, E. (1976) *Gender Advertisements*. London: Macmillan.

Gold, R. (1952) Janitors versus tenants: a status-income dilemma, *American Journal of Sociology*, 57: 486–93.

Gold, S. J. (1989) Ethical issues in visual fieldwork, in G. Blank, J. L. McCartney and E. Brent (eds) *New Technology in Sociology: Practical Applications in Research and Work*. New Brunswick, NJ: Transaction Publishers.

Gold, S. (1994) Israeli immigrants in the United States: the question of community, *Qualitative Sociology*, 17: 325–63.

Goldman, J. (1998) Political science: multimedia for research and teaching: the Oyez Oyez Oyez and History and Politics Out Loud Projects, *Social Science Computer Review*, 16: 30–9.

Goldman, R. (1992) *Reading Ads Socially*. London: Routledge.

Goodman, S. E., Press, L. I., Ruth, S. R. and Rutkowski, A. M. (1994) The global diffusion of the Internet: patterns and problems, *Communications of the ACM*, 37: 27–31.

Gottschalk, S. (1995) Ethnographic fragments in postmodern spaces, *Journal of Contemporary Ethnography*, 24: 195–228.

Gouldner, A. W. (1973) Romanticism and Classicism: deep structures in social science, in A. W. Gouldner (ed.) *For Sociology: Renewal and Critique in Sociology Today*. Harmondsworth: Penguin.

Goyder, J. (1987) *The Silent Minority: Nonrespondents on Sample Surveys*. Cambridge: Polity Press.

Gray, M. (1996) *Web Growth Summary*.
http://www.mit.edu/people/mkgray/net/

Greenbaum, P. E. and Greenbaum, S. D. (1981) Territorial personalization: group identity and social interaction in a Slavic American neighborhood, *Environment and Behavior*, 13: 574–89.

Groves, R. M. (1989) *Survey Errors and Survey Costs*. New York: Wiley.

Gumperz, J. J. (1972) Introduction, in J. J. Gumperz and D. Hymes (eds) *Directions in Sociolinguistics: The Ethnography of Communication*. New York: Holt, Rinehart and Winston.

Hagaman, D. (1993) The joy of victory, the agony of defeat: stereotypes in newspaper stories feature photographs, *Visual Sociology*, 8: 48–66.

Hakim, C. (1983) Research based on administrative records, *Sociological Review*, 31: 489–519.

Hall, E. T. (1959) *The Silent Language*. New York: Doubleday.

Hall, E. T. (1966) *The Hidden Dimension.* New York: Doubleday.

Hall, J. A. (1996) Touch, status and gender at professional meetings, *Journal of Nonverbal Behavior*, 20: 23–44.

Hansen, A. (1995) Using information technology to analyze newspaper content, in R. M. Lee (ed.) *Information Technology for the Social Scientist.* London: UCL Press.

Harper, D. (1986) Meaning and work: a study in photo elicitation, *Current Sociology*, 34: 24–46.

Harper, D. (1989) Visual sociology: expanding sociological vision, in G. Blank, J. L. McCartney and E. Brent (eds) *New Technology in Sociology: Practical Applications in Research and Work.* New Brunswick, NJ: Transaction Publishers.

Harper, D. (1997) Visualizing structure: reading surfaces of social life, *Qualitative Sociology*, 20: 57–77.

Hartnoll, R., Micheson, M., Lewis, R. and Byer, S. (1985) Estimating the prevalence of opioid dependence, *The Lancet*, 26: 203–5.

Hatala, M. N., Baack, D. W. and Parmeter, R. (1998) Dating with HIV: a content analysis of gay male HIV-positive and HIV-negative personal advertisements, *Journal of Social and Personal Relationships*, 15: 268–76.

Hatch, D. L. and Hatch, M. A. (1947) Criteria of social status as derived from marriage announcements in the *New York Times*, *American Sociological Review*, 12: 396–403.

Hayes, S. C., Johnson, V. S. and Cone, J. D. (1975) The marked item technique: a practical procedure for litter control, *Journal of Applied Behavior Analysis*, 10: 425–35.

Heath, C. (1988) Embarrassment and interactional organization, in P. Drew and A. Wooton (eds) *Erving Goffman: Exploring the Interaction Order.* Cambridge: Polity Press.

Hedges, B. (1987) Survey research for government, in M. Bulmer (ed.) *Social Science Research and Government: Essays on Britain and the United States.* Cambridge: Cambridge University Press.

Helmericks, S. G., Nelsen, R. L. and Unnithan, N. P. (1991) The researcher, the topic and the literature: a procedure for systematizing literature searches, *Journal of Applied Behavioral Science*, 27: 285–94.

Hermer, J. and Hunt, A. (1996) Official graffiti, *Law and Society Review*, 30: 455–80.

Herring, S. (1996) Linguistic and critical analysis of computer-mediated communication: some ethical and scholarly considerations, *Information Society*, 12: 153–68.

Hewson, C. M., Laurent, D. and Vogel, C. M. (1996) Proper methodologies for psychological and sociological studies conducted via the Internet, *Behaviour Research Methods, Instruments and Computers*, 28: 186–91.

Hill, M. R. (1993) *Archival Strategies and Techniques.* Newbury Park, CA: Sage.

Holsti, O. R. (1969) *Content Analysis for the Social Sciences and Humanities.* Reading, MA: Addison-Wesley.

Homan, R. and Bulmer, M. (1982) On the merits of covert methods: a dialogue, in M. Bulmer (ed.) *Social Research Methods.* London: Macmillan.

Hood, J. C. (1996) The lost art of theoretical sampling, paper presented at the Fourth International Social Science Methodology Conference, University of Essex, July.

Hornsby-Smith, M. P. (1987) *Roman Catholics in England: Studies in Social Structure since the Second World War*. Cambridge: Cambridge University Press.

Hox, J. J., de Leeuw, E. D. and Kraft, I. G. G. (1991) The effect of interviewer and respondent characteristics on the quality of survey data: a multilevel model, in P. P. Biemer, R. M. Groves, L. E. Lyberg and S. Sudman (eds) *Measurement Errors in Surveys*. New York: Wiley.

Huberman, B. A. and Lukose, R. M. (1997) Social dilemmas and Internet congestion, *Science*, 277: 535–7.

Huberman, B. A., Pirolli, P. L. T., Pitkow, J. E. and Lukose, R. M. (1998) Strong regularities in World Wide Web surfing, *Science*, 280: 95–7.

Humphrey, R. and Schuman, H. (1984) The portrayals of Blacks in magazine advertisements: 1950–82, *Public Opinion Quarterly*, 49: 551–63.

Humphreys, L. (1970) *Tearoom Trade: A Study of Homosexual Encounters in Public Places*. London: Gerald Duckworth.

Jackson, M. H. (1997) Assessing WWW communication structure, *Journal of Computer-Mediated Communication*, 3.
http: //cwis.usc.edu/dept/annenberg/vol3/issue1/jackson.html

Jacob, H. (1984) *Using Published Data*. Beverly Hills, CA: Sage.

Jacobs, J. (1967) A phenomenological study of suicide notes, *Social Problems*, 15: 60–72.

Jagger, E. (1998) Marketing the self, buying an other: dating in a postmodern, consumer society, *Sociology*, 32: 795–814.

James, L. (1994) Frankenstein's monster in two traditions, in S. Bann (ed.) *Frankenstein, Creation and Monstrosity*. London: Reaktion Books.

Jarman, N. (1997) *Material Conflicts: Parades and Visual Displays in Northern Ireland*. Oxford: Berg.

Jewitt, C. (1997) Images of men: male sexuality in sexual health leaflets and posters for young people, *Sociological Research Online*, 2.
http: //www.socresonline.org.uk/socresonline/2/2/6.html

Johnson, L. K. (1989) *America's Secret Power: The CIA in a Democratic Society*. New York: Oxford University Press.

Jones, R. A. (1980) Myth and symbol among the Nacerima Tsigoloicos, *American Sociologist*, 15: 207–12.

Jones, R. A. (1994) The ethics of research in cyberspace, *Internet Research*, 4: 30–5.

Jones, S. (1997) Using the news: an examination of the value and use of news sources in CMC, *Journal of Computer Mediated Communication*, 2.
http: //www.usc.edu/dept/annenberg/vol2/issue4/jones.html

Joseph, N. and Alex, N. (1972) The uniform: a sociological perspective, *American Journal of Sociology*, 77: 719–30.

Kaplan, E. H. (1991) Evaluating needle-exchange programs via syringe tracking and testing, *AIDS and Public Policy Journal*, 6: 109–15.

Katz, J. (1996) Families and funny mirrors: a study of the social construction and personal embodiment of humor, *American Journal of Sociology*, 101: 1194–237.

Keen, M. F. (1992) The Freedom of Information Act and sociological research, *American Sociologist*, 23: 43–51.

Keen, M. (1993) No-one above suspicion: Talcott Parsons under surveillance, *American Sociologist*, 24: 37–54.

Kehoe, C. M. and Pitkow, J. E. (1996) Surveying the territory: GVU's Five WWW User Surveys, *WWW Journal*, 3.
http: //www.w3journal.com/3/s3.kehoe.html

Kellehear, A. (1993) *The Unobtrusive Researcher: A Guide to Methods*. St Leonards, NSW: Allen & Unwin.

Kelman, H. C. (1982) Ethical issues in different social science methods, in T. L. Beauchamp, R. R. Faden, R. J. Wallace and L. Walters (eds) *Ethical Issues in Social Science Research*. Baltimore, MD: Johns Hopkins University Press.

King, S. A. (1996) Researching Internet communities: proposed ethical guidelines for the reporting of results, *Information Society*, 12: 119–27.

Kiser, E. and Drass, K. A. (1987) Changes in the core of the world-system and the production of utopian literature in Great Britain and the United States, 1883–1975, *American Sociological Review*, 52: 286–93.

Kitsuse, J. I. and Cicourel, A. V. (1963) A note on the uses of official statistics, *Social Problems*, 11: 135–9.

Klofas, J. and Cutshall, C. (1985) Unobtrusive research methods in criminal justice: graffiti in the reconstruction of institutional cultures, *Journal of Research in Crime and Delinquency*, 22: 355–73.

Kress, G. and van Leeuwen, T. (1996) *Reading Images: The Grammar of Visual Design*. London: Routledge.

Krippendorf, K. (1980) *Content Analysis: An Introduction to its Methodology*. Beverly Hills, CA: Sage.

Kruglanski, A. W. (1975) The human subject in the psychology experiment: fact and fiction, in L. Berkowitz (ed.) *Advances in Experimental Social Psychology, Volume 8*. New York: Academic Press.

Kruskal, W. (1981) Statistics in society: problems unsolved and unformulated, *Journal of the American Statistical Association*, 76: 505–15.

La Fontaine, J. (1990) *Child Sexual Abuse*. Cambridge: Polity Press.

Labov, W. (1972) *Sociolinguistic Patterns*. Oxford: Basil Blackwell.

Lamb, D. (1991) *Discovery, Creativity and Problem-Solving*. Aldershot: Avebury.

Larson, R. R. (1996) Bibliometrics of the World Wide Web: an exploratory analysis of the intellectual structure of cyberspace.
http://sherlock.berkeley.edu/asis96/asis96.html

Latané, B. and Darley, J. M. (1968) Group inhibition of bystander intervention in emergencies, *Journal of Personality and Social Psychology*, 10: 215–21.

Lawrence, S. C. and Bendixen, K. (1992) His and hers: male and female anatomy in anatomy texts for U.S. medical students, *Social Science and Medicine*, 35: 925–34.

Ledger, M. and Roth, A. (1977) Poems by chairpersons and their agents, *American Sociologist*, 12: 148–50.

Lee, R. M. (1981) *Interreligious Courtship and Marriage in Northern Ireland*. Unpublished PhD thesis, University of Edinburgh.

Lee, R. M. (1993) *Doing Research on Sensitive Topics*. London: Sage.

Lee, R. M. (1995a) *Dangerous Fieldwork*. Thousand Oaks, CA: Sage.

Lee, R. M. (1995b) Information technology for the social scientist: an introduction, in R. M. Lee (ed.) *Information Technology for the Social Scientist*. London: UCL Press.

Ley, D. and Cybriwsky, R. (1974a) Urban graffiti as territorial markers, *Annals of the Association of American Geographers*, 64: 491–505.

Ley, D. and Cybriwsky, R. (1974b) The spatial ecology of stripped cars, *Environment and Behavior*, 6: 53–68.

Lieberson, S. and Bell, E. O. (1992) Children's first names: an empirical study of social taste, *American Journal of Sociology*, 98: 511–54.

Lieberson, S. and Mikelson, K. S. (1995) Distinctive African American names: an experimental, historical and linguistic analysis of innovation, *American Sociological Review*, 60: 928–46.

Locke, K. (1996) Rewriting *The Discovery of Grounded Theory* after 25 years?, *Journal of Management Inquiry*, 5: 239–45.

Lofland, J. (1971) *Analysing Social Settings*. Belmont, CA: Wadsworth.

Lofland, L. H. (1973) *A World of Strangers: Order and Action in Urban Public Space*. New York: Basic Books.

Lundman, R. J. and MacFarlane, P. T. (1976) Conflict methodology: an introduction and preliminary assessment, *Sociological Quarterly*, 17: 503–12.

Macintyre, S. (1978) Some notes on record taking and making in an antenatal clinic, *Sociological Review*, 26: 595–611.

Macklin, R. (1982) The problem of adequate disclosure in social science research, in T. L. Beauchamp, R. R. Faden, R. J. Wallace and L. Walters (eds) *Ethical Issues in Social Science Research*. Baltimore, MD: Johns Hopkins University Press.

Manning, P. K. (1987) *Semiotics and Fieldwork*. Beverly Hills, CA: Sage.

Manning, P. K. (1988) Semiotics and social theory: the analysis of organizational beliefs, in N. G. Fielding (ed.) *Actions and Structure: Research Methods and Social Theory*. London: Sage.

Manning, P. K. and Cullum-Swan, B. (1994) Narrative, content and semiotic analysis, in N. K. Denzin and Y. G. Lincoln (eds) *Handbook of Qualitative Research*. Thousand Oaks, CA: Sage.

Marby, E. (1998) Frames and flames: the structure of argumentative messages on the Net, in F. Sudweeks, M. McLaughlin and S. Rafaeli (eds) *Network and NetPlay: Virtual Groups on the Internet*. Cambridge, MA: MIT Press.

Margolis, E. (1990) Visual ethnography: tools for mapping the AIDS epidemic, *Journal of Contemporary Ethnography*, 9: 370–91.

Market Research Society Working Group (1976) Response rates in sample surveys, *Journal of the Market Research Society*, 18: 113–42.

Marsh, C. (1985) Informants, respondents and citizens, in M. Bulmer (ed.) *Essays on the History of British Sociological Research*. Cambridge: Cambridge University Press.

Martin, P. and Bateson, P. (1993) *Measuring Behaviour: An Introductory Guide*. Cambridge: Cambridge University Press.

Marx, G. T. (1980) The new police undercover work, *Urban Life*, 8: 399–46.

Marx, G. T. (1984) Notes on the discovery, collection and assessment of hidden and dirty data, in J. W. Schneider and J. Kitsuse (eds) *Studies in the Sociology of Social Problems*. Norwood, NJ: Ablex.

Masterson, J. G. (1970) Consanguinity in Ireland, *Human Heredity*, 20: 371–82.

Mattera, P. (1985) *Off the Books: The Rise of the Underground Economy*. London: Pluto Press.

Maybury, K. K. (1996) Invisible lives: women, men and obituaries, *Omega: Journal of Death and Dying*, 32: 27–37.

Maynes, M. J. (1989) Gender and narrative form in French and German working-class autobiographies, in Personal Narratives Group (ed.) *Interpreting Womens's*

Lives: Feminist Theory and Personal Narratives. Bloomington, IN: Indiana University Press.

Mayo, E. (1933) *The Human Problems of an Industrial Civilization*. New York: Macmillan.

McCall, G. J. (1984) Systematic field observation, *Annual Review of Sociology*, 10: 263–82.

McKenney, J. L., Zack, M. H. and Doherty, V. S. (1992) Complementary communication media: a comparison of electronic mail and face-to-face communication in a programming team, in N. Nohria and R. G. Eccles (eds) *Networks and Organizations: Structure, Form and Action*. Boston, MA: Harvard Business School Press.

McNees, M. P., Egli, D. S., Marshall, R. S., Schnelle, J. F. and Risley, T. R. (1976) Shoplifting prevention: providing information through signs, *Journal of Applied Behavior Analysis*, 9: 399–405.

Medley, D. M. and Mitzel, H. E. (1963) Measuring classroom behavior by systematic observation, in N. L. Gage (ed.) *Handbook of Research on Teaching*. Chicago, IL: Rand McNally.

Melbin, M. (1978) Night as frontier, *American Sociological Review*, 43: 3–22.

Merton, R. K. (1957) Priorities in scientific discovery, *American Sociological Review*, 22: 635–59.

Merton, R. K. (1987) The focused interview and focus groups, *Public Opinion Quarterly*, 51: 550–66.

Michelman, S. O. (1997) Changing old habits: dress of women religious and its relationship to personal and social identity, *Sociological Inquiry*, 67: 350–63.

Midanik, L. (1982) The validity of self reported alcohol consumption and alcohol problems: a literature review, *British Journal of Addiction*, 77: 353–82.

Miles, I. and Irvine, J. (1979) The critique of official statistics, in J. Irvine, I. Miles and J. Evans (eds) *Demystifying Social Statistics*. London: Pluto Press.

Miles, M. B. and Huberman, A. M. (1994) *Qualitative Data Analysis: An Expanded Sourcebook*. Thousand Oaks, CA: Sage.

Milgram, S., Mann, L. and Harter, S. (1965) The lost-letter technique: a tool of social research, *Public Opinion Quarterly*, 29: 437–8.

Miller, D. C. (1991) *Handbook of Research Design and Social Measurement*. Newbury Park, CA: Sage.

Miller, H. (1995) The presentation of self in electronic life: Goffman on the Internet, paper presented at the Conference on Embodied Knowledge and Virtual Space, London, June.

Miller, N. and Morgan, D. (1993) Called to account: the CV as an autobiographical practice, *Sociology*, 27: 133–43.

Miller, P. V. and Groves, R. M. (1985) Matching survey response to official records: an exploration of validity in victimization reporting, *Public Opinion Quarterly*, 49: 366–80.

Mills, C. W. (1959) *The Sociological Imagination*. New York: Oxford University Press.

Mitchell, A., Sikka, P. and Wilmott, H. (1998) Sweeping it under the carpet: the role of accountancy firms in money laundering, *Accounting, Organizations and Society*, 23: 589–607.

Moller, H. (1987) The accelerated development of youth: beard growth as a biological marker, *Comparative Studies In Society And History*, 29: 748–62.

Molotch, H. L. and Boden, D. (1985) Talking social structure: discourse, domination and the Watergate hearings, *American Sociological Review*, 50: 273–87.

Molotch, H. and Lester, M. (1975) Accidental news: the Great Oil Spill as local occurrence and national event, *American Journal of Sociology*, 81: 235–60.

Mooney, K. M., Cohn, E. S. and Swift, M. B. (1992) Physical distance and AIDS: too close for comfort, *Journal of Applied Social Psychology*, 22: 1442–52.

Mooney, L. A., Brabant, S. C. and Moran, S. (1993) Gender and age displays in ceremonial tokens, *Sex Roles*, 29: 617–27.

Moore, M. (1983) Invisible offenses: a challenge to minimally intrusive law enforcement, in M. Caplan (ed.) *Abscam Ethics*. Washington, DC: The Police Foundation.

Morgenstern, O. (1963) *On the Accuracy of Economic Observations*. Princeton, NJ: Princeton University Press.

Morris, M. and Ogan, C. (1996) The Internet as a mass medium, *Journal of Communication*, 46: 39–50.

Mullins, L. S. and Kopelman, R. E. (1984) The best seller as an indicator as societal narcissism: is there a trend? *Public Opinion Quarterly*, 48: 720–30.

Musello, C. (1979) Family photography, in J. Wagner (ed.) *Images of Information: Still Photography in the Social Sciences*. Beverly Hills, CA: Sage.

Myers, J. (1992) Nonmainstream body modification: genital piercing, branding, burning and cutting, *Journal of Contemporary Ethnography*, 21: 267–306.

Nash, J. E. (1990) Working at and working: computer fritters, *Journal of Contemporary Ethnography*, 19: 207–25.

National Commission for the Protection of Human Subjects (1978) *Ethical Principles and Guidelines for the Protection of Human Subjects of Research.* (The Belmont Report.) Washington, DC: US Government Printing Office.

Newhagen, J. E. and Rafaeli, S. (1996) Why communication researchers should study the Internet: a dialogue, *Journal of Communication*, 46: 1–38.

Noakes, J. A. (1995) Using FBI files for historical sociology, *Qualitative Sociology*, 18: 271–86.

Norris, C., Fielding, N., Kemp, C. and Fielding, J. (1992) Black and blue: an analysis of race on being stopped by the police, *British Journal of Sociology*, 43: 207–24.

O'Donnell, I., Farmer, R. and Catalan, J. (1993) Suicide notes, *British Journal of Psychiatry*, 163: 45–8.

Omori, Y. (1995) The first videotheque, in P. Hockings (ed.) *Principles of Visual Anthropology*. Berlin: Mouton de Gruyter.

Orne, M. T. (1962) On the social psychology of the psychological experiment: with particular reference to demand characteristics and their implications, *American Psychologist*, 17: 776–83.

Paccagnella, L. (1997) Getting the seat of your pants dirty: strategies for ethnographic research on virtual communities, *Journal of Computer Mediated Communication*, 3.
http: //www.asusc.org/jcmc/vol3/issue1/paccagnella.html

Padfield, M. and Procter, I. (1996) The effect of the interviewer's gender on the interviewing process: a comparative enquiry, *Sociology*, 30: 355–66.

Palmer, J. and Maguire, F. L. (1973) The use of unobtrusive measures in mental health research, *Journal of Consulting and Clinical Psychology*, 40: 431–6.

Parnell, A. M. and Rodgers, J. L. (1998) Seasonality of induced abortion in North Carolina, *Journal of Biosocial Science*, 30: 321–32.

Parsons, H. M. (1974) What happened at Hawthorne? *Science*, 183: 922–32.

Peters, S. (1998) Finding information on the World Wide Web, *Social Research Update*, 20: 1–4.

Pfaffenberger, B. (1995) *The USENET Book: Finding, Using and Surviving Newsgroups on the Internet*. Reading, MA: Addison-Wesley.

Philip, C. E. (1995) Poems and journal entries from 'Lifelines', Journal MSS, 1988–1994, *Journal of Aging Studies*, 9: 265–322.

Phillips, D. J. (1996) Defining the boundaries: identifying and countering threats in a Usenet newsgroup, *Information Society*, 12: 39–62.

Piliavin, I. M., Rodin, J. and Piliavin, J. A. (1969) Good samaritanism: an underground phenomenon? *Journal of Personality and Social Psychology*, 13: 289–99.

Pinch, T. and Clark, C. (1986) 'Patter merchanting' and the strategic (re)-production and local management of economic reasoning in the sales routines of market pitchers, *Sociology*, 20: 169–91.

Platt, J. (1981) Evidence and proof in documentary research: I: Some specific problems of documentary research, *Sociological Review*, 29: 31–52.

Plummer, K. (1983) *Documents of Life: An Introduction to the Problems and Literature of a Humanistic Method*. London: George Allen and Unwin.

Pratt, L. (1981) Business temporal norms and bereavement behavior, *American Sociological Review*, 46: 317–32.

Pratt, M. G. and Rafaeli, A. (1997) Organizational dress as a symbol of multilayered social identities, *Academy of Management Journal*, 40: 862–98.

Pratt, W. C. (1992) Using FBI records in writing regional labor history, *Labor History*, 33: 470–82.

Press, L. (1997) Tracking the global diffusion of the Internet, *Communications of the ACM*, 40: 11–17.

Presser, S. and Traugott, M. (1992) Little white lies and social science models: correlated response errors in a panel study of voting, *Public Opinion Quarterly*, 56: 77–86.

Price, D. H. (1997) Anthropological research and the Freedom of Information Act, *Cultural Anthropology Methods Journal*, 9: 12–15.

Prosser, J. (1998) The status of image-based research, in J. Prosser (ed.) *Image-based Research: A Sourcebook for Qualitative Researchers*. London: Falmer.

Prost, J. H. (1995) Filming body behavior, in P. Hockings (ed.) *Principles of Visual Anthropology*. Berlin: Mouton de Gruyter.

Rabow, J. and Neuman, C. E. (1984) Garbaeology as method for cross-validating interviewer data on sensitive topics, *Sociology and Social Research*, 68: 480–97.

Rafaeli, S. and Sudweeks, F. (1998) Interactivity on the Nets, in F. Sudweeks, M. McLaughlin and S. Rafaeli (eds) *Network and NetPlay: Virtual Groups on the Internet*. Cambridge, MA: MIT Press.

Rathje, W. L. (1979) Trace measures, in L. Sechrest (ed.) *Unobtrusive Measurement Today*. San Francisco, CA: Jossey-Bass.

Rathje, W. and Murphy, C. (1992) *Rubbish! The Archaeology of Garbage*. New York: HarperCollins.

Reid, E. (1996) Informed consent in the study of on-line communities: a reflection on the effects of computer-mediated social research, *Information Society*, 12: 169–74.

Reiss, A. J., Jr. (1971) Systematic observation of natural social phenomena, in H. L. Costner (ed.) *Sociological Methodology 1971*. San Francisco, CA: Jossey-Bass.

Reuter, P. (1982) The irregular economy and the quality of microeconomic statistics, in V. Tanzi (ed.) *The Underground Economy in the United States and Abroad*. Lexington, MA: D. C. Heath.

Reynolds, P. D. (1982) *Ethics and Social Science Research*. Englewood Cliffs, NJ: Prentice-Hall.

Rice, R. E. and Love, G. (1987) Electronic emotion: socioemotional content in a computer-mediated communication network, *Communication Research*, 14: 85–108.

Ridgeway, C., Berger, J. and Smith, L. (1985) Nonverbal cues and status: an expectation states approach, *American Journal of Sociology*, 90: 955–78.

Riesman, D. and Watson, J. (1964) The Sociability Project: A chronicle of frustration and achievement, in P. E. Hammond (ed.) *Sociologists at Work: Essays on the Craft of Social Research*. New York: Basic Books.

Robinson, D. E. (1976) Fashions in shaving and trimming the beard: the men of the *Illustrated London News*, 1842–1972, *American Journal of Sociology*, 81: 1133–41.

Roethlisberger, F. J. and Dickson, W. J. (1939) *Management and the Worker*. Cambridge, MA: Harvard University Press.

Rolston, B. (1987) Politics, painting and political culture: the political wall murals of Northern Ireland, *Media, Culture and Society*, 9: 5–28.

Romm, C. T. and Pliskin, N. (1998) Electronic mail as a coalition-building information technology, *ACM Transactions on Information Systems*, 16: 82–100.

Rosenthal, R. and Rostow, R. L. (1975) *The Volunteer Subject*. New York: Wiley.

Rosenthal, R. (1976) *Experimenter Effects in Behavioral Research*, enlarged edition. New York: Irvington.

Rosenthal, R. and Rubin, D. B. (1978) Interpersonal expectancy effects: the first 345 studies, *Behavioral and Brain Sciences*, 3: 377–415.

Rosnow, R. L. and Rosenthal, R. (1997) *People studying People: Artifacts and Ethics in Behavioral Research*. New York: Freeman.

Rossi, A. S. (1965) Naming children in middle class families, *American Sociological Review*, 30: 499–513.

Rosswurm, S. and Gilpin, T. (1986) The FBI and farm equipment workers: FBI surveillance records as a source for CIO union history, *Labor History*, 27: 485–505.

Rothschild, N. A. (1981) Pennies from Denver, in R. A. Gould and M. B. Schiffer (eds) *Modern Material Culture: The Archaeology of Us*. New York: Academic Press.

Ruback, R. B. and Snow, J. N. (1993) Territoriality and nonconscious racism at water fountains: intruders and drinkers (Blacks and Whites) are affected by race, *Environment and Behavior*, 25: 250–67.

Rubinstein, R. P. (1995) *Dress Codes: Meanings and Messages in American Culture*. Boulder, CO: Westview.

Sanders, C. R. (1989) *Customizing the Body: The Art and Culture of Tattooing*. Philadelphia, PA: Temple University Press.

Schaeffer, J. H. (1995) Videotape: new techniques of observation and analysis, in P. Hockings (ed.) *Principles of Visual Anthropology*. Berlin: Mouton de Gruyter.

Schiano, D. J. (1997) Convergent methodologies in cyber-psychology: a case study, *Behaviour Research Methods, Instruments and Computers*, 29: 270–3.

Schneider, S. M. (1996) Creating a demographic public sphere through political discussion: a case study of abortion conversation on the Internet, *Social Science Computer Review*, 14: 373–93.

Schonfield, A. (1980) In the course of investigation, in M. Bulmer (ed.) *Social Research and Royal Commisssions*. London: George Allen and Unwin.

Schramm, L. (1995) Framing the debate: ethical research in the information age, *Qualitative Inquiry*, 1: 311–26.

Schratz, M. and Steiner-Löffler, U. (1998) Pupils using photographs in school self-evaluation, in J. Prosser (ed.) *Image-based Research: A Sourcebook for Qualitative Researchers*. London: Falmer.

Schroeder, R. (1996) *Possible Worlds: The Social Dynamic of Virtual Reality Technology*. Boulder, CO: Westview.

Schuman, H. and Converse, J. (1971) The effects of Black and White interviews on Black responses in 1968, *Public Opinion Quarterly*, 35: 44–68.

Schuman, H. and Presser, S. (1981) *Questions and Answers in Attitude Surveys: Experiments on Question Form, Wording and Context*. New York: Academic Press.

Schwartz, M. F. and Wood, D. C. M. (1993) Discovering shared interests using graph analysis, *Communications of the ACM*, 36: 78–89.

Schwartz, T. P. (1993) Testamentary behavior: issues and evidence about individuality, altruism and social influences, *Sociological Quarterly*, 34: 337–55.

Schwarz, N. and Hippler, H. J. (1985) Response alternatives: the impact of their choice and presentation order, in P. P. Biemer, R. M. Groves, L. E. Lyberg and S. Sudman (eds) *Measurement Errors in Surveys*. New York: Wiley.

Schwimmer, B. (1996) Anthropology on the Internet: a review and evaluation of networked resources, *Current Anthropology*, 37: 561–8.

Scott, J. (1990) *A Matter of Record: Documentary Sources in Social Research*. Cambridge: Polity Press.

Sechrest, L. and Phillips, M. (1979) Unobtrusive measures: an overview, in L. Sechrest (ed.) *Unobtrusive Measurement Today*. San Francisco, CA: Jossey-Bass.

Shanklin, E. (1979) When a good social role is worth a thousand pictures, in J. Wagner (ed.) *Images of Information: Still Photography in the Social Sciences*. Beverly Hills, CA: Sage.

Sheehan, N. (1971) *The Pentagon Papers: As Published by the New York Times*. London: Routledge & Kegan Paul.

Shlapentokh, V. (1987) *The Politics of Sociology in the Soviet Union*. Boulder, CO: Westview Press.

Shrum, W. and Kilburn, J. (1996) Ritual disrobement at Mardi Gras: ceremonial exchange and moral order, *Social Forces*, 75: 423–58.

Shulman, D. (1994) Dirty data and investigative methods: some lessons from private detective work, *Journal of Contemporary Ethnography*, 23: 214–53.

Sieber, J. E. (1991) Introduction: sharing social science data, in J. E. Sieber (ed.) *Sharing Social Science Data: Advantages and Challenges*. Newbury Park, CA: Sage.

Sigelman, L., Dawson, E., Nitz, M. *et al.* (1990) Hair loss and electability: the bald truth, *Journal of Nonverbal Behavior*, 14: 269–83.

Silverman, I. (1975) Nonreactive methods and the law, *American Psychologist*, 30: 764–9.

Simmel, G. (1902) The number of members as determining the sociological form of the group, *American Journal of Sociology*, 8: 1–46.

Simon, A. and Boyer, E. G. (1974) *Mirrors for Behavior III: An Anthology of Observation Instruments*. Wyncote, PA: Communication Materials Center.

Simón, A. (1981) A quantitative, nonreactive study of mass behavior with emphasis on the cinema as behavioral catalyst, *Psychological Reports*, 48: 775–85.

Simpson, C. (1994) *Science of Coercion: Communication Research and Psychological Warfare, 1945–60*. New York: Oxford University Press.

Sluka, J. A. (1992) The politics of painting: political murals in Northern Ireland, in C. Nordstrom and J. Martin (eds) *The Paths to Domination, Resistance and Terror*. Berkeley, CA: University of California Press.

Smith, C. B. (1997) Casting the Net: surveying an Internet population, *Journal of Computer-Mediated Communication*, 3.
http: //www.ascusc.org/jcmc/vol3/issue1/smith.html

Smith, M. (1997) Measuring and mapping the social structure of Usenet, paper presented at the 17th Annual International Sunbelt Social Network Conference, San Diego, CA, February.

Smith, M. A. and Leigh, B. (1997) Virtual subjects: using the Internet as an alternative source of subjects and research environment, *Behaviour Research Methods, Instruments and Computers*, 29: 496–505.

Smith, T. W. (1983) The hidden 25 percent: an analysis of nonresponse on the 1980 General Household Survey, *Public Opinion Quarterly*, 47: 386–404.

Smith, T. W. (1995) Trends in non-response rates, *International Journal of Public Opinion Research*, 7: 157–71.

South African Truth and Reconciliation Commission (1998) *Final Report of the Truth and Reconciliation Commission*. Cape Town: Groves Dictionaries Inc.

Sproull, R. F. (1991) A lesson in electronic mail, in L. Sproull and S. Keisler (eds) *Connections: New Ways of Working in the Networked Organization*. Cambridge, MA: MIT Press.

Stanley, L. (1984) *The Diaries of Hannah Cullwick, Victorian Maidservant*. London: Virago.

Stanley, L. (1992) *The Auto/Biographical I*. Manchester: Manchester University Press.

Stanley, L. (1993) On auto/biography in sociology, *Sociology*, 27: 41–52.

Starr, P. (1987) The sociology of official statistics, in W. Alonso and P. Starr (eds) *The Politics of Numbers*. New York: Russell Sage Foundation.

Starr, P. and Corson, R. (1987) Who will have the numbers? The rise of the statistical services industry and the politics of public data, in W. Alonso and P. Starr (eds) *The Politics of Numbers*. New York: Russell Sage Foundation.

Steeh, C. G. (1981) Trends in non-response rates, 1952–1979, *Public Opinion Quarterly*, 45: 40–57.

Stoffle, R. W., Halmo, D. B., Wagner, T. W. and Luczovich, J. J. (1994) Reefs from space: satellite imagery, marine ecology and ethnography in the Dominican Republic, *Human Ecology*, 22: 355–78.

Stone, G. P. (1962) Appearance and self, in A. M. Rose (ed.) *Human Behavior and Social Processes*. London: Routledge & Kegan Paul.

Strauss, A. L. (1987) *Qualitative Analysis for Social Scientists*. Cambridge: Cambridge University Press.

Suchar, C. S. (1997) Grounding visual sociology research in shooting scripts, *Qualitative Sociology*, 20: 33–55.

Sudman, S. and Bradburn, N. M. (1982) *Asking Questions: A Practical Guide to Questionnaire Design*. San Francisco: Jossey-Bass.

Sullivan, G. L. and O'Connell, P. J. (1988) Women's role portrayals in magazine advertising: 1958–83, *Sex Roles*, 18: 181–8.

Sussman, R. W., Green, G. M. and Sussman, L. K. (1994) Satellite imagery, human ecology, anthropology and deforestation in Madagascar, *Human Ecology*, 22: 333–54.

Swindells, J. (1989) Liberating the subject? Autobiography and 'Women's History': a reading of the *The Diaries of Hannah Cullwick*, in The Personal Narratives Group (ed.) *Interpreting Womens's Lives: Feminist Theory and Personal Narratives*. Bloomington, IN: Indiana University Press.

Synnott, A. (1987) Shame and glory: a sociology of hair, *British Journal Of Sociology*, 38: 381–413.

Tang, P. (1998) How electronic publishers are protecting against piracy: doubts about technical systems of protection, *Information Society*, 14: 19–31.

Tanzi, V. (1982) A second (and more skeptical) look at the underground economy in the United States, in V. Tanxi (ed.) *The Underground Economy in the United States and Abroad*. Lexington, MA: D. C. Heath.

Taylor, A. J. W. (1970) Tattooing among male and female offenders of different ages in different types of institution, *Genetic Psychology Monographs*, 81: 81–119.

Taylor, S. (1989) How prevalent is it?, in W. S. Regers, D. Hevey and E. Ash (eds) *Child Abuse and Neglect: Facing the Challenge*. London: B. T. Batsford.

Thang, N. M. and Swenson, I. (1996) Variations in Vietnamese marriages, births and infant deaths by months of the Julian calender and years of the Vietnamese and Chinese astrological calendars, *Journal of Biosocial Science*, 28: 367–77.

Thomas, J. (1996) Introduction: a debate about the ethics of fair practices for collecting social science data in cyberspace, *Information Society*, 12: 107–12.

Thomas, J. J. (1988) The politics of the black economy, *Work, Employment and Society*, 2: 169–90.

Thomas, J. J. (1990) Measuring the underground economy: a suitable case for interdisciplinary treatment, *American Behavioral Scientist*, 33: 169–90.

Thomas, R. (1996) Statistical sources and databases, in R. Sapsford and V. Jupp (eds) *Data Collection and Analysis*. London: Sage.

Thomas, W. I. and Znaniecki, F. (1918) *The Polish Peasant in Europe and America. Vol. 1 Primary-Group Organization*. Boston: The Gorham Press.

Thompsen, P. A. (1996) What's fueling the flames in cyberspace: a social influence model, in L. Strate, R. Jacobson and S. B. Gibson (eds) *Communication and Cyberspace: Social Interaction in an Electronic Environment*. Cresskill, NJ: Hampton Press.

Tourganeau, R. and Smith, T. W. (1996) Asking sensitive questions: the impact of data collection mode, question format and question context, *Public Opinion Quarterly*, 60: 275–304.

Towler, R. (1984) *The Need for Certainty: A Sociological Study of Conventional Religion*. London: Routledge & Kegan Paul.

Turkle, S. (1995) *Life on the Screen: Identity in the Age of the Internet*. New York: Simon and Schuster.

Turner, V. (1986) *The Anthropology of Performance*. New York: PAJ Publications.

Valentine, G. (1998) 'Sticks and stones may break my bones': a personal geography of harassment, *Antipode*, 30: 305–32.

Van den Hoonaard, D. K. (1997) Identity foreclosure: women's experiences of widowhood as expressed in autobiographical accounts, *Ageing and Society*, 17: 533–51.

Van Zoonen, L. (1994) *Feminist Media Studies*. London: Sage.

Vaughn, T. R. (1967) Governmental intervention in social research: political and ethical dimensions in the Witchita jury recordings, in G. Sjoberg (ed.) *Ethics, Politics and Social Research*. London: Routledge & Kegan Paul.

Vernon, G. M. (1960) Bias in professional publications concerning interfaith marriages, *Religious Education*, 55: 261–4.

Veroff, J., Hatchett, S. and Douvan, E. (1992) Consequences of participating in a longitudinal study of marriage, *Public Opinion Quarterly*, 56: 315–27.

Wales, E. and Brewer, B. (1976) Graffiti in the 1970s, *Journal of Social Psychology*, 99: 115–23.

Walsh, B. M. (1970) *Religion and Demographic Behaviour in Ireland*. Dublin: Economic and Social Research Institute.

Walter, S. L. and Adler, A. R. (1991) Fees and fee-waivers, in A. R. Adler (ed.) *Litigation under the Federal Open Government Laws*. Washington, DC: American Civil Liberties Union Foundation.

Walter, T., Littlewood, J. and Pickering, M. (1995) Death in the news: the public invigilation of private emotion, *Sociology*, 29: 579–96.

Waterman, S. and Kosmin, B. (1986) Mapping an unenumerated population, *Ethnic and Racial Studies*, 9: 484–50.

Waxer, P. H. (1985) Video ethnology: television as a data base for cross-cultural studies in nonverbal displays, *Journal of Nonverbal Behavior*, 9: 111–20.

Webb, E. J., Campbell, D. T., Schwartz, R. D. and Sechrest, L. (1966) *Unobtrusive Measures: Nonreactive Research in the Social Sciences*. Chicago: Rand McNally.

Webb, E. J., Campbell, D. T., Schwartz, R. D., Sechrest, L. and Grove, J. B. (1981) *Nonreactive Measures in the Social Sciences*. Dallas: Houghton Mifflin.

Webb, E. and Weick, K. E. (1983) Unobtrusive measures in organizational theory: a reminder, in J. Van Maanen (ed.) *Qualitative Methodology*. Beverly Hills, CA: Sage.

Weber, R. P. (1985) *Basic Content Analysis*. Beverly Hills, CA: Sage.

Webster, C. J. (1996) Population and dwelling unit estimates from space, *Third World Planning Review*, 18: 155–76.

Weick, K. E. (1968) Systematic observational methods, in G. Lindzey and E. Aronson (eds) *Handbook of Social Psychology*. Reading, MA: Addison-Wesley.

Weitzman, E. A. and Miles, M. B. (1995) *Computer Programs for Qualitative Data Analysis*. Thousand Oaks, CA: Sage.

Wellman, B., Salaff, J., Dimitrova, D. *et al.* (1996) Computer networks as social networks: collaborative work, telework and virtual community, *Annual Review of Sociology*, 22: 213–38.

White, H. (1970) *Chains of Opportunity: System Models of Mobility in Organizations.* Cambridge, MA: Harvard University Press.

White, N. R. (1998) 'The best years of your life': remembering childhood in autobiographical texts, *Children and Society*, 12: 48–59.

Williams, F., Rice, R. E. and Rogers, E. M. (1988) *Research Methods and the New Media.* New York: Free Press.

Williamson, J. (1978) *Decoding Advertisements: Ideology and Meaning in Advertising.* London: Marion Boyars.

Witmer, D. and Katzman, S. (1998) Smile when you say that: graphic accents as gender markers in computer-mediated communication, in F. Sudweeks, M. McLaughlin and S. Rafaeli (eds) *Network and NetPlay: Virtual Groups on the Internet.* Cambridge, MA: MIT Press.

Wolfinger, N. H. (1995) Passing moments: some social dynamics of pedestrian interaction, *Journal of Contemporary Ethnography*, 24: 323–40.

Woodruff, A., Aoki, P. M., Gauthier, P. and Rowe, L. A. (1996) An investigation of documents from the World Wide Web, paper presented at the Fifth International World Wide Web Conference, Paris, May.

Wrench, J. and Lee, G. (1982) Piecework and industrial accidents: two contemporary case studies, *Sociology*, 16: 512–25.

Wuthnow, R. (1977) A longitudinal, cross-national indicator of societal religious commitment, *Journal for the Scientific Study of Religion*, 16: 87–99.

Wyatt-Brown, A. M. (1995) Creativity as a defense against death: maintaining one's professional identity, *Journal of Aging Studies*, 9: 349–54.

Wynn, E. and Katz, J. E. (1997) Hyperbole over cyberspace: self-presentation and social boundaries in Internet home pages and discourse, *The Information Society*, 13: 297–327.

Yancey, G. and Yancey, S. (1998) Interracial dating: evidence from personal relationships, *Journal of Family Issues*, 19: 334–8.

Zelwietro, J. (1998) The politicization of environmental organizations through the Internet, *Information Society*, 14: 45–56.

Zerubavel, E. (1987) The language of time: toward a semiotics of temporality, *Sociological Quarterly*, 28: 343–56.

Zube, E. (1979) Pedestrians and wind, in J. Wagner (ed.) *Images of Information: Still Photography in the Social Sciences.* Beverly Hills, CA: Sage.

Index

SOCIAL RESEARCH: SECOND EDITION
ISSUES, METHODS AND PROCESS

Tim May

Review of the first edition:

> . . . a wide ranging text . . . provides a thorough coverage of official sta-
> tistics, questionnaires, interviewing, documentary research and com-
> parative research.
>
> *Journal of Social Policy*

This revised and expanded edition of a bestselling text incorporates the latest
developments in social research. Additions to each chapter do further justice to
ideas on the research process in general and aspects of its practice in particular.
Chapter summaries, questions for reflection and signposts to further reading
are incorporated into a new textbook format. The aim of the book, however,
remains the same: to bridge the gap between theory and methods in social
research, each of which is essential to understanding the dynamics of social relations. The style remains clear and accessible and the basic structure, similar.

Part 1 examines the issues in social research and Part 2 the methods available.
The topics covered in Part 1 include an overview of perspectives and their
relationship to research – such as realism, positivism, empiricism, feminisms,
poststructuralism, postmodernism and idealism – and an examination of both
the way theory relates to data and the place of values and ethics in social
research. These issues are then linked into a discussion in Part 2 on the actual
methods and process of social research with chapters on official statistics,
survey research, interview techniques, participant observation, documentary
research and comparative research. These chapters follow a common structure to enable a clear understanding of the place, process and analysis of each
research method. This allows the reader to compare their strengths and weaknesses in the context of discussions in Part 1.

This book will have wide appeal as an introduction for undergraduates studying the methods and techniques of social science, as well as for postgraduate
courses in research methods. In addition, it will enable those practising and
teaching social research to stay abreast of key developments in the field.

Contents

240pp   0 335 20005 2 (Paperback)   0 335 19806 0 (Hardback)

SIMULATION FOR THE SOCIAL SCIENTIST
Nigel Gilbert and Klaus G. Troitzsch

- What can computer simulation contribute to the social sciences?
- Which of the many approaches to simulation would be best for my social science project?
- How do I design, carry out and analyse the results from a computer simulation?

Simulation for the Social Scientist is a practical textbook on the techniques of building computer simulations to assist understanding of social and economic issues and problems.

Interest in social simulation has been growing very rapidly world-wide as a result of increasingly powerful hardware and software and also a rising interest in the application of ideas of complexity, evolution, adaptation and chaos in the social sciences. This authoritative book outlines all the common approaches to social simulation at a level of detail which will give social scientists an appreciation of the literature and allow those with some programming skills to create their own simulations.

Social scientists in a wide range of fields will find this book an essential tool for research, particularly in sociology, economics, anthropology, geography, organizational theory, political science, social policy, cognitive psychology and cognitive science. It will also appeal to computer scientists interested in distributed artificial intelligence, multi-agent systems and agent technologies.

Contents
Preface – Simulation and social science – Simulation as a method – System dynamics and world models – Microanalytical simulation models – Queuing models – Multilevel simulation models – Cellular automata – Multi-agent models – Learning and evolutionary models – Appendix – Bibliography – Index.

288pp   0 335 19744 2 (Paperback)   0 335 19745 0 (Hardback)